The Opinionated Middle Ground

The Opinionated Middle Ground

Consensus is Possible and Polarization is Curable

John Scott Cowan

sh.
SUTHERLAND
HOUSE
Toronto, 2023

Sutherland House
416 Moore Ave., Suite 205
Toronto, ON M4G 1C9

Sutherland House and logo are registered
trademarks of The Sutherland House Inc.

First edition, November 2023

If you are interested in inviting one of our authors to a live event or
media appearance, please contact sranasinghe@sutherlandhousebooks.com
and visit our website at sutherlandhousebooks.com for more
information about our authors and their schedules.

We acknowledge the support of the Government of Canada.

Manufactured in China
Cover designed by Jordan Lunn

Library and Archives Canada Cataloguing in Publication
Title: The opinionated middle ground : consensus is possible and polarization
is curable / John Cowan.
Names: Cowan, John Scott, author.
Identifiers: Canadiana (print) 20230458351 | Canadiana (ebook) 20230458416 |
ISBN 9781990823534 (softcover) | ISBN 9781990823541 (EPUB)
Subjects: LCSH: Conflict management. | LCSH: Civil society.
Classification: LCC HM1126 .C69 2023 | DDC 303.6/9—dc23

ISBN 978-1-990823-53-4
eBook 978-1-990823-54-1

TABLE OF CONTENTS

PREFACE

YOU CAN BLAME THE Covid pandemic for this book. The interruption of all travel and most social life, starting in March 2020, liberated time for reflection and writing that had long been planned and long been procrastinated. So, while others were doing home renovation (and, yes, we did a bit of that too), I accelerated my rate of writing articles, some of them rather lengthy, for *Ottawa Life Magazine*.

Even before the pandemic I had written five articles for that magazine, with some appearing in both the online and print version and some in the online version only. I had two reasons for choosing that magazine. One was that the editor/publisher already knew my writing style, and liked it, so he had instructed his staff to leave my text alone. As I enter curmudgeonhood, I really appreciate not having my text altered by others. Like most authors, I've had all the usual hypertensive experiences of being edited by semiliterate thirty-somethings, and it has been a great relief to sidestep that process. The second reason was that Ottawa is where some decisions are taken in Canada. Yes, I know that the decision-making process in Canada is slow and turgid, and that many decisions are half-measures, but, nonetheless, if one wants to influence decisions, one needs to be intellectually present in Ottawa.

The publisher and editor of that magazine, my friend Dan Donovan, was so welcoming to my long rants, and gave them such prominent display and promotion, that I have joyously produced more than two dozen since the spring of 2020. The longest gap between them was in the summer of 2021, when I took time out to write and publish my short, lighthearted book, *From Bad to Verse: Seriously Unserious Pieces in Verse and Short Story Form, Plus Something in the Air: A Short Memoir of My First 22 Years of Flying.*[1]

Looking back now, I realize that, despite the wide range of topics, all those strongly worded essays in Dan's magazine shared a common characteristic; furthermore, that same characteristic could be found in my articles in that magazine as far back as 2014 and, similarly, in some others that I had written for *Queens' Quarterly Magazine*, including one as early as 2007. That persistent characteristic was almost a Canadian joke. The essays were, each in their own way, very "middle of the road." (Old joke: "Why did the Canadian chicken cross the road?" Answer: "To get to the middle.") The writing consistently reflected my intense abhorrence of extremism of all types. And yet the arguments I advanced did not feel like pandering to soulless compromise. It felt to me like there was a genuine intellectual basis for my adherence to the middle ground. But the full rationale for that drive to the centre becomes easier for me to articulate when I add some context to the stances that I expressed in those articles covering such a wide range of subjects over that 15-year period from 2007 to 2022. That consolidation of my "centrism" is my hope for this book, which is a new exploration of context that has some elements of anthology. It also explains the title of the book.

Note to Reader

In each section of this volume, the narrative is continuous, but portions of the continuous narrative are, in fact, the text of the previously published articles and essays. To clarify which portions are those articles, in each case they are initiated with a note about the title of the piece and the date of publication, and, in each case, a wider left margin is maintained to the end of the original piece.

CHAPTER I

The Middle Ground

THE MIDDLE GROUND SUFFERS from a perpetual identity crisis. You would too, if you were defined by two other points over which you had no control. In the middle of what? And yet the middle ground is where the most productive human discourse takes place, whether it be political, social, economic, or cultural. It puts the "civil" into civil society. And given its abovementioned identity crisis, it needs all the help it can get. We see what happens when it collapses: highly polarized politics, lack of empathy and social cohesion, and ultimately violence or even organized armed conflict.

When the middle ground is thriving, politicians treat their opponents with respect, so their adherents do the same. This is true in other arenas as well. I did a lot of labour relations work over about 40 years, including plenty of negotiation, mediation, and arbitration, and learned plenty of little tricks to keep people focused on problem-solving rather than fighting. And the solutions were never found at the extremes.

How then can a writer of op-ed type articles and essays help to amplify and reinforce the middle ground and weaken the influence of the extremes? How will the articles help others to find, appreciate, adopt, and benefit from the middle ground?

There appear to be a number of ways. The ones that I prefer include

(a) properly describing the middle ground on individual issues and its advantages;

(b) finding and publicizing innovative middle ground ideas;

(c) showing the failings of the extremes, but always using humour or compassion to avoid exacerbating division;

(d) explaining where the middle ground is and how we might help it to prevail; and

(e) where a given polarization has its roots in history, finding interpretations of that history that encourage convergence.

Some of the articles do not specifically address the extreme stances being countered but merely mount evidence-based arguments for the preferred position, which is not explicitly labelled a "middle ground." But readers know a middle ground argument when they see it.

In this chapter my intent is to provide a sampler of some of the above techniques. I applied them to four tasks, as follows: (i) to set out a sort of manifesto of the middle ground; (ii) to show how, sometimes, false middle grounds can exist; (iii) to show two examples of middle ground arguments in two very divisive areas of public policy; and, lastly, (iv) to ridicule an opponent of the middle ground with gentle humour and a bit of compassion.

Six later individual chapters will group arguments all related to six broad topic areas. They are the Covid pandemic, the state of our universities, international relations and conflicts, the politics of democracies, domestic public policy, and society.

1.1 A Middle Ground Manifesto

All public policy is somehow related to politics. It can cause political activity by being the feedstock from which a political position is built, or it can, in turn, be a product of a political urge. And sometimes it is just the plaything of politics. Clearly, if there is to be a strong middle ground in public policy, it must be reflected in a persuasive middle ground in politics.

By the time Donald Trump became the Republican candidate for president in July 2016, it had become clear that the political middle ground had become badly eroded, not only in the United States but in the United Kingdom as well, with the Brexit referendum (June 2016) and the election of Jeremy Corbyn as leader of the Labour Party (September 2015). The middle ground had also been disappearing for some time in many parts of Europe, with the rise, on the one hand, of strong conservative populist parties tainted with antidemocratic tendencies and rhetoric, while at the same time much of the democratic left in Europe and North America was becoming anti-scientific, socially dogmatic, censorious, and negative, with most of their policy stances involving punishing those they didn't (at that moment) like.

I had written about bits and pieces of these phenomena from 2015 onward, but it was only after the rise of "Le mouvement des Gilets jaunes" in France in late 2018 that I turned my reflection to the more general problem of the rising tide of polarization and extremism. Or I should say, turned back to such reflection. I was born during the Second World War and grew up in an informed, centrist household in which there was constant discussion of the extreme polarizations of the first half of the twentieth century. In early 2019, I wrote a short piece entitled "The Curvature of Political Space." At first it was accepted by the *Globe and Mail*, but we disagreed on the editing, so I withdrew it and sent it to *Ottawa*

Life Magazine. Published on April 8, 2019, it now represents for me a sort of manifesto of the middle ground.[2] It sets out not only my objections to the extremes but also the role of the middle ground in the advancement of humankind. What I wrote was as follows:

The Curvature of Political Space

One of the triumphs of 20th century physics was the proof that space is curved. But whilst the great swaths of interstellar space are indeed seen to be curved, on the smaller earthly scale, political space of the 20th century was routinely viewed as linear, with left and right being the bookends of a convenient spectrum, with everything else in between.

It seems we were wrong. The political space is also curved, and, as the radius of that arc in front of us diminishes, and the ends are no longer in plain view, the extreme left and the extreme right are comingling surreptitiously behind our backs.

So, it should surprise no one that the yellow vest movement in France has fulminating elements of both. And it is not just that both extremes are willing to employ the most arbitrary methods, to eschew real debate and to use violence, intimidation, or feigned outrage to silence opponents. Much of the world is seeing the rise of so-called populist movements that tend to share certain common features. While usually, but not always, employing rhetoric of the hard right, these movements also demand benefits from government or action by government that have been notable touchstones of the left. On the other hand, the traditional left, which has always had an admirable penchant for supporting and encouraging underdogs, has of late been inclined to back some admittedly disadvantaged underdogs who regrettably espouse the most fervent reactionary, racist, discriminatory, and even feudal views. The ends of the curve flirting with each other is disconcerting indeed.

Even in academe, where open debate has been protected for about three generations, there is now a persistent effort by so-called progressives to enforce a new orthodoxy using the traditional methods of the far right. Again, the ends of the curve meet.

What is common ground to both ends of the political spectrum is that the adherents of both extremes harbour a deep resentment of the power of so-called "privileged elites" and a deep suspicion of any information emanating therefrom. And while there is a noble aspect to the attempt to wrest some power from "elites," the most disturbing feature of the mindset of those at the apex of this new fusion of the two extremes is the profound and palpable contempt for expertise.

Yes, the elites have had it their own way for a damned long time, even if those who comprise the elite changed with each era. But within those bastions of privilege, be they economic, social or academic, are stored the accumulated knowledge that humans have amassed over a few thousand years. To believe that all this knowledge is really conspiracy, and that there are "alternate truths" just a click away, scripted by a fantasist in a basement, perhaps, but just as good as knowledge tested in the fires of debate or experiment, of peer review and reconfirmation, is to throw away civilisation and any chance of improvement in the human condition or uplifting of the spirit.

But today's extremists, in occupying the pretend moral high ground, are inclined to insist that the discourse of virtually every public official, every scientist or scholar or other expert, and every person of means is suffused with blatant self-interest, and indeed conflict of interest, and that there are no facts, only opinions. Thus, facts can, in the new parlance, be countered by "alternate facts." Hence the anti-vaccine movement and the like. Such folk cannot dare to believe that those with special expertise, even if privileged, might speak actual truth out of genuine public interest, out of concern for others, and out of a sense of public duty, because it clashes with their world view. The idea that those with special expertise and/or exceptional insight could have produced something called "progress" undermines the revolutionary agenda of the fused extremes.

Nonetheless, progress exists. And it was made, and will continue to be made, by the people with open minds, not closed ones. The trick is where to find them. As one contemplates again our no longer linear, but now hopelessly curved opinion spectrum, one is far more likely to find them by striding forward towards the center of the arc than going backward to the confederation of the extremes.

While that short piece from 2019 was clear enough in setting out my antipathy toward extremism and, to that extent, might serve as a "middle ground manifesto," the title of this book hints that perhaps not all middle ground stances are equal. The word "opinionated," as a modifier of "middle ground," suggests that some middle grounds don't qualify. And the ones that don't meet my arbitrary test are those that are devoid of real analysis and just reflect an automatic assumption that compromise is always appropriate. As we will see below, that isn't always logical, and false middle grounds can exist.

1.2 An Example of a False Middle Ground

It is not enough, however, to just make a mad dash for the middle on any issue and automatically assume that the truth will be found there. A desire to avoid the extremes and a conviction that solutions usually involve finding common ground in the middle are admirable. But the middle ground is not just some arithmetic midpoint between the extremes. That sort of soulless interpolation can sometimes yield dangerous results. This is especially true when the competing views arise from entirely different ethical systems.

The admirable tradition of free speech and open debate in the liberal democracies has sometimes given rise to calls that we "need to understand the views and desires of the other side," even if the other side holds strongly to particularly repugnant views, including the view that the liberal democracies should not even exist. Such calls sometimes come from groups that, under the guise of reform movements, have degenerated into elaborate exercises in self-blame. These situations are rare, but they do arise from time to time.

Sometimes they result from a characterization of the two disparate positions as "the two extremes," when, in fact, one is an extreme position and the other is not. As I write these lines in 2022, I take note of those voices outside of Russia and Belarus that seek to explain Russia's invasion of Ukraine as a manifestation of Russia's "legitimate concerns" about the imperial aims of the liberal democracies, and it reminds me of an analogous time some years ago when some commentators in the liberal democracies were making excuses for the extreme views and toxic practices of the Islamic State (ISIS). The refrain usually exhorted us to "understand the root causes of such a movement," usually attributing the origins of the problem to Europe's colonial past or the outsized influence of the United States on world affairs since 1945. Their arguments seemed to me to have a faint echo of arguments heard in the 1930s and underscored the profound dangers of moral relativism. In December 2014 those calls for a false middle ground prompted me to write a piece entitled "Why ISIS and Its Friends Must Be Opposed." It was published on January 27, 2015, in the online version of *Ottawa Life Magazine*;[3]

in the print edition, January/February 2015; and in *On Track Magazine*. What I wrote was as follows:

Why ISIS and Its Friends Must Be Opposed

On the eve of the outbreak of the Second World War, and even for a while in its early stages, many in Canada were opposed to going to war. While amongst them there were a few proto-Nazis and Nazi sympathizers, the vast majority were merely isolationists, pacifists and some on the left who viewed the entire conflict as a collision of capitalist regimes, and unworthy of their attention. These folks wished Canada to avoid the great tragedy of another European war, and saw events an ocean away as beyond our concern. The reaction of the left had also been complicated by the Hitler-Stalin Pact, which for a time put the majority of the Canadian communists (but not all) in the anti-war camp, and some socialists followed suit.

In the aftermath of the war and of the holocaust, these early opponents of our involvement were routinely characterized as despicable and deeply venal. They carried the stigma of their implicit association with great evil for the rest of their lives, often resulting in family estrangement and social isolation.

Most of these folk were not evil (though some were). Most were just wrong. In the banality of their analysis, they misjudged both the great resolve and the great evil of the opponent. The judgement of history lies harshly upon them, perhaps too harshly. Surely most of them would have wished to stop the Nazis early if they had been able to imagine what was to come.

That was three quarters of a century ago, and almost all of those folks are gone now. But today a new generation of moral relativists, isolationists, pacifists and a sprinkling of other well-intentioned naïve folk are engaged in setting themselves up for the same sort of disastrous misjudgement. But this time the analysis is even more difficult and the setting murkier, because of the breakdown of the Westphalian system and the rise of proto-states and broadly distributed non-state actors who nonetheless do share a common worldview, broadly defined. At this moment, the apex of this new great evil is the proto-state known variously as IS, ISIS or ISIL. Whilst it is the most brutal, active and visible local franchise of a trans-national movement, there are plenty of other less flashy foci. That movement is an anti-democratic and totalitarian one, espousing ethnic cleansing and genocide, and which considers armed force to be the political tactic of choice, even (or especially) where voting is an alternative. Like the Nazis, it claims to be bringing into effect a natural destiny, but in this instance mounts a religious justification for its evil policies and programs, by aligning them with an extreme interpretation of Islamic law and belief.

Furthermore, much of the Islamic world has, until recently, been of two minds about actively and vocally opposing such views, which can have at least minor resonance with their own history, traditions and current practices.

In Canada, our legitimate desire to be tolerant and inclusive, which has become a Canadian political touchstone (though of very recent origin), has given succor to the moral relativists who see all belief systems as notionally equal. They aren't. Variants of belief systems which are anti-human will eventually fail, but they must be opposed. However, to do so requires first the acceptance of the idea that evil actually exists. Some have trouble with that idea.

But most accept that, in this era of undeclared wars and near-wars, Canada is at war with IS (or whatever we call it) and its clones, analogues and enthusiasts. It is popular in some circles to be stylishly pessimistic about any action in the Middle East, and this stylish pessimism ("That area will never change") is reinforced by a subtle racism which hints that the Kurds, or perhaps the Iraqi Yazidis, Christians, Shia and moderate Sunnis, are less worthy of our help in their fight against IS than were the French, Belgians, Dutch, British, Poles, etcetera, in their fight against the Nazis.

So, we are in a state of proto-war against a proto-state which fronts for a world-wide movement seeking to expunge democracy, pluralism, and any sane view of human rights. But that proto-war is acceptable to some of us only in so far as no Canadian is lost and it fits within a peacetime defence budget. Neville Chamberlain and the Cliveden set would be so proud.

But it will soon become apparent that we must become more resolved, or later generations will view us as appeasers too.

When I wrote this, ISIS was nearing its zenith. It has since collapsed, but the broader movement from which it sprang is very active and has been reinvigorated by the success of the Taliban in Afghanistan. The Canadian contribution to the demise of the ISIS proto-state was small, but at least, as the excesses of ISIS became more blatant, the voices in Canada asking us to "understand" ISIS largely died away.

1.3 Two Middle Ground Arguments on Two Divisive Topics

Few issues of public policy are more divisive in North America than carbon taxes and gun control. Admittedly, the polarization on both of these is vastly greater in the United States than in Canada. That being said, the polarization on both issues, in both countries, is enormously complex.

There is, of course, the obvious political right/left fracture line, with those to the right much more likely to oppose both carbon taxes and increased gun control than those on the left. But there are other interesting fracture lines. On gun control, in both Canada and the United States, there is a rural/urban fracture line, especially with respect to long guns, as many rural residents consider a long gun to be a normal tool for pest control or hunting. On carbon taxes, there is also something of a rural/urban fracture line, as those who have to drive further or use fuel to run machines for their business tend to be more concerned about fuel price increases.

There is also an age fracture line, especially on carbon taxes, with the young tending to be more idealistic and enthusiastic. And scepticism about the current climate change orthodoxy is more widespread among older folk.

The Canada/US difference is substantial, as most Canadians accept a tax level on carbonaceous fuels that would cause riots in the United States, and most Canadians are comfortable with a level of gun control that would be viewed as an extreme posture in the United States. Of course, Canada is not burdened with a constitutional provision that, if interpreted in a semiliterate way, would appear to guarantee easy access to firearms.

But, for both of these issues, careful reflection can reveal a middle ground that is not merely a compromise but that actually reflects a higher truth.

On the question of carbon taxes, somehow the debate about imposing them became inextricably linked with climate change and CO_2 emissions. Consequently, those who hold to a less apocalyptic view of the effects of rising atmospheric CO_2, including those who want a more adaptive approach, are inclined to oppose carbon taxes. The opposed-to-the-tax tent also includes a considerable grab bag of conspiracy theorists, plus those on the economic right who oppose all new taxes as a normal reflex. On the other side, those most alarmed by the anthropogenic contribution to climate change tend to treat the suppression of carbon-based fuel use as a goal pursued with a degree of fervour normally only associated with religious extremism.

However, the opposing camps missed two important points. First, there were already plenty of carbon taxes, but we just called them something else, like road taxes or fuel taxes, so the debate was only about their level, not their existence. And secondly, and more importantly, a carbon tax was and is a damned good idea, completely aside from the climate change debate. There is a middle ground that all could support, but it had been missed in the snowball fight over climate change.

This prompted me to write a piece in June, 2019, entitled "Carbon Taxes: Fine Idea, Terrible Marketing." It appeared on June 11, 2019, in *Ottawa Life Magazine*.[4] What I wrote was as follows:

Carbon Taxes: Fine Idea, Terrible Marketing

"Carbon tax" is a bit of a misnomer. It is in fact a carbon combustion tax. Or more precisely, a tax on the combustion of carbonaceous fuels recovered from beneath the surface of the earth. The idea behind such taxes is that, by increasing the fuel cost, they cause folk to either reduce the activity for which the fuel is burned, or, where possible, shift to energy substitutes sooner than they might otherwise have done.

Most politicians and others advocating for such taxes invariably focus exclusively on reducing such combustion (and hence CO_2 release) in order to slow or stop the warming trend of the planet. While this is indeed a perfectly valid reason for a carbon tax, it is by far not the best reason to cite in any campaign for carbon taxes. In fact, it barely makes third place amongst the list of valid reasons.

There are four main reasons why climate change (formerly known as global warming) is a divisive and ineffective political argument for instituting or increasing carbon taxes:

(a) First, it is very long term. The western liberal democracies work on a short electoral cycle, and no issue which is longer than about three electoral cycles has much traction either at the ballot box or in politicians' hearts, because, if the good effects of any decision take a few electoral cycles to be felt, current players will get no credit during their term of office.

(b) Secondly, there is vast uncertainty about some aspects of the problem. The halving of the IPCC estimate of the climate sensitivity to CO_2 concentration is a case in point. On the other hand, some other gasses have a huge greenhouse effect, and are rarely discussed or addressed. Reforestation has made greater gains on the CO_2 front than any fuel reduction measure in recent years. Issues of orbital mechanics now also appear important, as does the behavior of the sun. So, while there is no doubt about an anthropogenic component to climate changes, within the scientific world there are lots of uncertainties about the weight of each sub-component and the fix.

(c) Thirdly, vast numbers of folk have been persuaded, perhaps foolishly, to doubt the entire climate story, and are unlikely to endorse immediate action.

(d) Lastly, the nasty, usually unspoken truth about such warming is that there are winners and losers. Of course, with a populous society built upon the way things are now, any thermal deviation from the status quo will have substantially more losers than winners, but there are some winners. And Canada would very likely be a net winner. And yet, we are exhorted to do our utmost to prevent it to help other lands that will be less fortunate, but which themselves may seek exemption from the solutions.

As it happens, there are vastly better and vastly more immediate reasons for imposing carbon taxes. The very best reason is that burning such fuels currently kills about 10 percent of all people who die. The aerosolized particulates from such combustion make up the greatest part of human-produced harmful aerosols. Yes, there are plenty of natural aerosols, but they are mostly salt in the atmosphere from the oceans, and, interestingly, salt is soluble in water, so if one breathes it in, it just dissolves into our interstitial fluid, adding a bit more salt to the blood, to be excreted by the kidneys. The human-made particulates are the vast bulk of the dangerous ones, and, of those, most come from burning carbon-based fuels. Lesser amounts come from other industrial processes.

According to WHO data for 2016, of the 55.3 million people who died that year, more than 7 million were killed by these human-made aerosols, implying that perhaps 4–5 million a year are killed by the particulates from burning oil, coal and gas. That's two holocausts every three years! I have reviewed the WHO methodology for making these estimates, and while, like most epidemiological research, it does have some conjectural aspects, the methodology is generally sound and not slanted. So broadly, the figures are likely fairly accurate. That is a damned good reason to cut back on burning those fuels right away. Furthermore, particulate distribution tends to be concentrated near the originating source, so if we cut back, the improvement in health and longevity will be greatest near the point of cutback. That means our actions will differentially benefit us and our near neighbors, rather than being uniformly distributed worldwide.

The second-best reason for avoiding burning those fuels is that they are also the feedstock for making enormously useful chemicals, polymers and plastics, and we'll likely have a need for these things for thousands of years. Burning up the feedstock for them in the short run to heat our houses is a bit like burning your antique furniture in your fireplace to heat the living room, which is perfectly reasonable in an extreme emergency, but a truly stupid plan for a normal routine.

These latter two reasons for a carbon tax are more obvious, more saleable and less divisive that the one folks mostly talk about. Why are our politicians and other public figures focussing on the only reason that is a hard sell? My guess is because they are scientific illiterates, but I'm sure there is a more charitable explanation somewhere.

In this instance, finding the middle ground was accomplished by broadening the range of arguments for increased carbon taxes, and not just relying upon the climate change argument. That being said, the anthropogenic contribution to climate change is real. It's just more complex than some of the campaigners think it is. It certainly makes sense to dramatically reduce the use of carbonaceous fuels for any non-mobile purpose, as the conversion away from carbon combustion is dramatically easier for fixed installations than for things that move. For vehicles of all types, it's more problematic, as it is still difficult to match the energy density of gasoline, diesel fuel, or jet fuel. Electric vehicles will fill some needs, but not all, at least not until the energy density of electricity storage systems is vastly better than it is now.

But there is plenty that can be done, and eliminating the least efficient fuels like wood and coal for all fixed uses would be a start, followed by vastly improved electrical infrastructure and more reliable methods of generating electricity, including not only solar but also nuclear and tidal generating systems. Electricity is, after all, not an energy source but merely an energy transport system.

Gun control is another matter. Finding the middle ground on gun control, at least in Canada, involves facing the awkward fact that placing further restrictions on legal gun ownership has reached a point of very much diminished returns in terms of further reducing gun violence. But that doesn't make the regulatory and registration system either unnecessary or irrelevant. It just means that it cannot be expected to make the further gains that its most vocal advocates hope for. The largest part of the problem lies elsewhere.

In early 2020 the Government of Canada introduced legislation to ban some (but not all) semi-automatic rifles, based on their style, as opposed to their actual capabilities. This presented me with a golden opportunity to let the facts point the way to the middle ground. In late April, 2020, I took advantage of that opportunity and wrote an article entitled "Gun Crime, Gun Tragedies and Gun Control." It appeared on May 4, 2020, in *Ottawa Life Magazine*.[5]

What I wrote was as follows:

Gun Crime, Gun Tragedies and Gun Control

Will the new Canadian initiative in banning certain styles of semi-automatic rifles reduce gun crime and gun tragedies? The best answer, based on data and logic, is maybe, but only slightly, and only if the measure reduces overall gun ownership, which is not necessarily a predicted outcome of the change.

In 2017, there were 7660 violent firearms crimes in Canada. The vast majority were committed with firearms that were not legally registered, and the vast majority were committed with handguns.

Of those violent crimes, 267 were murders committed with guns (the other 393 Canadian murders that year did not involve guns). Of the gun murders, most were committed with illegal handguns. Only 65 were committed with (mostly unregistered) long guns (the term for rifles or shotguns). The fraction of those 65 involving the style of rifle recently banned is not known. (The newly-banned rifles are long guns styled to look like, but not function like, military assault rifles. True fully-automatic assault rifles have long been banned in Canada.)

On the other hand, there were 4157 suicides in Canada that year, and about 665 were gun suicides, about 80% of which were carried out with long guns (rifles or shotguns). These were almost all legally registered weapons.

So, banning legal ownership and registration of assault-style semi-automatic rifles, while permitting others that work the same way, but look different, can only help in the following minor ways:

1. Some fantasists, who imagine themselves as "warriors" of some type, who see assault-styled weapons as important to their bizarre persona may be discouraged, and may find other outlets for their fantasies. A small fraction of such fantasists might have become violent, and if this legal change makes such a person less likely to go on to commit a violent act, so much the better.

2. If the total number of registered weapons drops somewhat (and this is not certain to occur), there may be a slight drop as well in the number of weapons stolen from registered owners and falling into criminal hands,

though this source accounts for only a small fraction of illegal street weapons in Canada.

3. If a result was indeed a modest reduction in the total numbers of registered long guns, it probably would also mean fewer gun suicides. Experts suggest that while less availability of long guns may in some cases simply result in other methods of suicide, it would still be likely to reduce the number of suicide deaths.

However, most violent gun crime will be unaffected.

So, what *can* be done to reduce violent gun crime? The answer comes in two parts.

1. For the minority of violent gun crimes perpetrated with guns legally owned by the person committing the crime, gains may come from stricter vetting of owners. The relevant act currently mandates assessment based upon of four aspects of an applicant's history: criminal activity, mental health, addiction, and domestic abuse. Arguably, some initial assessments may have been too lenient, and revocations too infrequent.

2. The vast majority of violent gun crimes are committed with illegal guns. The most effective way to reduce violent gun crime is to make illegal guns vastly more costly and dangerous for people to trade or own. There is only one civilized way to do this, and that is to change the law to make the penalties for owning or having care and control of an illegal gun very similar to the penalties for using that illegal gun in a violent crime. If this were the case, those who buy and resell illegal guns would be taking much greater risks in order to ply their trade, and therefore the price of what they sell would go way up. On the street, only gang

leaders would be able to afford such a status symbol, which would be beyond the reach of the rank and file criminals. Furthermore, many of the rank and file might wonder about the wisdom of owning and carrying such a status symbol, if the penalties for just having it are as high as if they used it.

This may not directly address the problems of violence and violent criminal behavior, but it takes illegal guns, and the false courage they give, largely out of the equation. Without affordable illegal guns, the criminals may not be nearly as bold. That's what real gun control is about.

Thus, we can see that, in Canada, the middle ground on this issue has two parts, with the smaller part related to the control of legal firearms and the larger part related to discouraging the importation, distribution, and use of illegal firearms.

For the first (and smaller) part of the middle ground solution, the key remedy suggested for reducing crimes and tragedies related to legally acquired firearms is to actually bother to enforce the regulations that we already have. That enforcement requires the assistance of the public in identifying and bringing to the attention of the authorities those situations where permit revocation ought to occur. It seems more than likely that the inquiry into the mass shooting in Nova Scotia of April 18–19, 2020, will make it abundantly clear that Gabriel Wortman had frequently exhibited behaviours that should have had his firearms permits revoked.

I have had some exposure to a number of analogous cases in university settings. The first was the Fabrikant case. On August 24, 1992, an engineering faculty member, Dr. Valery Fabrikant shot five people at Concordia University in Montreal, killing four.

He remains in prison. About a year later I was appointed by the Board of Governors of Concordia University to conduct a Board of Inquiry into the institution's 13-year handling of Dr. Fabrikant. My report was presented to the board in May 1994 and was entitled "Lessons from the Fabrikant File" and was described as "An independent review of the employment history of Valery Fabrikant at Concordia University, with particular emphasis on concrete measures to enhance the future ability of the University to deal with a wide range of issues raised by the case in question." It was one of the earliest documents to find its way onto the internet and can still be found.[6]

Usually referred to as the Cowan Report, it is still a relevant and interesting read. Only a small portion of it, however, dealt with the firearms question. But the mistake that was made by the university on that score was catastrophic. In the months before the murders, many people at Concordia were aware that Fabrikant owned firearms, including handguns, practiced with them, and had threatened violence against colleagues. As matters came to a head as summer approached in 1992, the university slowly and reluctantly instructed that a letter be drafted and sent to the Sûreté du Québec (SQ), the provincial police force in the Province of Quebec, asking for Fabrikant's firearms permits to be revoked and the guns removed. The letter was finally sent just under six weeks before the murders and had not yet resulted in any action by the police. But it ought to have gone much earlier. The reason it had not was because it had languished for quite a time awaiting translation into French, and some temporizing also caused it to lose its two most energizing and alarming paragraphs. My report had 14 recommendations, and only the last one, number 14, bears on this question. In the report, all my recommendations were followed by brief explanatory comments. My recommendation and comment were as follows:

RECOMMENDATION 14: If you have an emergency, don't send it to translation.

The supposedly emergency letter to the S.Q. on the issue of the permit to transport a handgun was sent on July 14, 1992. Assistant Legal Counsel had drafted that letter on June 29. All that happened in the interval was translation into French, which took a full week, and the deletion of the two best paragraphs. The S.Q. has occasion to read in both languages and does it very well.

But if the Concordia tragedy just missed being nipped in the bud, I do know of a number of other cases where tragedy was averted. During the period from July 1992 to July 1994, I was on sabbatical leave from the University of Ottawa and was serving as the first Senior Advisor on Labour Relations to the Association of Universities and Colleges of Canada (since renamed Universities Canada). In that capacity I became aware of a situation somewhat analogous to the Concordia one, but this time at a prairie university. After some discussions with me, the president of that university decided to act earlier and more forcefully than he had initially intended and moved expeditiously to confront the faculty member involved, who, in exchange for not being disciplined, voluntarily gave up his firearms licence, turned the firearms over to a firearms dealer, who would sell them on his behalf, and agreed to psychiatric assistance. I do know, from comments received from various university officials around the country, that the tragedy at Concordia, plus my report, did help raise the consciousness of the community to these types of risks and consequently made it easier to be proactive when risks began to mount.

Some years later, in the late 1990s, when I was VP at Queen's University in Kingston, Ontario, I recall that a law student used a hunting knife to pin a violent threat to the door of another student, and in that case the institution immediately involved the police, who provided a tactical team that entered the home of the perpetrator of the threat and removed a variety of legal weapons from his residence.

From incidents like this, even a sector like higher education, which is notorious for its tendency to temporize and delay action, has learned that, when in doubt, it is better to act. Better to be slightly embarrassed now than deeply sorry later.

All this taught me that it makes sense to enforce the laws you have, before trying to create even more elaborate versions of them.

As noted earlier, the second (and larger) part of the middle ground solution, in the Canadian context, is to use all reasonable means to stop the importation of illegal weapons and their distribution and use. On the one hand, we are fortunate that there is no Canadian manufacturing of small arms for the civilian market, so all small arms other than ones for military use are imported. But the truth is that we have a very long, very porous border with the United States, which is awash with guns. Hence, my suggestion in the article quoted earlier that curbing the spread of these illegal firearms largely requires setting conditions such that the risk of having illegal weapons outweighs any advantage or status they might confer. As I write this at the end of May, 2022, I note that the Government of Canada has just announced that it will introduce legislation that further limits handguns and that also increases the penalty for trading in or holding illegal weapons. These proposed measures seem logical, in light of the data that I cited in the piece above, written just over two years earlier.

If all that seems a somewhat palatable middle ground on this issue for the Canadian setting, the problem is vastly more difficult in the United States. But interestingly, the principal difficulty is not the very odd contemporary spin being given to their Second

Amendment on the right of states to have an armed reserve (militia) force (though that contemporary spin, which implies that the right belongs to individuals, is bad enough). It is that much of the world's gun manufacturing capacity is in the United States, so the supply there is essentially unlimited. As a result, there are some 410 million small arms in the hands of private citizens in the United States. Consequently, all that reasonable gun control legislation can achieve in that setting is to tackle the issue of the misuse of legally acquired firearms and prevent those who are already seen to be untrustworthy or unstable from acquiring them.

That is a decent step, but it cannot even begin to address the carnage caused by illegal guns. And, even with the best legislation possible, it could take a couple of generations to flush out and remove a large fraction of the illegal guns. Politicians normally cannot wait generations for validation of their decisions, which is why middle ground opinion in that country is now talking a fair bit about "culture change" as a gradualist strategy. Personally, I would find it hard to be an American searching for their middle ground on this issue. I am quite aware of the fact that my Canadian middle ground stance on this issue places me so far from the middle ground in the United States that I rarely feel that I can even discuss it there, unless my interlocutor has already signalled sympathy for vastly better control of firearms.

What this example tells us is that middle grounds are not necessarily the same everywhere. Fortunately, the variations in the location of the middle ground are not usually quite so extreme as in the example above. The gun control issue is a bit of an outlier. But the middle ground does vary from country to country and from society to society. It is important to recognize this and to notice when it occurs, because generations of catastrophic foreign policy mistakes have been made by assuming otherwise. Furthermore, just because the middle ground is different in one setting than in another does not mean that seeking the middle ground is unimportant. Finding and reinforcing the middle ground, even if it is one that does not apply to the whole planet, is often still important for social cohesion and civic peace. Of course, not all middle grounds are admirable. Earlier in this chapter I cited an example of a false middle ground. But there are also some genuine middle grounds that are distasteful or even immoral. They are largely found in societies that have not yet adapted to modern thought about human rights. But, for the most part, middle grounds are a damned sight better than the local extremes they compete against.

1.4 The Gentle Roasting of an Extremist

Most people, including many with fairly extreme views, are susceptible to middle ground arguments, provided that those arguments are well presented, fact-based, and respectful. But there are inevitably a handful of influential persons who are intentionally polarizing, often for personal advantage. That personal advantage may be power, or adulation, or wealth, or any combination thereof. For the most part, they are self-centred and care little about any adverse impact of their discourse on others, and, in some cases, their hatred of "the other" (whatever group that may be) is an additional motivator.

When such individuals rise to prominence, they can do significant harm to all attempts at coalescing opinion around the middle ground. But countering them is tricky. It is important not to do so in such a strident fashion that the supporters of that polarizing figure are immediately repelled, even if their support for that figure had been due to naiveté or a lack of exposure to the facts. Humour can be a useful vehicle, provided that it is not coarse.

One such intractable opponent of the middle ground is Donald J. Trump, former president of the United States.

Throughout 2016 I had never imagined that, if elected, he would not begin to moderate his bizarre utterances. But he did not, and within less than four months of his inauguration, it seemed to me that his stances and statements were so extraordinary and counterfactual that he would either have to soon become more truthful in his posture or be forced out. (And, indeed, the fact that he managed to complete his term without moderating his communications was remarkable.) I decided that the only contribution I could make to reinforcing centrist opinion in our neighbour to the south was through humour.

The opportunity to do so was aided by my recollection of a story told to me by Dr. Geza Hetenyi Jr., who had been my PhD supervisor at the University of Toronto and who remained my close friend for 30 years thereafter, until his death in 1999. It seemed that I could honour him by retelling his tale, with an updated twist, and take a gentle swipe at contemporary counterfactual nonsense at the same time. On May 21, 2017, I wrote it up as an article entitled "The Archduke Game." It appeared on May 23, 2017, in *Ottawa Life Magazine*.[7]

What I wrote was as follows:

The Archduke Game

My PhD supervisor was an elegant Hungarian who had grown up in the wreckage of the Austro-Hungarian Empire. He completed his advanced study by the late 1940s and fled Hungary during the revolution. Arriving in Canada in 1957, he joined the faculty at Toronto. He was a terrific mentor and a lifelong friend, and in his brilliant, mirthful and compassionate way taught me high science, low cunning, philosophy, humour, and lots of European culture. Amongst the salad of cultural tidbits that he had salvaged from the rubble of the Kingdom of Hungary was a cynical little game about oral examination boards and favoritism, played by graduate students. It was called "The Archduke Game."

In the game, a small group were the Examining Committee, while another graduate student played the Archduke. The Examining Committee was required to ask the Archduke an easy question, and task of the Archduke was to give the most outrageously wrong answer he could imagine. The Examiners were then required to explain to the audience and to the judges why that answer was actually correct, and even brilliant and especially perceptive, because it had exposed interesting alternate meanings of the question, or special circumstances, or little-know new knowledge. The judges then decided that either the Archduke had won, by making an answer nobody could polish, or that the Examiners had won by making a plausible argument for the peculiar answer.

A chilling variant of the Archduke game is now being played in earnest in the United States. The role of the Archduke is being played by President Trump, but the easy questions arise spontaneously from the normal daily events in the political milieu or are posed at press conferences. The explanatory task of the Examiners is being carried out by Sean Spicer, Paul Ryan, Kellyanne Conway, and a host of folk sympathetic to the President. The judges are variously the political classes, the electorate, and the world. No-one wants mayhem, so it is natural, sitting in front of a TV, to surmise that surely he meant something just slightly different, as we try, whether we agree with him or not, to impose a framework of rationality on the world about us.

And it is very likely that at least in some cases, he did mean something a bit different than how it came out. But the Archduke-style answers guarantee a lot of caprice and unpredictability.

So dialogue in some quarters, including within the President's camp, has turned to how to "manage" the President. To be fair, anyone carrying out the busiest job in the world probably needs some "management" to be effective.

But this time around the discussions about such managing have taken on disturbing tone, as Republicans discuss the difficulty/impossibility of giving the President bad news, or the likelihood of being fired if your advice or guidance doesn't match some pre-existing and not fully rational prejudice. Discourse on how to stop the tweets or make him less inclined to lash out sound less like how to manage an overloaded senior government figure and more like how to manage a performing, semi-tame carnivore.

Imagine, if you will, the discourse of the handlers on a movie set trying to get set up to film the scene where they want their fairly tame grizzly bear to break into the cabin, while making sure he doesn't eat the prospector inside. Walt Disney, where are you when we really need you?

Chuckle if you will, but the handling being discussed now sounds a lot like how to deal with a sentient creature for which you may have some sympathy, but which is clearly not a fully capable person. This is an unstable and dangerous state of affairs.

The Archduke game must end very soon, and there are only two routes from the game back to reality. Either the President must dramatically re-invent himself or he must go. His allies will be watching desperately for signs of the former in the next few weeks. If they don't see those signs, their thoughts will start to drift to the latter.

Was the Riyadh speech a start on re-invention or just a blip on the graph? Today only the Archduke knows, but soon the Examiners will know, and then the judges will judge.

I had mentioned above that I wrote this piece on May 21, 2017. That was the date that President Trump had made the speech in Riyadh, to which I referred in the concluding sentence of the article. It was a reasonable speech and the first such that I had heard him deliver. That is why I had wondered in my article if it was the beginning of a transition toward a more conventional style or just a blip. It turns out that it was, indeed, just a blip.

Clearly, my expectation that Mr. Trump's allies would turn on him for his persistent and rather loopy prevarication, even while he was president, was unfounded. In the end, they were more interested in the benefits he could confer on them than they were in the greater good. But now, in mid-2022, with his preferred candidates doing poorly in some Republican primaries, my hope is that there will be a gradual drift back toward a more measured discourse and that the recent custom, on both extremes, of using pejorative labelling against anyone daring to tread the middle ground will gradually fade.

But, back to the use of humour. It is, in my view, one of the most effective devices for making a bit of chiding or cajoling palatable. For adherents of the middle ground, it is an article of faith that success is defined by persuading a clear majority to compromise a bit and converge toward the centre. Well, it's hard to converge with someone when you are angry with them. But someone who made you laugh, well, it might be easier to try to see some merit in their point of view. In the following chapters of this book, I have felt the need to use the humour option quite often, especially when writing about some of the sillier aspects of the Covid-19 pandemic or about some of the odd posturing in the international arena. Similarly, some of the less felicitous consequences of the rapid pace of technological progress and some electoral politics are best seen through the humorist's lens. The use of a bit of humour does not mean that the subjects are inherently trivial. Quite the contrary. On complicated stuff, sometimes the only way to get people to let go of their customary mantras is to get them first to have a chuckle.

CHAPTER II

The Covid-19 Pandemic

THE COVID-19 PANDEMIC HAS been a defining event of recent years, altering economic models, accelerating progress in molecular biology and immunology, changing habits, social patterns, ways of working, and a whole host of personal preferences. It has also been a great tragedy, made worse by the (predictable) ineptness of various governments. And, as we inch, incrementally, toward the oft-touted "new normal" in this third year of the pandemic, one of the most troubling aspects of the voyage from early 2020 to the present has been the massive amount of polarization about things that ought to have been relatively straightforward and objective matters of fact.

On the other hand, in an odd way, the tragedy of the pandemic may have had a modest silver lining because it has largely banished cynicism and complacency about the possibility of pandemics in the modern world and put in place somewhat durable systems for reacting rather faster and better next time. If you wanted to imagine a suitably vivid warning for humankind to be ready to deal with pandemics, a novel disease that spreads easily but has a lethality, even in the absence of a vaccine, of less than 2 per cent (though much higher for some age groups) is a memorable wake-up call. But we could have done a lot better dealing with it.

Infectious disease experts had been warning us of risks for decades. While it will never be known if SARS-Cov-2, the virus that causes Covid-19, originally crossed into humans in the "wet market" in Wuhan, everyone knew that such markets selling untested wild animals for food were dangerous, but the will to stamp them out was lacking. Zoonoses were always viewed as the greatest infectious disease risk to humans. But even the scare of SARS in 2003 did not make for much steadfastness in preparation, as governments of developed states let their emergency stockpiles of personal protective equipment go out of date, and allowed the evolution of creaky and stretched supply chains, trying to eke out the last nickel of savings from the fragile doctrine of "just-in-time delivery." The problem was that we were almost too lucky with SARS, with well under 1,000 deaths worldwide. Of course, it is possible even to bungle the containment of a not-too-easily spread pathogen like the original SARS virus. The city of Toronto demonstrated that quite nicely, which is why about 5 per cent of all the people in the world who died anywhere from SARS in 2003 did so in Toronto. In 2003, the Toronto metropolitan area was home to only 0.08 per cent of the people on earth.

2.1 There Are Many Ways to Fail

In the first days of the Covid-19 pandemic, a variety of national governments did exactly what you would expect, given their respective characters. Dictatorships did public denial and obfuscation very well, while sometimes using their great control over their populations to some effect in controlling the spread, while the liberal democracies dithered and worried more about appearances and mild inconveniences than about fast reaction. In the developed world, the whole debate about imposing travel restrictions got mired in secondary issues of implied blame and the risk of restricting a variety of nonexistent travel "rights," while missing the importance of buying an extra month or two of a grace period in order to shorten the time between extensive disease spread and vaccine availability. Had we been more expeditious in slamming the door shut, considerably fewer lives would have been lost because the initial wave would have been delayed a while, and slightly blunted, while the vaccine development timeline would not have been altered.

By the beginning of May 2020, it seemed to me that, with both China and the United States bungling the early phases of the pandemic and covering their own errors by sniping at each other, it might be useful to write something about the very different routes by which each would eventually get to the other side of the new crisis. The piece was called "Two Nations, Two Systems, One Pattern." (The title was, of course, also intended, secondarily, to be a play on words that was a bit of a wry criticism of China's abrogation of its deal over Hong Kong, where the slogan of "One nation, two systems" was taking a terrible beating as China systematically eroded the Hong Kong system.) This first article of my series on Covid was published on May 12, 2020, in *Ottawa Life Magazine*.[8]

What I wrote was as follows:

Two Nations, Two Systems, One Pattern

To no-one's very great surprise the United States of America handled the first few stages of the Covid-19 pandemic badly. After a period of dithering, denial, and poor attention to expertise, the various levels of government began to act, but unevenly, with poor messaging, fulminating partisanship, and the disadvantage of a thoroughly decayed and resource-poor public health system. The delays have been costly in lives and treasure. But now the United States is picking up steam somewhat, testing more and doing somewhat more, though the lack of even-handedness continues to grate. Eventually, the Americans will solve this problem as they have every other, which is to say by dumping huge amounts of money, scientific talent and industrial power on the problem until it succumbs, which might indeed be a year or two from now.

In any major crisis, the United States is always late-to-task, and not very sure-footed at the outset, but succeeds in the end by bludgeoning the problem to death with overwhelming financial, industrial and intellectual might. This was true of two world wars and a variety of other significant challenges since it became a major power.

The reasons why it always does this are somewhat beyond the control of individuals, because they are rooted in the structure of American democracy. The structure is cumbersome and complex beyond belief. Newcomers to Washington take decades to learn where all the buttons are. And it is not accidental that it is so. The Founding Fathers wanted to create a system where it was nearly, but not quite impossible to get something done from the centre. This appealed to them, because most of them held to the view that they had just finished fighting a seven year long war against over-government, and in the slower-moving times of the 18th century, a structure where all the balanced parts might eventually agree on something was all they really needed at the centre. Most of the immediate decisions could be made at the periphery, ie in the state or local democratic institutions.

In modern times, when coordinated and speedy action has often been needed, even the most skilled presidents could only make the delicately balanced system work with a modest degree of urgency and coherence at the outset of any challenge. Even to do this, they needed to be able to persuade and coopt a wide range of legislators, office holders and other powerful players. They did so by building trust and commitment by engaging in vast numbers of one-on-one or small group meetings where they were eloquent and understanding, and could build bridges with their interlocutors. Many presidents have not been especially good at this juggling act. The current incumbent[9] shows little inclination and even less capacity to plow that particular furrow.

Structural reform in the US is nearly unthinkable, because its current structure and constitution have become a religion for secular times. But its good fortune is in the accomplishments of its people, institutions and corporations, which have equipped it to face almost any challenge once the needed way ahead becomes blindingly obvious. It lacks alacrity, but it has power.

China, on the other hand, is as far from a democracy as one could reasonably imagine. In the classic style of a dictatorship dressed in the clothes of a democracy, it holds pretend elections within a single party to use as a thin veil over a thugocracy which exercises exquisite control of every aspect of life of the people. In such systems it is often hugely dangerous to tell truth to power, especially if that truth is unpleasant, unwelcome, or threatening.

Little wonder that officials in Hubei province were reluctant to advise the centre of the early stages of the presence and spread of Covid-19. After all, denial was plausible for a while, and, following that phase, coverup for local mistakes is virtually a tradition. Eventually, but too late, the centre understood what was happening, and it is likely that the centre too had a period of denial, after which point it was too late to prevent the Covid-19 genie from getting out of the China bottle. This is how and why totalitarian structures like that in China are also almost always late-to-task in certain types of emergencies.

But it is often said that what makes us bad also makes us good, and a thugocracy is damned good at making its citizens do what it wants, so China instituted the mother of all lockdowns, accompanied by a maximum effort use of traditional public health techniques, including remarkably coercive ones, and it worked. Meanwhile, China, like the US, is a major scientific, industrial and financial powerhouse, and it too is now well engaged in the titanic struggle to bludgeon Covid-19 to death. Indeed, the race for treatments and vaccines is also a race for kudos and influence.

One could hardly imagine more different political systems or more different notions of personal liberty than in the United States of America and the Peoples Republic of China. But ironically, both systems share a pattern: the human tragedy and extra cost of always being late-to-task, and the eventual success that comes with the concerted exercise of vast intellectual, financial and industrial power.

The tale of guaranteed early bungling made inevitable by the dreadful flaws in both governing systems aside, the prognostication made in May of 2020 was reasonably accurate. As I write these words in the summer of 2022, it is true that a mighty effort has produced rather good vaccines (with better to come in due course) and a stunning leap forward in our abilities to respond quickly to future pathogens. And, in addition to the vaccines, some quite effective therapeutic drugs are becoming available.

What I did not anticipate was the extent to which hyper-nationalism would drive China (and its president) to eschew the most effective vaccines in favour of the dramatically less effective homegrown ones, which, even today, leaves China rather too vulnerable to a potential surge of the Omicron variant of Covid-19, which could do considerable harm because the two principal vaccines used in China do not slow it down much.

Nor did I fully anticipate how the actions of President Trump might end up so politicizing the science being used to counter the pandemic that, in the end, the United States was unable to effectively use the toolbox it had to fully counter the pandemic. That being said, the optimism of my prediction did turn out to be largely justified, just in a more chaotic and uneven fashion than I had expected. I had somehow expected the middle ground to hold better.

2.2 At First, Canada Was Unsteady

And, indeed, in some places the middle ground held quite well, but not without the occasional slip-up. As a Canadian, I naturally have a preoccupation with how the land of my birth handles challenges. And at the beginning of the pandemic, in Canada some of the behaviours of our leadership were not promising, mostly due to dithering and half-hearted action, but lots of other countries were doing no better.

What compounded the problem was the ineffectual nature of communication from Ottawa on key pandemic issues. The most frustrating aspect of early communication from the prime minister and his cabinet or from the public health officials of the federal government was the blindingly obvious political slant to all statements. This was counterproductive in ways the government had not anticipated. At a time when the public needed accurate, definitive, and scientifically credible advice, the official pronouncements were manipulative and sometimes obscure. Admittedly, the manipulation was obviously intended to be reassuring, but it very often contained guidance that was ambiguous at best and sometimes simply scientifically massively unlikely.

Having spent a generation as a professor (and later department chair) in a faculty of medicine, I was able to deconvolute the various official statements, but I would hear from many people how confusing the chop-and-change messaging was for those further removed from the biosciences.

Finally, in late May of 2020, I wrote a piece with the intention of encouraging the government to be more candid and less political when it came to public health issues. The title was "Telling Half-truths Never Ends Well." It appeared on May 29, 2020, in *Ottawa Life Magazine*.[10]

What I wrote was as follows:

Telling Half-Truths Never Ends Well

Canada's handling of the first phase of the Covid-19 pandemic, up to late May, has been moderately good compared to other developed nations. I would rate it at perhaps just at the lower edge of the top 20% in that comparison, if taking into consideration testing, public health practices and strictures, clinical adaptation, and speed and even-handedness of economic assistance. But there have been some things that ought to have been done, or done sooner or better, and these significant lacunae and failures have non-trivially exacerbated the harm done.

The reasons for these errors are sometimes obscure, but what is clear is that in virtually every case they were signalled by absurd official pronouncements. A wonderful mentor of mine, now sadly gone, had some marvelous aphorisms. One of them was especially apt for the way officialdom has handled this crisis. It was, "If someone doesn't want to do something, one reason is as good as another."

In Canada, with our fairly high customary standards of public probity, official pronouncements are rarely complete untruths. So, the favorite deflection technique, when officialdom wants to somewhat mislead, is to answer a question rather different from the one implicitly posed by those advocating some action that the government (for whatever reason) wishes to sidestep. Thus, a slightly related truth becomes a convenient half-truth that meets the "one reason is as good as another" test.

The first notable application of this technique to pandemic issues came in February, when various folk called upon the government of Canada to close off the entry of non-residents to Canada and to institute a fairly rigorous quarantine or self-quarantine system for citizens and permanent residents returning from abroad. Most of those advocating this step had no illusions that it would prevent eventual transmission of the disease here, but rather that it would reduce the initial seeding from known and unknown hot-spots and consequently reduce the size of the wave we'd have to deal with.

But the government really didn't want border closures and quarantines, for a variety of reasons including a desire to appear internationalist, and to sidestep any appearance of ethnic discrimination. So, the official pronouncement was that we would not impose these suggested constraints "because they would not prevent the disease from coming here in due course." The government response was a retort to a hypothesis no-one had advanced. It did not address the legitimate mitigation strategy of entry constraints.

Eventually, in mid-March, the government did adopt a softer version of the measures asked for in February, and that delay probably multiplied the phase one peak here by at least a factor of five, and put the infection numbers beyond the ability of traditional public health techniques to contact trace and isolate.

But this was not the only occasion on which government had to eat its words and do a U-turn. The lessons of SARS forgotten, the provinces and the feds had let their guard down on pandemic planning, and were short of lots of critical supplies. One supply of great interest to the public was masks, rated or otherwise. The shortage was exacerbated by the culture of disposability for convenience embraced by the health care field. (When I was a young medical researcher half a century ago, very little was disposable. Almost everything got sterilized and re-used.)

Governments urgently wanted to safeguard the limited supply of masks for clinical settings. But lots of folk, including any with a modicum of scientific education, were suddenly reflecting upon how masks could reduce (not eliminate) their chances of contracting Covid-19. The official pronouncement used to deflect this tendency was that "masks would not completely protect someone from catching the virus," and therefore should not be worn when going out in public. Again, answering a question no-one had asked. No one had expected complete protection. This statement was reinforced with the insulting addendum that the public, untrained in such use, would either do it wrong, or be emboldened to have close contacts they would otherwise avoid, vitiating any benefit. Apparently, the general public, many of whom have considerable scientific or technical training, are viewed as incapable, despite all the evidence that, with a modicum of instruction, they operate all manner of vehicles and computers, cook without poisoning themselves, use dangerous chemicals safely, etc.

Eventually, the governments did have to backtrack on the mask issue, though even today some officials claim that the mask you wear protects others, but not you. A simple porous filter as a one-way valve? I think not. Yes, containing droplets near their source is a good idea, but any filter is better than none, in either direction.

And there have been myriad other dubious pronouncements, ranging widely from weasel-worded comments on some of the scores of clinical trials underway to explaining how airports have (not) adapted. Again, in most instances the pronouncements bear the twin burden of intentional slight misdirection and condescending oversimplification.

All these half-truths were promulgated for "a good public purpose." But the problem is that taming a pandemic can only be accomplished with a huge amount of voluntary compliance by the public, once it is given direction. There can never be enough enforcement in a democratic society to compel the level of compliance needed, nor should there be. But a high degree of voluntary compliance will only be given by people who feel they can trust implicitly that they are being told the truth. The uttering of half-truths and condescending caveats, even for "a good public purpose" thoroughly undermines that trust. Prevaricating by halves and talking down to the people won't end well. Just tell the damned truth.

To be fair, expert opinion was initially genuinely divided on the travel restriction question, but those experts who fully understood that the challenge of the moment was the race between the spread of the pathogen and the rapid development of vaccines all pretty much agreed that shortening the time between the peak of the first wave and the availability of vaccines by even a few weeks would be valuable in saving quite a few lives. Some "experts" who should have known better, however, had initial doubts about whether a vaccine was even possible. I addressed that naiveté in a more predictive later piece.

As things progressed through the rest of 2020 and into 2021, the same pattern has persisted. On the whole, the actions of the governments of Canada and its provinces were reasonable, with effective economic crutches and somewhat too slow and incomplete public health measures, but overall, I would give them a solid "B." What never got much better was the tone-deaf communication. By way of example, the on-again/off-again endorsements and cautions from Ottawa about the Astra-Zeneca vaccine, with constantly shifting groups that could receive it, certainly cranked up vaccine hesitancy and was a godsend for the nuttier anti-vax elements. And the pattern of dodging hard questions by answering a slightly similar sounding but inherently different question persists. That's a valid technique of debate when lives are not at stake. But when they are, it is cowardly.

Fortunately, with one notable exception, ill-informed opposition to public health measures in Canada has been substantially milder than in the United States. It seems that most stereotypes have a tiny grain of truth in them. Mining the stereotypes, you'd guess that if you told a typical Canadian to go and stand in the corner, the usual response would be, "Oh, sorry to bother you with a question, but how long do you think I'll need to do that?" Tell an American stereotype to do the same, and what you'd likely hear would be, "No way! Who made you God?"

2.3 Some Lucky Guesses

By June of 2020, I noted that many of the people that I knew were not coping terribly well with the pandemic. It seemed to me that what most troubled many of them was the uncertainty of what was to come. I wondered if I could do anything useful for them and, incautiously, decided to try my hand at prediction.

Predicting the future is almost always a dumb idea. But the temptation was too great. If you think back to June 2020, vaccines against Covid-19 were merely a future hope, and therapeutic experiments were still disappointing.

But with time on my hands and a strong biosciences background, I was reading everything I could find, whether as peer-reviewed articles, pre-prints, of just press releases and news stories, and it felt to me like a picture was emerging. I tried to imagine where we would be by the summer of 2021, and the process of getting there. I didn't see the summer of 2021 as an abrupt end to the pandemic, but I did think it would be the end of many of the uncertainties, and that, thereafter, Covid-19 might be handled systematically like any other unpleasant pathogen, to be avoided (through immunization and behaviours) whenever possible and treated when unavoidable.

Toward the end of June, 2020, I took the bold step of writing a long, two-part piece on the year to come. On re-reading it now, I can only conclude that it was a once-in-a-lifetime gift from the gods to anyone foolish enough to try to predict the future. By some strange stroke of fortune, it almost reads like an after-the-fact account of that turbulent year from June 2020 to the summer of 2021. It was entitled "Covid-19: Reflections on the End Game," and it appeared on June 30, 2020, in *Ottawa Life Magazine*.[11] What I wrote was as follows:

Covid-19: Reflections on the End Game

Part 1: The Time before a Vaccine

Now half way through 2020, having spent a few months with the drawbridge raised, most of us are becoming deeply curious about how the Covid-19 crisis ends. There have been flocks of somewhat superficial articles about how the world will be different after, with oodles of speculation about telework and changes in real estate values and travel patterns. But the portrait of the next 12 months has not been very finely drawn.

The lockdown roller-coaster: Some jurisdictions have been better than others at using lockdowns to blunt the rise in Covid-19 cases. The most effective have even reduced the numbers of active cases to such a low level that traditional public health techniques of identification and contact tracing can actually control the spread of infection. The less competent ones have merely converted what would have been an exponential rise in active cases into a linear one. In between these lie the majority of jurisdictions, which have produced a near steady state of a largish number of active cases, too many to use classical methods to finish off the job, but few enough to be tempted to stick their heads above the parapet again.

Some will over-do the relaxation of restrictions. The public needs to know that the easing up doesn't mean its over. It only means that there's room for you in the ICU. The titration of the opening up, both in timing and extent, has been better handled in some jurisdictions than others. We watch some parts of our southern neighbour in horror as ideology rather than science drives the speed, the extent, and the style of the re-opening. The roughly two-month lag between the return of incautious behaviour and very high death rates makes informed leadership even more critical.

Errors in failing to impose restrictions early enough, hard enough and long enough to restore the ability to use contact tracing and testing for the few remaining flare-ups arose in part from a facile but false early assumption that the restrictions were, in effect a balancing act between the risks to health and life on the one hand and doing economic harm on the other. This notion of a balancing act has been a mainstay of media coverage of the crisis, but it is unlikely to be true. It was based upon early, oversimplified short-term modeling. Such simplified modelling fails to cover the economic effects during the entire period till a vaccine becomes available, including repeated secondary lockdowns if the primary one was inadequate or interrupted too soon. It also fails to consider the long-term economic impact of impaired future health among many and the economic losses associated with myriad premature deaths. Furthermore, it neglects to take note of the cost of waiting too long before locking down, and further neglects losses during any extended recovery which follows the roller-coaster ride of repeated lockdowns. When more elaborate modelling methods are used that include these missing elements, the results tend to support the view that earlier and tougher measures reduce *both* the disease burden *and* the total economic cost.

It seems that we may now be in for a series of peaks and valleys where restrictions need to be re-imposed from time to time. But by now, at least in Canada, the public knows the drill, and each re-imposition is likely to be effective more quickly than the first time, and therefore not last as long. Improved widespread readily available testing for the virus and for antibodies will also help to get new outbreaks under control faster and with less damage.

The media have been unhelpful in another respect, because of their love affair with the term "second wave." Their incessant speculation about whether or not there will be a "second wave" has been an enabler for the "let's re-open fully" lobby. News flash: This is all still first wave, and will be for a long time. The first wave may have had the Monty Python foot dropped on it, but the modified first wave is still here.

The key to all management of Covid-19 in the period before there is a profound revolution in therapeutics or a vaccine for it is in managing the tricky little parameter called Ro.

The tweaking of Ro: Ro is the symbol for the rate at which Covid-19 infections multiply. It is not an inherent parameter of the virus, but rather a reflection of the interaction of the virus with the totality of behaviours of a given society. For our society as it was last January, various epidemiologists have estimated Ro to be 3.0–3.4, meaning that each case at that time gave rise on average to 3.0–3.4 new cases. But our moderate lockdown changed those dynamics, and seemed to drop Ro to about 0.6–0.8. This is important, as any sustained Ro below one will eventually see the disease die out, while any sustained Ro above one will see it rise. The amount above or below 1.0 determines the slope of the rise or fall of active case numbers.

The key to successful partial re-openings is to allow enough return to normalcy to allow people some freedom to get on with life without allowing Ro to exceed 1.0. This is a tricky calibration, and many jurisdictions will overshoot the 1.0, forcing new restrictions for a while. Nonetheless, a few factors are encouraging.

First of all, on average, behaviours are now more cautious than they were before the crisis. Yes, there are a non-trivial number of fools, knaves and simpletons, but most folk have developed some new infection avoidance reflexes that even if we did open up fully, which we won't, the new Ro would likely be closer to 2.0 than to 3.0. That implies that a partial opening has a real chance of keeping Ro below 1.0 most of the time.

Another small factor in our favour is that, for a time at least, a handful of our neighbours may be immune. As I write this, less than a third of one percent of Canadians have tested positive for Covid-19, but few scientists believe that everyone who has been infected has been tested, given that some of those infected may experience either no symptoms or minor ones easily rationalized as something else. So, it may well be that one or two percent of Canadians now represent a minor bulwark against the disease, in that, at least for now, they can't get it or spread it. This is very far from any "herd immunity" concept, but it does tweak the effective Ro slightly downwards.

Progress in therapeutics for Covid-19: There is a vast array of work underway to identify and verify treatments for Covid-19. There have been a few successes amongst the horde of trials, experiments, and revisions of care practices.

A major thrust has been to identify likely candidates among existing drugs, and to try to ameliorate Covid-19 with this "off-book" use of them. While anecdotal small-scale studies hinted at many possibilities, so far there is only a degree of certainty about a few:

(a) Remdesivir, an anti-viral drug which is a nucleotide analog type antiviral, has been shown to shorten the course of the disease. It is still in short supply, is given intravenously over either 5 or 10 days, and is therefore given in hospital, so far only to quite ill patients. However, considering its mode of action, one would expect it to be even more useful if it could be given somewhat earlier in the course of the disease. I could imagine eventual outpatient administration of this drug.

(b) Dexamethasone, a glucocorticoid, is an anti-inflammatory, which, when given to the sickest patients (those being ventilated), appears to prevent about a third of the deaths. For patients receiving supplemental oxygen, but not on a ventilator, loss of life is reduced by about a fifth. This drug can only be used late in the course of the disease, at the point where the major risk is overreaction of one's own immune system, but when the original virus has already mostly cleared. If given too early, it would likely worsen the disease by enabling easier reproduction of the virus.

(c) In the most severely ill patients with Covid-19, the disease seems to trigger dangerous blood clots in many parts of the body. Anti-coagulants such as heparin are now being used to prevent the formation of these blood clots. How much of the mortality and morbidity of Covid-19 is due to this clotting is not yet entirely clear.

Another major thrust is the race to make brand new drugs to counter the virus. Amongst the most promising lines of work are the attempts to identify, test and mass-produce antibodies that could be injected into a patient to counter the virus until the patient's own defences become fully engaged. One would not expect to see significant availability of such newly tailored antibodies until at least a few months from now.

And some gains are being made, boringly enough, by simply improving care. By way of example, less damaging ways of using ventilators show promise, as does a greater reliance on other, less drastic ways to improve oxygenation.

Dozens of clinical trials are due to be completed between now and October. They will likely produce some incremental improvements in treatment. But early progress reports from many of them do not hint at any spectacularly effective treatments.

Therapeutic improvements are a critical part of the struggle against Covid-19, but, in the period from now to the availability of a vaccine, they are unlikely to reduce the risk from this disease to the more familiar levels of seasonal influenza. Bear in mind that up to this point Covid-19 has been considerably easier to catch than the flu and possibly as much as twenty or thirty times as lethal for those that do get it. Therapeutics will help considerably, but a vaccine is the gold standard.

Part 2: Vaccines and beyond

Why a vaccine is a near-certainty: It has become commonplace for the media to interview medically-trained folk who intone things like, "There is no certainty that a vaccine can be made. After all, there have been no vaccines against other human coronaviruses." Such a statement underscores the narrowness of their thought processes, and is almost certainly misleading.

Before SARS-CoV-2, the virus that causes Covid-19, there were only six known human coronaviruses. Four of these cause cold-like symptoms, and may be responsible for about a quarter of the minor illnesses we call colds. The other three quarters of colds are caused by rhinoviruses. Just imagine a researcher approaching a drug company and saying "Please invest hundreds of millions of dollars in development and validation of our proto-vaccine which can prevent up to 25% of colds." You can guess the outcome. There is zero market for a vaccine which will prevent only a small fraction of a minor annoyance.

The other two previously known human coronaviruses are SARS and MERS. Outstanding work was done on candidate vaccines for both, but when it came time to move to Phase 2 trials, both diseases had been controlled. No phase 2 trial can possibly be done when you know in advance that the placebo will be just as effective as the vaccine in preventing the disease, because no-one is getting the disease anyhow. The work was recorded and shelved.

The brilliant work on those vaccines in fact became the foundation for the rapid work today on some of the candidate vaccines against Covid-19.

The role of economics and demand in vaccine creation, including vaccines for coronaviruses, can be seen most clearly if we look at the animal world. We know of over 30 animal coronaviruses, and there are eight of them for which vaccines are commercially available right now. The ones available now include vaccines for cats, dogs, pigs (2 different coronaviruses), cattle, chickens and turkeys. Unsurprisingly, there are as yet no vaccines for the coronaviruses that infect Asian leopard cats, antelopes, giraffes, bats, rats, mice, belugas and pangolins. Thus, the obvious becomes clear. The existing vaccines for coronaviruses are the ones for which there was a real market, justifying their development.

A case could be made that the SARS-CoV-2 coronavirus may be somewhat more of a problem, as it is a beta-coronavirus, and all but three of the vaccines noted above are for alpha-coronaviruses. It is worth noting however, that the bovine coronavirus is a beta-coronavirus, and yet there is an available vaccine against it, since cattle are an economically important species. (The two avian coronavirus vaccines I mentioned are against gamma-coronaviruses).

I taught medical students for more than 15 years. I have enormous respect for their dedication and hard work. But many of them were so focussed on the great mass of material they needed to absorb that they had little time for learning about other fields. So, when they later appear clueless about animal diseases and vaccines, or about economics, or many other fields of human endeavor, have some sympathy for what they missed between the ages of 21 and 27. But it does often make them less than perfect seers when it comes to some broad-spectrum human endeavor.

The expedited vaccine approval process: There has been concern expressed by some that vaccine approvals are being rushed, and that safety may be compromised as a result. These comments give succor to the conspiracy theorists and to the anti-vaccine movement (there is an overlap between them). In fact, quite the opposite is true. It is enormously likely that any vaccine produced for widespread use against Covid-19 will be one of the safest medications ever produced.

The vaccine approval process has been in sore need of an overhaul and some streamlining for at least 15 years, because it is an artifact of a time before many of the stunning developments of the past generation in molecular medicine.

Vaccine development traditionally was part science and part art, a bit like making beer. But today, with rapid sequencing of genetic materials, the ability to build biologically active materials from scratch, instead of growing them, and the ability to accurately assay minute amounts of biological substances, the vaccine building and testing process is considerably altered. Rather than working with the pathogenic virus, killed or weakened, most vaccines are now made either by placing a suitable sequence from the pathogen into a known harmless adenovirus, or by going the all-synthetic route by making a synthetic mRNA related to one tiny part of the pathogenic virus against which ones wishes to raise an immune response.

Many of these modern vaccine platforms are already so well known in terms of their effects on humans that animal trials can be truncated or skipped entirely. Furthermore, the phase 1 human trials, which are to demonstrate safety, rather than effectiveness, can also be used to collect precise data of the raising of appropriate antibodies in vivo, and thus can be logically added to phase 2 data. Similar eliding of phase 2 and 3 data is equally logical, given what can now be measured.

So the current move to streamline the vaccine approval processes in a number of developed nations is a triumph of logic over bureaucracy. A small bit of good fallout from a nasty crisis.

How good does a vaccine need to be? A vaccine against Covid-19 does not need to be an especially good one to defeat the pandemic. It just needs to be good enough to push the effective Ro (remember that term from Part 1) of the disease to anything less than 1.0. Given a modicum of good sense on the part of the population, a vaccine that protects anything over half the population would likely see the disease die out in a season. It is also likely that those in whom the vaccine did not entirely prevent infection would experience a much milder form of the disease than they would have otherwise.

It is also likely that more than one vaccine for Covid-19 will come to market in the next year or so. Given that there are over a hundred candidate vaccines, and that some 15 are moving along quite expeditiously, multiple approved vaccines may be inevitable. This is not a bad thing, in that different vaccines can block the infective process in slightly different ways. The first vaccine may not be the most effective, but that should not cause people to wait for a better one. I usually explain this to folk in my age group by pointing out that even if they had the Zostavax vaccine for shingles (moderately effective), their doctors will still encourage them to get the now available two-shot Shingrix vaccine (very effective). One does not preclude the other.

It will go badly for the anti-vaccine lobby: The anti-vaccine movement has been enabled by social media. No surprise there, in that countless loopy fads have been so enabled. But up till now, its adherents have had a free ride, because objecting to established vaccines for long-present illnesses enabled them to hide behind the immunized majority. As vaccines for Covid-19 come on line, they will argue before the courts that they have the right to refuse inoculation, in the same way that they have the right to decline any medical treatment. And in this they will succeed.

The big disappointment will come when they find that a bunch of other things that they thought were rights are not seen by the law as rights, but as qualified privileges. Thus, they may find that they cannot be accorded the privilege of working in a job that involves meeting the public. They may find that their children will need to be home-schooled. In highly litigious jurisdictions, like the US, they may experience civil liability for those they infect. But on the whole, it will be crucial to message precisely, accurately and compassionately in order to extend acceptance of the vaccines and to minimize the harm that such poorly informed folk will do to themselves and others.

What are the possible spin-offs from all this work on vaccines? There will be as yet unimagined future developments that will have had their genesis in the flood of science being done because of Covid-19, but one can certainly guess at three.

First, the new-found techniques for fast vaccine production will likely mean that the lowly annual flu shot will get better. At this point the guess as to which influenza strains to immunize against is made so far in advance that it's often a poor guess. Going forward, that guess will only need to be made much closer to when the vaccine is needed than it is now, with the lag between the guess and the delivery being reduced by a half to two-thirds. That will make it a better guess. It's like looking at a weather forecast. Are you more likely to believe the forecast for two days from now than you are for a week from now? You bet you are.

Secondly, generic vaccine platforms will have been developed that can quickly be adapted for use against new threats. With some investment, this could be the last pandemic, as we could see the lag times from identification of a pathogen to a vaccine shortened so much that the new pathogen never gets a real foothold.

Thirdly, it opens the door to using the new technologies for vaccinating against a number of common cancers, a notion that was already gaining traction in some scientific circles.

The shock waves from Covid-19 are far from over. The voyage to summer 2021 will be awkward and complicated. But when we get there, it will be worth tallying not only what we've lost, but also what we've learned and what we've gained.

A friend of mine from Newfoundland has a wry comment that he frequently deploys when someone has an unlikely win. And any successful prognostication during a pandemic is probably an unlikely win. The comment is, "Even a blind squirrel finds the occasional nut." Truthfully, I was darned lucky with that piece, but it did what I wanted it to do, which was to persuade those who read it that systematic, orderly solutions to the crisis would, over time, become available. Now, two years after it was written, I can see that the extrapolations I made were entirely reasonable.

Of course, there have been other advances that were a mere glimmer on the horizon in June of 2020. The Pfizer therapeutic combination called Paxlovid is clearly a significant step forward in the prevention of hospitalization and death. I also have considerable optimism about the gradual appearance of better vaccines, including, in due course, multivalent vaccines and possibly a pan-coronavirus vaccine. Indeed, some candidate pan-coronavirus vaccines are in testing now.

But the article did what I wanted, which was to calm down those who read it and get them to converge on a common understanding of the way ahead. In that sense, it was a defence of the middle ground. The feedback that I got was that it was very useful and answered many troubling questions for some people.

The task of proselytizing for the middle ground, as it applies to the pandemic, however, has turned out to be a good deal easier in Canada than in our neighbour to the south. It may have been inevitable, given the uneven approach to health care and education about health care in the United States, that consensus would not evolve and hold on any of the following: vaccination, therapeutics, or public safety measures imposed based upon public health findings. But that the complete opposite of consensus has arisen—indeed, a divergence so profound that it has become a civil war fought with invective rather than guns—is due largely to former POTUS Donald Trump and those of his ilk, who have found an effective route to power by vigorously purveying stances that they know are counterfactual in order to gain and hold influence. But more on that later.

As a Canadian, my first concern was that there was a natural spillover of some of the same nonsense into Canada. Canadians are steeped in US culture and news via television and the internet. Conspiracy theories, counterfactual pseudo-scientific babble, and bizarre legal concepts may not have had the same uptake in Canada as in the United States, but their penetration in Canada is not zero.

As of the date when I write this, in June 2022, more than 82 per cent of Canadians are fully vaccinated, versus less than 67 per cent of Americans, and Canada has administered 225.7 doses of Covid vaccines per 100 people, while the United States has administered 178.4 doses per 100 people. Since, as of this writing, only about 95 per cent of the population of each country was old enough to be vaccinated (5 years or older), these differences tell us that loopy ideas of resisting public health measures are found in Canada but only about one-third as frequently as in the United States. How could I cajole some of my fellow citizens to make rational choices and to trust real expertise?

2.4 It's Easier If You Make Them Laugh

As I noted in Section 1.4, advice that someone doesn't really want to hear is sometimes better received if you can make the recipient laugh a bit. But criticizing someone's views can easily be heard as ridicule. How, then, to make someone see humour in an argument directed against their current view and make them more receptive to revising their stance? For me, the thing that always does it is doggerel. (I should note that I hold to a rather rigid notion of doggerel; to me, it almost always has to be rhyming couplets in iambic tetrameter. And it cannot be nonsense rhymes but must tell a story of some sort).

So, on June 27, 2021, I wrote some doggerel, aimed squarely at the substantial group of people who were reluctant to get vaccinated, for a whole raft of somewhat odd reasons. The piece was partly inspired by W. H. Auden's poem, "Under Which Lyre," published in 1946. I entitled it "Covidiots, and Their Cure." It first appeared on July 2, 2021, in *Ottawa Life Magazine*[12] and later appeared in an anthology, which is still in print.[1] What I wrote was as follows:

Covidiots, and Their Cure

Ideas make the world go 'round,
But some ideas are not sound.

In days of yore it was hard work
To spread falsehoods to every jerk
Who can't tell shit from carrot cake
And cannot tell when something's fake.

It's gotten simpler recently,
As access to the web is free,
So anyone can trumpet views
That they disguise as real news.

Fact-checking is a fading art,
Because, to check, before you start,
You need to know a bit about
The subject of the "fact" in doubt.

And getting facts from social media
Is vastly worse than Wikipedia;
Even that needs constant checking
To counter vandals' tries at wrecking.

Thus, it comes as no surprise
That lots of folk are not that wise.
One cause is fads in education
That have paralyzed the nation.

Higher ed has moved its goal
Towards a mass job-training role;
"How to think" takes a back seat
To "How to get to easy street."

Pushing training over thought
Is a decision very fraught

With consequences for good choices,
Drowned out by chaotic voices.

Nor have the twelve years from grade one
Fared better, with the things they've done;
Schools today have put their focus
On a very different locus -
The pace of learning counts for less;
The main concern's avoiding stress.

Learning stuff has been subsumed,
And teachers' thoughts are now consumed
By fears of recognizing merit,
Figuring that folks won't wear it,
If their dummy kid can't get
A prize as big as any, yet
He still can't spell or count or think;
We'll let him pass—just give a wink,
Because to slow him might cause harm
To self-esteem, that glorious charm
That dominates preoccupations
Of touchy-feely delegations.

They don't care what kids don't know
As long as they can feel the glow
Of fulsome praise for feeble tries -
Who cares if they can't analyze?

Then into this maelstrom of fluff
A challenge comes that's rather tough:
A nasty virus that can spread
From droplets coming from the head

Of anyone, who having caught
The virus, then still breathes a lot.

But, unlike plagues of bygone days,
We've had good luck in many ways,
With science marching to our aid
In record time, because we've made
Such great advances recently
In cellular biology.

The miracle of the vaccines
To push aside those awful scenes
Of hospitals in parking lots,
And mobile morgues in many spots,
Has certainly persuaded most
To get the shots, and they do boast
That they have done just what they must
To crush the plague into the dust.

But there are others who adhere
To nutty views or awful fear
Of plots bizarre, of tracking chips,
Or rumours, myths and backroom tips
That vaccines make your hair fall out,
Or make you thin, or make you stout.
Among them there are quite a few
Who hold onto the wacky view
That the pandemic is a hoax
Designed to scare us, by some folks
Who want control of all our wealth,
And plan to get it, using stealth.

It is a shame that these damned fools
Now flaunt those customary rules
That used to guide us when in doubt
On things we don't know much about.

That older system worked much better:
Run your questions through a vetter
Who has real expertise,
And will not lie, or try to please
Some fat dyslexic idiot
Who would be king, but knows he's not.

The real experts test their view,
Subjecting it to peer review,
'Cause science is a funny beast -
It doesn't matter in the least
How loud you shout a false conclusion;
In the end, you'll still be losin',
Because others check on you
With fancy tools that let them view
The real data, not polemic,
On how to halt the epidemic.

Anti-vaxxers need to know
That actors shouldn't steal the show;
No special insight can they claim
By having entertainment fame.

They know about a camera angle,
Or a big, outrageous bangle,
But don't take medical advice

From vapid folk who won't think twice
About the costs the fans may bear,
Because the actors do not care.
They'll ham up any sort of lie,
So they stay in the public eye.

There are some nervous nellies, too,
Who want to wait till me and you
Have had our vaccines for a year
And haven't grown an extra ear.

They think their risk of a vaccine
Outweighs the benefits we've seen;
Innumerate as they may be,
We need to help them learn to see
That risk from vaccination pales
When Covid and its long-term tails
Are tallied up for their true cost
Of years of happy living lost.

Plus, doubters need to realize
The place where real duty lies;
Protect yourself *and* others too -
Your duty isn't just to you.

Of course, there are a few who see
An issue about liberty
In their refusal to pitch in,
Because they're certain it's a sin
To try to pressure all of us
To get the shot and make no fuss.

They're half-right, in one simple way,
As courts already had their say:
One can refuse a medication;
That is true across the nation.
But then comes the big surprise:
There is no right, in the court's eyes,
To hold a job or go to school,
If you decide to shun a rule
Made properly, about a fix
That may be needed if you mix
With folks together and indoors,
So that disease transmission soars.

Indeed, we may need to replace
Those ant-vaxxers, who can't face
The public, with some certainty
That they'll not give the pox to thee.

No jab, no job! Oh, what to do?
They'll have to think the matter through,
And at that point, most will record
A change of heart, and come on board.
No crazy US situation
Is likely to afflict our nation:
I think that most of them will come
To see the shot as not so rum.

Of course, those already vaccinated found it chuckle-worthy indeed, but what surprised me was how it opened the door to reasonable discussion with a number of acquaintances who had heretofore not been vaccinated. A number of them subsequently did get vaccinated. Gentle teasing evidently works better than shouting at someone. It's not the answer; it just gets the process of reasoned discussion started.

But that method of persuasion doesn't work for everyone. Why might that be? Because humour only works on those who, while perhaps not yet fully admitting it to themselves, have already largely figured out that they need to make a modest change of course. For the others, it's more complicated.

2.5 Why Have So Many Been Silly?

Well before the so-called Truckers Convoy movement blockaded Ottawa and some border crossings, it had become clear that some odd conspiracy theories, mixed with some junk science, had captured the imagination of some Canadians, though a far smaller fraction of the population than in the United States. In Section 2.2, I used vaccination rates as a surrogate indicator to estimate the comparative ratios of the population that had bought into such foolishness. But the fact that the ratio was perhaps 1/3 that of our southern neighbour was only soothing to a degree.

That is still a large number of people, and only a small minority of them fit the stereotype that the rest of us imagined for them. Yes, there are a few who could best be described as "wacky" or worse, but most of them are people who seem entirely conventional in most other aspects of their lives. The temptation to demonize them is strong, especially since their actions risk the health and lives of others. But, for the committed centrist, sometimes it is worthwhile to reflect a while upon the dichotomy between what such people say and what they actually mean (even if, in some cases, they have not yet understood what they mean).

As a long-time labour relations negotiator and mediator, I did get used to trying to "listen between the lines," because what really bothers people is sometimes a bit different from what they are prepared to say is bothering them. When I taught labour relations to university deans and VPs, I made up a few vivid aphorisms to help them understand the interactions at the bargaining table, and I called them "Cowan's Laws." One of my laws related to the appearance at the bargaining table of very odd, seemingly quirky, demands from either side. I quote it here:

> *Cowan's Law of Weird Bargaining Proposals*: **Unsuccessful grievances reappear later at the bargaining table as weird union proposals; successful grievances reappear later at the bargaining table as weird employer proposals.**

The little truth behind that "law" is that bizarre stances often emanate from some unspoken stress that is not necessarily obvious from observing the bizarre stance itself. It caused me to ponder the real drivers behind the resistance to reasonable public health measures. In early November 2021, I wrote a piece entitled "Unspoken Causes of Vaccine Avoidance and Public Health Noncompliance," and it was published on November 12, 2021, in *Ottawa Life Magazine*.[13]

What I wrote was as follows:

Unspoken Causes of Vaccine Avoidance and Public Health Noncompliance

In Canada we are fortunate, in that a vast majority of our population take public health rules and guidance very much to heart. Most of us have availed ourselves of the offered vaccines, and most make a pretty decent effort to comply with distancing, masking rules, and gathering sizes.

Nonetheless, public health experts and other knowledgeable folk remain puzzled by what makes some of the public so very fearful of the vaccines or, in some cases, avid consumers of conspiracy theories, snake oil cures, or extreme views of their "rights" to harm others. It has become standard to blame such nuttiness on poor public education in the sciences, or the leverage which social media provides to charlatans, loopy propagandists and mischief makers, both local and international.

But that isn't the whole story. Indeed, a more scientifically literate public which placed greater reliance on tested and trusted portals when surfing the net would be a good thing, but a bit of reflection reveals that there are some other causes too. To understand these unspoken causes, we need to start by stepping back in time a bit.

I grew up in the aftermath of the Second World War, and finished secondary school in 1960. All the adults around me when I was growing up had lived, worked and fought through the dangerous and stressful six years of that war, and they all had a well-honed ability to assess risk. They understood that everything in life has some risk, and were, for the most part, extremely well practiced at looking at every choice, every fork in the road, and assessing which choice had the greater risk, and which had the smaller risk. The sane ones routinely selected the choice with the smaller risk.

And then a strange thing happened. I saw it happen, because, even as a child, I had an unquenchable interest in science, which is what led me to become a medical researcher for the first couple of decades of my working life. Science in the period of my youth was moving fast; every year it became possible to measure smaller and smaller amounts of just about anything. And it was this new-found ability to measure concentrations of elements, molecules and compounds that were so small as to be negligible (a few parts per million or even billion) that gave rise, in the minds of non-scientific but vocal advocates, to the idea of "zero risk." It started with efforts to expunge "all" contaminants in food (though quality control folk know perfectly well that there is still a specification for how much rodent hair or feces is allowed in flour).

There is, of course, no true "zero risk," nor is avoidance of all risk a guarantee of long life, or even a happy one. But the zero risk movement captured the imagination of much of the public, who quite properly figured that we could do better than in the past. Once the "zero risk" movement picked up enough steam, however, it led to movements to stop fluoridating municipal water supplies, to ban GMO foods (despite the fact that we have been genetically modifying crops for 10,000 years), and ultimately led to helicopter parenting. I recall in the 1970s, during the most active part of my aviation career, that some campaigners started talking about "zero risk" aviation. I would gently point out to such folk that zero risk in aviation was easy. All you had to do was bolt the aircraft to the tarmac, and then forbid anyone from walking under the wings, because there was an infinitesimal but non-zero chance that the wing would, at that moment, fall off and crush them.

Now, two generations later, there have been unquestionable benefits from the zero risk movement, including much safer cars and remarkably good food safety. But there has been a downside as well. A substantial minority of the population can no longer make a comparative risk assessment. The mere mention of any risk produces a stasis rather akin to a rabbit caught in the headlights of a car. They just cannot cope with the idea that they must voluntarily assume some risks, and that, in doing so, they can likely avoid greater risks. Thus, the litany of worries about vaccine side effects that spew from such folk, with no attempt to balance that risk, against the vastly greater risk of Covid. And that's without getting into the discussion that is yet to come about the possible shortening of the lifespans of those who have had Covid and recovered, because we all know that, for example, all lung scarring is correlated to shorter life spans (not always, but certainly on average), when compared to similar folks with no lung scarring.

We have, as a people, partly lost the ability to parse risk. We've had it so good for so long that some of us fail to recognize or quantify a serious and immediate risk when it marches onto the stage.

An old friend of mine, the late Dr. Bill Delaney, had a favorite expression, which for years I have been citing as "Delaney's Law." The expression is, "If somebody doesn't want to do something, one reason is as good as another." At its heart, it means that the reasons a person gives for not doing a thing may bear no relationship whatsoever to the underlying source of the reluctance. And that is where the zero risk movement melds with an even more potent force, which I call the "fallacious freedom" movement.

It seems that the favorite narrative these days for many of those who do not wish to adhere to social distancing dicta and size limits for gatherings, who resist mask wearing when recommended or required, and who eschew vaccination for Covid and decry vaccine mandates, is that such public health measures are an attack upon their freedom. Some are so vehement on this score that their discourse and related public demonstrations verge on revolution, or at least sustained public disorder. Appeals to them about their duty to protect others seem to enrage them even further.

But logically, the stance that the cited public health measures are a substantial curtailment of some pre-existing freedom doesn't hold up to serious scrutiny. All those "freedom" advocates grew up surrounded by entirely accepted limitations that they never took as infringement on their freedoms, even though those accepted restrictions were and are greater than the new ones. Those entirely accepted restrictions included vaccinations of various sorts for school attendance and for practicing various professions and trades, gathering size limits for safety, whether on a boat, in an elevator, or in a restaurant or pub, and explicit clothing restrictions. They willingly obey the "No shirt, no shoes, no service" notices on restaurant doors. And as youngsters, they were surely told by their mothers that, "You can't run out into the street without your pants! Get back in here!"

If they are so keen on resisting constraints on "freedom," why focus on the public health based constraints? Why not take on some of the older constraints? May I suggest to such folks that they try to exercise their "freedom" by slipping out to the supermarket with no clothing on between the waist and the ankles and see how that works out for them?

But you and I both know they won't do that. Deep down, their talk about freedom is really about change. They can not cope with change. The new constraints alarm them, not because they are significant, but exactly because they are new.

Yes, there is a non-trivial subset of society that cannot cope with change, even minor change. We have lived through such a good period that these folk never experienced a major war, a major famine, a major pandemic or deep privation. They have become so wussy that any sudden change from what they know scares them shitless. That is why they sound so strident. That's what scared people sound like.

They are so scared, in fact, that any appeal to them for compliance with public health measures based upon their duty to protect others is guaranteed to fail. They can't think of others just now, because they are terrified about themselves and that their lives are changing.

Further evidence that fear is driving that particular train is what happens when the occasional vocal vaccine critic does get pressured into getting vaccinated in order to keep a job or go on a desired trip. Do they continue afterwards stridently campaigning against such measures? No, they don't. For the most part, they just leave the debate. They got vaccinated. They didn't die. They didn't grow an extra ear. End of story.

And, for those who remain attracted to the "fallacious freedom" movement, in their terror, they act in ways that are inimical to their own self-interest. Watching them, we are, of course, tempted to wonder how so many of our compatriots got so soft, so stupid, and so lacking in their duty of care for others. That is a valid and interesting question, but also an unworthy thought. We should also reflect on how to help them get out of their funk. Anyone who has had children knows a lot about how best to steer them out of a hissy fit and back under the guidance of their better angels. Most of those tricks work just as well on frightened adults.

After all, they are not without some coping mechanisms. They can usually cope with very gradual change. For example, many have made the leap from flip phones to smart phones. Some read their newspapers on line. They have adjusted to our see-through plastic banknotes.

Most of them will eventually learn to live with most of the needed public health measures, but not immediately. The process will be slow, and we can help by celebrating the gradual normalization and institutionalization of those changes that must, of necessity, become permanent. And in due course, we can hope that, psychologically, they may be better equipped to handle the next pandemic, if not this one.

But for the moment, they are in a wilderness. They are on the wrong side of history, and not coping well with that fact.

If we don't over-react to their fervor and their extremist rhetoric, many of them will eventually adapt. Or at least, their children will. Sometimes I take the long view.

The last quip notwithstanding, I genuinely believe that most people can be persuaded to adapt. But the persuasion must be both respectful and replete with actual facts. It must come from many sources and will always be better received if the political class does not make a meal of small variations in the tale. After all, there is a gradual accretion of knowledge, so the best advice changes somewhat with time.

As the Covid-19 pandemic edges into a gradual new status as an endemic, managed disease, a look back reminds the developed world that it has so far neither failed nor excelled in the handling of the crisis. It has muddled through. That's not the "middle ground" one hopes for in such a crisis. The scientists mostly did a pretty commendable job. They get an A minus. The Government of Canada gets a B minus, mostly for effective, if delayed, vaccine purchasing and some useful economic bridging programs. On most other fronts, it didn't do that well.

The US situation is well known to all. At the outset of the pandemic, the Trump administration did well with pushing vaccine development but completely failed in every conceivable aspect of public communication or consensus building. The follow-on Biden administration inherited the end stage of that dumpster fire and, absent any talent whatsoever for charismatic speech, have decided to call it a barbeque.

While one would hope that we would handle "the next one," whatever it is, somewhat better, the outlook for considered planning and real consensus in the liberal democracies is not promising.

For any committed centrist, the lesson learned should be a heightened enthusiasm for actually preparing in advance for predictable but infrequent dangerous or catastrophic events. In politics, the urgent usually trumps the important (no pun intended). But a dedicated adherent of the middle ground has an obligation to brave the slight unpopularity associated with preparation for serious but infrequent challenges, especially those related to the security of the state and its citizens, so that, if in due course, they do arise, the response, carefully crafted in advance, will be coherent and logical, and the messaging associated with the response will not cause the people to lose confidence in the truthfulness, probity, or basic competence of government.

CHAPTER III

An Awkward Time for the Universities

I ENTERED THE UNIVERSITY OF Toronto as an undergraduate student of mathematics, physics, and chemistry in 1960. In 1969 I received a PhD from the same university in physiology. Four other universities later, I retired from full-time university work in 2008, having been a professor, department chair, VP (at two different universities), and, for more than nine years, a university principal. Now, in 2022, I'm still on the Program Advisory Committee of one US university. That is 62 years of exposure to universities, drawing university pay for forty-three of them. During one two-year period in the 1990s, as Senior Advisor on Labour Relations to AUCC, I handled crisis management in 21 universities. It would be fair to say that I feel at home in the university world and have had a ringside seat for most of the evolution of the North American universities since the post-Sputnik boom that started in the late 1950s.

Universities are designed to be mired in controversy. It's actually part of their job. And, yes, some denizens of the universities are pretty eccentric. After all, if you can't have eccentrics in the universities, where can you have them? But, while the post-1960 university world has always been a roiling mass of enthusiasms, interests, oddities, discoveries, controversies, and biases, it does have a pattern. If we take it that the purpose of the modern university is both the teaching of the knowledge of humankind and the creation/discovery of additional new knowledge, then we can imagine a sort of overall scorecard.

Over the period since the end of the Second World War, my sense is that the pattern has been something of an asymmetric arc. The North American universities got better and better for quite a while, but then experienced a fairly flat, long apogee before beginning to decline. It is my view that the decline can be halted and reversed and that, in any event, it is neither a uniform decline nor a very steep one. It affects some disciplines more than others and some levels of study more than others. But it is real. It is also not irreparable.

There is a dubious old adage that troubles normally appear in sets of three. If this superstition has any merit, then our universities have had bad luck indeed, because their present swarm of difficulties seem to fall into four bins, rather than three. The sorting into the four bins might look something like

(a) issues surrounding free speech, academic freedom, and concerns over "acceptable" speech,
(b) misconceptions about the various purposes and utility of higher education,
(c) a gradual decline in the quality of undergraduate education, and
(d) a profound misunderstanding of how to make the most effective use of university research capacity.

The universities of the developed world have been the epicentre of knowledge generation since the Second World War, and so have been instrumental in the dramatic improvement in wellbeing and standard of living experienced by the citizens of those lands. If they are in trouble, we are all in trouble.

In 2020, after reflecting at length on this suite of concerns, I agreed to organize an event, spanning two days, at the Charleston Library Society to explore these issues. Since retiring from full-time work, we usually spend the worst part of the winter in Charleston, SC. I know that Canadian snowbirds often go further south, but Charleston has such a rich cultural life that we got used to going there, and now have many friends there. The Charleston Library Society was founded in 1748. It is the oldest cultural institution in the southern states and the second-oldest surviving subscription library in the United States. It organizes and hosts about 200 talks, conferences, musical events, exhibits, and other types of events a year.

3.1 If You Can't Have Eccentrics in the Universities, Then Where Can You Have Them?

On returning to Canada in early March 2020, at the beginning of the Covid-19 pandemic, I set out to write about these matters. In my commitment to the middle ground, I resolved that I would not expound on any problem without proposing a solution and that my proposed solutions needed to respect, to the extent possible, the range of forces and views that had given rise to the problems in the first instance.

I decided to write first about free speech and academic freedom, in part because there is so much public confusion over the (very different) meanings of the two terms. Academic freedom, as a concept, was not thoroughly codified and institutionalized in

North America until the middle of the 20th century. Most of the famous early cases of struggles over academic freedom revolved around attempts to suppress leftist speech in the United States and, to a lesser extent, in Canada. To some limited extent, the academic freedom struggles of today relate to the other end of the spectrum. But not that often. Sometimes the "approved" doctrine isn't especially left or right but is surprisingly exclusionist.

One of the norms of the middle ground is that discourse about problems should also include logical solutions. Given my commitment to not citing a problem without offering a solution, the piece I wrote was entitled "Free Speech and Academic Freedom in Universities: Challenges and a Solution," and it first appeared on August 10, 2020, in *Ottawa Life Magazine*.[14] It has been reprinted in a subsequent print edition of *Ottawa Life Magazine* and has appeared in French in the Quebec-based academic quarterly *Argument* in late 2021.[15] What I wrote was as follows:

Free Speech and Academic Freedom in Universities: Challenges and a Solution

Our universities are designed and funded to be more than institutions for teaching. They have long served as the incubators and testing grounds for ideas. But now, in much of the developed world, the universities are experiencing some challenges in maintaining the practices of free speech, open debate and academic freedom, all of which are needed to allow ideas to be tested in the crucible of experimentation, peer review, open discourse and reconfirmation.

And some of the controversy over what can and cannot be said on campus these days is due to the confusion between and conflation of two different concepts: free speech and academic freedom. They are not the same at all.

Free speech is not confined to the universities, but rather is the notion, throughout a free society, that the government cannot punish you for speaking your mind. Exceptions to this rule are very narrow, largely prohibiting speech which is an incitement to physical harm of others or damage to their property. Free speech, however, is not without consequences for the speaker. You can be fired for its exercise if your employer feels that a loyalty line has been crossed, and you certainly may risk being sued, shunned, and/or insulted or otherwise disadvantaged from its exercise. But that is as it may be. You cannot be jailed for it. The consequences of free speech for the speaker, if any, are all in the civil or social domain.

Parenthetically, the idea that the exercise of free speech may have consequences for the speaker was always based on the notion that the speaker was identifiable. There never was the concept of free speech while wearing a disguise, which is why we struggle so to deal with many of the platforms on the internet which purport to be providing for free speech, but which are really just vehicles for intimidation, since they are indeed amplified speech with no identifiable originating speaker.

Academic freedom is different, in that it applies only to scholars employed by institutions of learning, and does bar the employer from taking action against its employed faculty members for exercising it. To be fair, the universities of North America have not always been entirely receptive to and protective of the broadest reasonable range of discourse. Academic freedom was actually institutionalized quite late. Its formalisms derive from the AAC/AAUP declaration of 1940, which is the originating root of all academic freedom policies in universities in both the USA and Canada. In Canada, the principles of that declaration underlay the reactions to the cases of Frank Underhill (1941) and Harry Crowe (1958), which are the most cited Canadian early cases. Academic freedom is the freedom to research, publish, and speak publicly in one's area of expertise without institutional constraint or sanction, and hence goes further than free speech, but only for a limited group of people. It also implies its twin, academic responsibility, which includes an obligation to eschew provable falsehoods, to use reasoned arguments and actual data, and to avoid purporting to speak for the institution unless delegated to do so.

There is quite a bit of useful jurisprudence about academic freedom in the US, and much of it derives from the Pickering case and its sequelae (Pickering vs Board of Education 391 US 563 (1968) SC). Essentially, the Pickering Test means that academic freedom can even be used to protect speech which does some harm, provided that the matter being spoken of is a matter of public interest. In this it differs from ordinary free speech, which, if it does harm can readily be a cause of action at law. Since the inception of the Charter of Rights and Freedoms in Canada, it is reasonably easy to argue for the applicability this sort of US precedent in Canadian courts, but a number of high-profile post-Second World War academic freedom cases in Canada had already laid a solid groundwork.

In the three generations since academic freedom became a touchstone value of the North American Universities, it has caused those institutions to become the clear world leaders in the generation of new knowledge. A cursory look at the distribution of Nobel Prizes would be a pretty convincing indicator.

But today academic freedom and open debate are experiencing some non-trivial setbacks, though mostly not in the experimental disciplines. The targets in the cross-hairs are largely in the encyclopedic disciplines. Debate in the humanities and social sciences is becoming more and more constrained by a new orthodoxy which has developed an interesting technique for protecting itself from challenge. It is the technique and culture of the taking of offence, or perhaps the feigning of the taking of offence, at the expression of views different from one's own. And indeed, sometimes the taking of offence extends to claiming that the "offending" speech is itself violence. This hugely trivializes real violence.

We now see speakers who are scholars being shouted down for holding to "unapproved" views, or being prevented from speaking on campuses because university administrators, fearing repercussions, impose vast "extra security" costs on the entity wishing to invite the speaker, and therefore using economic clout to prevent such discourse.

It was not always thus. I fondly recall my time as an undergraduate and graduate student at the University of Toronto in the 1960s. A debate was arranged in Convocation Hall between Wm F. Buckley Jr. and David Lewis. For those who don't recall, David Lewis was Canada's leading socialist, a former Rhodes Scholar and former head of the Oxford Debating Union, and later the leader of the social democratic party he had helped to found, the New Democratic Party. I was a Lewis fan, and he was a personal friend and mentor as well, and Buckley was considered by most Canadians to be extraordinarily far to the right. That being said, the audience was entirely respectful and it was a brilliant debate between the two best debating stars of their generation. Though agreeing with most of what Lewis said, my take on the event was that Buckley won the debate on points. It was a damned good lesson for me. Listen to the other side. Even in your disagreement you will likely learn something.

Another interesting event during that time was the mass teach-in held by the University of Toronto and York University at Varsity Arena in Toronto in the fall of 1965. The teach-in movement had begun in the US as an intellectual activity of the anti-war movement opposing the Vietnam War. But despite the fact that all the organizers were anti-war, the Toronto organizing committee opted for a non-partisan exchange of expert views. Before an audience of up to 6,000, the speakers all got a respectful hearing. The long roster of speakers was blue-ribbon all the way. We were charmed, of course, by Chester Ronning, the very progressive, very articulate Canadian ex-diplomat and China expert, who had been born in China. But we listened attentively as well to the "realist" Polish-American strategist Zbigniew Brzezinski, who, despite his brilliant career in US foreign policy, was a hawk on the subject of the Vietnam War, and on that score ended up on the wrong side of history. Nobody was shouted down.

But today that would not happen. And it is not only voices of the hard right which are shouted down, chased off and stigmatized. Even social scientists near the center who may have adopted an intentionally strident style are routinely given the same treatment. Dr. Jordan Peterson is the current obvious example of this. Similarly, pro-Israel speakers or even just Israeli visiting scholars also often get the bum's rush, and Jewish student organizations get dropped from lists of student-government-approved university clubs. And with the abortion debate, especially in the US, it is even more chaotic, with some venues driving out speakers advocating access to abortion and others driving out speakers favoring bans on abortion. Somehow, it appears that our institutions of higher learning have become terrified of the injury that their students and researchers may suffer if they accidentally hear the voices of "the other," whatever that other may be at any given moment. But appearances may mislead.

For those leading the movements and demonstrations which suppress speech, they do so not out of fear but as a calculated tactic in an ideological battle. They have no stake in free speech, academic freedom or open debate. They are committed campaigners, happy warriors with certainty in their hearts and confident in their righteousness. In their minds, the suppression of the offending speech is their duty. Tomas de Torquemada would be proud of them.

This determined attempt by committed campaigners to silence those who disagree with them by disruptive protest does not make the political and social opinions of the protesters automatically wrong. Indeed, in some cases the political and social views of the protesters are quite progressive and have much to commend them. But their methods and tactics are completely wrong, and threaten to destroy the universities. Why do the universities themselves not resist more forcefully the current popular tactics of suppression of speech?

The short answer to that question is failure of administrative courage when faced with disruptors in the academy. There are good cultural reasons why this occurs with frightening regularity. Some of the factors which tend to trap university senior administrators into inaction are dealt with in a report I wrote in 1994, and which remains relevant. In that year I was commissioned by Concordia University to conduct an inquiry into Concordia's long-term handling of Dr. Valery Fabrikant in the 13 years before he committed the murder of four colleagues. The report[6] is widely available (just enter "Lessons from the Fabrikant File" into your browser). I conducted the inquiry and wrote the report in the months after Fabrikant's conviction for the murders, but it focused on the problems the institution experienced with him in the many years leading up to those events. In retrospect, it is a case study in how very accomplished good people with good values can fail to appropriately constrain disruptors in the academy.

That report touches upon one of the two key factors which hampers decisive action by senior university administrators, and that is that most of them have little training to administer. They frequently were elevated into their administrative roles for being fine scholars and teachers, and the above-mentioned report does set out why they sometimes do not acquire the skills, conditioning and ethos that they will need in their administrative roles. Yes, despite their intelligence, integrity and good intentions, senior university administrators can sometimes look like the laboratory exercise for teaching the Peter Principle. No surprise, then, that many hesitate when faced with some chaos on campus.

The second key factor is, regrettably, how university boards have been selecting university leaders of late. I've spent much of my career amongst university presidents and principals, and, while the group is blessed with plenty of extraordinary people, there has been a recent trend to select folk who have never offended or annoyed anyone. Interestingly, people fitting that description may either be highly articulate extraordinary peacemakers blessed with powers of persuasion, or folk who are uncourageous and determined to do nothing controversial. One always hopes to appoint people from the first bin, but the supply is limited, and sometimes those from the second bin are selected. Hence today a non-trivial fraction of such senior administrative posts go to people who are determined to please everyone. It can't be done. A determination to respect everyone would go further. And that sort of determination would lead to university senior officers who would have no regrets about barring from campuses those who challenge rights to speech, open debate and academic freedom. I personally barred plenty of folk who were disruptive or intimidating from the three universities where I had that authority, and not only kept my job, but found that some of the disruptors then adopted more fitting tactics as a result and, when I allowed them to return, they became markedly better members of the academic community. On rare occasions they even thanked me for steering them in a better direction.

I do understand, however, that even the best university leaders have some concern that if they show an even-handed resolve to maintain order on campuses while allowing the maximum expression of views to the extent permitted by law, their boards may not back them up. A good plan might be to talk through that possibility with the governing board before any incident has occurred, so that there is an understood consensus on a suitable response. And then boards must give the university leaders some maneuvering room, rather than having a plan of action that is too rigid and constrained.

Furthermore, if university leaders as a group, at the national or provincial/state level, resolved collectively to act similarly on such matters, so as to create a common front, boards would be more inclined to back them to the hilt, because for explanation they could properly attest that they were merely adhering to a widespread sectoral policy. Such collective reinforcement could help to restore administrative courage.

Shouting down or physically intimidating or attacking scholars in order to prevent them from speaking in any venue is bad enough. On a university campus, it is analogous to the burning of books that was a signature act of the Third Reich and of other intolerable regimes. Any university administration that thinks this is the new normal has lost its soul, and in the process has lost any reasonable claim to support from the public purse.

I have every confidence that what is happening now to discourse in the universities is not a permanent transformation and that free and open debate will, in due course, be restored. It remains unclear, however, if it will be decorous debate, and it would be vastly better for the institutions if it were. But the absence of decorum may not be the fault of the universities, as much of society seems to be drifting toward a more rancorous style of airing differences of opinion.

But that's only the first of the four bins of university problems. Indeed, if it were the only problem the universities were currently facing, they might be able to re-inculcate some of the lost values fairly speedily. But it's not their only problem. As I noted earlier, there are three more bins of problems to reflect upon. In the next section we will explore misconceptions about the various purposes and utility of higher education.

3.2 It's Not Just Training for Employment

At the very centre of the crisis in the university world is a vast misunderstanding of what education is actually for. As the universities in Canada became more complex and expensive to operate, they persuaded governments to expand their funding by promising not only social but also economic impacts. Over time, the idea of seeking higher education to get a better job came to dominate all policy decisions about, and sometimes within, universities. In the United States, with essentially two systems, one private and one public, the debate was more complex but similar.

When I set out to address this narrowness of mind, I realized that the discussion could not be restricted to educational policies alone because the broader health of the polity of the liberal democracies was intertwined with the educational piece. I realized that the portal into this part of the reflection upon higher education was not education but democracy. I conceived of a fairly complex rant entitled "Education, Information and Democracy." It appeared on October 12, 2020, in *Ottawa Life Magazine*.[16] It is my take on the second bin of university problems. What I wrote was as follows:

Education, Information and Democracy

Fretting about the health of democracy has recently moved from being an esoteric activity of academics to a widespread preoccupation across much of the developed world. We treasure the ideal of democracy for good reason. While there are many forms of democracy, some more direct than others, some more secular than others, some with broader franchises than others, with widely varying constitutional frameworks and checks and balances, they *all* are forms of collective decision making.

The fretting is understandable, as we observe low voter turnouts, cynicism about political choices, and oversimplification or outright misrepresentation of important issues of public policy by both elected representatives and media.

We know that democratic forms don't always produce the right decision, and they frequently fail to take timely decisions, but at least we're masters of our own fate, and we do continue to hope that the choices made by the majority have a reasonable chance of being good decisions for the great majority. And they probably will be, if that majority has a clue. But there are challenging forces at play.

Meanwhile, the issues get more difficult. All politics may be local, but the last century of scientific and social change has guaranteed that the problems to be solved are neither local nor simple. Indeed, even the issues highlighted in a single election usually span most of human knowledge, including both the scientific and technological disciplines and the humanities and social sciences.

Now we need to mine the past a bit, to understand the present. Since the end of World War II, North Americans have witnessed an explosion in higher education. Once the province of a privileged few who were either wealthy or especially talented and determined, university attendance steadily grew to the present state of affairs, in which it has become a near-normal expectation for those who finish high school well.

Along the way it went through phases. In the 1950s, degrees were few enough that possession of one, regardless of field of study, was usually a ticket to a better than average economic future. But during the 1960s we saw the first signs of a clear shift towards a noxious mythology that holds sway in many quarters today. It appeals particularly to folk who describe themselves as "pragmatic."

Thus, it has become alarmingly fashionable to know a great deal about a single field, but quite unfashionable to have a solid basic grounding in many. This fashion rests on five false assumptions made by governments, and by many parents and students about the taxonomy and purpose of higher education.

The five false assumptions are:

1. A specialized technical, commercial or professional education which provides immediate access to a good job is the main reason for going on to higher education.
2. Such specialized education is more desirable than a less marketable one, but is also inherently more difficult.
3. For those who feel especially driven towards one of the other less practical disciplines, intense specialization in it may be acceptable, as one can always work as a

teacher and scholar in that discipline, in which case the rest of society will support you, albeit grudgingly.

4. A liberal education consists of a buffet style selection of the humanities and social sciences. It is good for something, in that it makes you a well-rounded person so you can enjoy the world around you more and think beautiful thoughts during your leisure time.

5. Since a liberal education is not good for getting a job, it is a good choice only for the slightly less energetic children of the well-to-do whose families can afford to support those beautiful thoughts. Others, however, may pursue a liberal education while still finding themselves, provided that they then move on.

The holder of a so-called liberal education is therefore viewed as rather a dilettante, and the primacy of specialized, professional education as the *real* higher education is reinforced.

But the myth of the impractical, beautiful, self-indulgent liberal education is persuasive only to those who know little of the past and think little about the future.

In the Middle Ages, the pillars of liberal education were the subjects of the trivium and the quadrivium. The trivium of three logical and linguistic disciplines, which were grammar, logic (usually called dialectic) and rhetoric, formed the basic platform, sort of the BA of medieval times. The quadrivium of four mathematical disciplines, which were arithmetic, music, geometry and astronomy was the advanced program, more or less the MA of its day. These more advanced subjects were not viewed from a theoretical perspective at all, but rather were taken as descriptive of and explaining the actual world.

There was an eighth core subject implied but not stated, and that was the second language requirement, a concept familiar to Canadians. In the Middle Ages, that second language was Latin, as all instruction, spoken and written, was given in Latin. University students were required to speak Latin when not in class as well, with penalties for failing to do so.

These were the "liberal arts"; they were so heavily laced with mathematics that it makes one chuckle to think of the occasional modern student who flees to the mistaken modern notion of the liberal arts because of a fear of math. The trivium and the quadrivium were called the liberal arts because they were viewed as the minimum suite of subjects necessary for "liberi"—"free men." This is an important concept, that there is a broad educational requirement for those who would be free, and that there is a way of defining what that reasonable minimum might be.

We speak easily of living in a free society, but have given little thought to what the citizenry of a free society need to know to meet their obligations. Indeed, society is so free that individuals are free to know nothing, while still having an equal vote and an equal say in our affairs of state.

So, what risks do we run by accepting the primacy of specialized, professional education? In some ways we don't know, as we haven't run the experiment all that long. The scientist was also a natural philosopher and often an artist not only in Leonardo Da Vinci's time, but right up to the dawn of the 20th century. Until that point, we placed a very high value on knowing a reasonable amount about almost everything. The idea of the Renaissance man or woman as the epitome of education did not end with the Renaissance, but it may have died on the battlefields of the First World War.

Now it may be that we will be lucky, and can just barely muddle through as a free society with a citizenry that often hasn't a clue, except in a narrow domain. After all, during the

SARS crisis of 2003 the World Health Organization survived Toronto mayor Mel Lastman's surprise at its existence, and the Canadian Alliance leader Stockwell Day was ultimately unsuccessful in reversing the flow of the Niagara River. And, so far, the US has survived the spectacle of prominent politicians misplacing various foreign lands, or thinking that in Latin America one speaks Latin, and is coping moderately well with countering a leader who routinely repeats as fact any number of easily verified falsehoods, especially in the area of science.

Furthermore, people like to learn broadly, and will do so on their own, given half a chance. They take pride in knowing something that others may not, and the popularity of the television show "Jeopardy" is not just because of one slightly jug-eared contestant who had a winning streak of 74 games, but because an enormous fraction of the viewers will try to beat the contestants to the answers. Somehow, viscerally, knowledge matters.

This natural desire to know things, right down to the smallest detail, is enormously valuable in a democracy, a society committed to collective forms of decision-making. For any collective decision-making process to produce good decisions, many of those participating need to have a reasonable grasp of the facts of the matter at issue, and at least some of those who are knowledgeable need to have access to the tools used to communicate with and persuade others.

But, despite (or perhaps because of) the communications revolution, in some ways the flow of real information in Canada and the US on questions of public policy is drying up. This is a grave threat to any functioning democracy. And it's related to some disturbing trends in dissemination of news.

There are multiple causes for the remarkable dumbing-down of news dissemination in Canada over the past 40 years.

The process has gone through two distinct stages. The first stage was the growth of television news, which saw the need to compress complex issues into 10—30 second sound bites. The higher visibility of the reporters and news readers also created a bit of a news celebrity culture, leading to a sort of journalistic narcissism of portions of the media who report incessantly on themselves.

The print media, struggling with declining market share, especially in the period before they went heavily on line, tried to imitate television by trying for the print version of attractive sound bites and a gradual underweighting of news in favour of opinion columns, some of which became infected with the same narcissism as the TV news.

Interestingly, during this first stage decline in the handling of news in Canada a generation ago, one effect was related to market size. As critical as we are of US media, during the stage one shift in technology, one could find some thoroughly brainy specialized commentary in the US. This was because it was a huge market, so that through syndication a journalist could then actually make a living understanding issues in economics, or science, or geopolitics. But not here in the smaller market of Canada, where you were the science reporter the week after you were the society reporter, and the week before you became the constitutional issues reporter. Generalist journalists know that they haven't the time to learn enough to deal with the full complexity of the issues, and this pressure has only gotten worse. Thus, they have little choice but to fall back on the double-barrelled stock in trade of any articulate journeyman writer under time pressure, human interest and scandal. Hence almost all Canadian news has for decades been covered as human interest or scandal.

Then came the second, and more destructive stage of the decline in news dissemination: the rise of social media.

Social media enable the immediate mass distribution of images and text without any accountability. While some responsible disseminators use these tools, they are generally overwhelmed by a flood of unedited, mislabelled, silly or malicious drivel which often has the effect of countering or diluting actual knowledge. As a source of news, it erases the middle ground and leaves many users going exclusively to sites that they are comfortable with, greatly amplifying confirmation bias, stoking divergence and crushing the middle ground. Amongst the greatest victims is science, which is often being politically distorted or misconstrued to an extent not seen since Galileo's time. The notion of free speech was always attended by the assumption that the speaker would be known and could be held accountable. It was never imagined as free speech wearing a disguise, and that's what much of social media activity has become.

In the absence of responsible and accountable editing and fact checking, citizens must do all the editing and verification for themselves. To do so one must already know quite a bit in order to judge which sources to trust or to be able to sniff out nonsense when one hears it. A broad liberal education is a crucial enabler of the good judgement needed to do that.

We now live under a constant waterfall of mere snippets of news, so that a complex subject never gets the comprehensive and reflective treatment it deserves. Even key televised political debates are nothing of the sort. They are joint news conferences, with snappy talking points. I've known quite a few political leaders, and, surprisingly, in private some of them are genuinely impressive.

One of my fantasies is to imagine a properly conducted election campaign debate not moderated by journalists putting a string of tendentious questions to the campaigners.

Imagine the people we might elect debating each other in long enough blocks to be coherent, and on subjects which *they* think we might wish to hear about before we judge their fitness to govern. Contemplate the possibility of political discourse not broken up every minute or two by a new question from a moderator whose only real role ought to be to keep order and keep track of time.

We might get political discourse appropriate for a free people, and, by chance, some listeners would have the "liberal" education to assess it properly.

I was very fortunate to be involved in an interesting experiment about liberal education that began 22 years ago. In 1998 I was appointed to chair the committee charged with developing a renewed core curriculum for the Royal Military College. At the time I was still a VP at Queens' University, about a year before I became principal at RMC. The college knew that it could not leave liberal education to chance. H. G. Wells described the history of humankind as "a race between education and catastrophe." Nowhere is this truer than for the modern profession of arms.

Today, a young officer may be called upon to be a skilled leader, a technical expert, a diplomat, a warrior, and even an interpreter and an aid expert, all at once. And while remarkable acceleration of technological change and the growth of knowledge are vast multipliers of the effectiveness of numerically small military forces, they also amplify the need for complexity of thought and maturity of judgement to avert catastrophe, and drive that requirement further down the chain of command than ever before. Complexity of thought and maturity of judgement are the products of a strong liberal education, and its application to the interpretation of experience. Indeed, while experience is important, experience without education is a form of tourism.

In September 1999 RMC implemented that new core curriculum of subjects deemed essential for officership in the 21st century, and specifically set certain minima in all programs for knowledge of: ethics, psychology, leadership, Canadian history, Canadian civics, politics, law, military history, international affairs, cross-cultural relations, mathematics, logic, information technology, physics, chemistry, English and French. This list was not arrived at in the customary university fashion, which is to say by assembling the collective biases of the members of a committee. Instead, and in the grand military tradition of rigor tinged with bureaucracy, we had returned to the then current version of the Officer General Specification (OGS), and tried to determine from the list of required competences what studies would get us there.

On top of the core curriculum, students still had their chosen specialty, be it electrical engineering, French literature, economics or whatever. Of course, it caused the academic portion of an RMC degree to be a bit long; an RMC undergraduate degree has 10–20% more course credits than the same degree at a good civilian university. This was unavoidable if the needed breadth is going to be there, while still getting the specialization that society has come to expect.

The RMC core curriculum that was implemented in 1999 was the modern equivalent of the trivium and the quadrivium, so much so that, for example, the minimum physics requirement in Arts could be met with a course on the physics of music. But the liberal education core was not nostalgia or someone's pipe dream. No committee was captured by a philosopher with a hankering for the Middle Ages. We got there by working backwards from what we needed on the ground in the Balkans or Afghanistan, on ships engaged in blockade, and in air operations around the globe. Strange as it seems, the liberal education needed to be truly free is pretty much the same one needed to defend freedom in an ethical manner.

Liberal education is not just the humanities and social sciences. It is not just to think beautiful thoughts. It is not just for the idle rich. It is not second-class education. It is what helps people make good choices. And it is the collective making of those good choices that will determine our collective future, and our persistence as a free people. It is what makes democracy tick.

Of course, concerns about the health of democracy do not normally play especially well with the government of the day (regardless of party), as the government in power generally feels that democracy has been working just fine. After all, it put them into power, didn't it?

But I remain confident that our political masters (who are, after all, also our political servants) would be delighted to be able to boast of any awards or publicized indicators of high quality that our provincially funded institutions of higher learning garner. So, in that very real sense, we, the users and operators of the system of higher learning, are in the driver's seat, if we choose to move gradually away from the exaggerated emphasis on the trade school aspects of our universities in order to reach that middle ground where students learn with the dual purpose of becoming learned and becoming employable.

The reaction from my university colleagues to this piece and some related earlier ones has been most heartening. And, to my considerable joy, I do hear occasionally from current students about their desire to learn and not just their desire to be trained up for employment.

But even if we can make some gains in the struggle for breadth of education, there is another strong tide running against us.

In the conclaves of university presidents, and in the halls of government, it is discussed only in the most muted tones. It is the quintessential "elephant in the room." In the next section, we face that elephantine problem and, in true centrist fashion, discover that it too has remedies that are not too pyrrhic.

3.3 The Elephant in the Room

There is a problem in the university world that almost every university professor and administrator sees, but many fear the consequences of any comprehensive public rumination about it. But truth be told, it is not entirely the universities' fault, and it may not be intractable. Nonetheless, fixing it does require facing up to it.

It is absolutely customary for any older generation to insist that the generations that follow them are less good at various things or less assiduous in seeking to learn. As far back as we have written histories, there are accounts of the fecklessness of the young in the face of tasks or challenges of various sorts. It is the subject of jest, sometimes turned back at the elders, like the trope that, in their day, they walked five miles through the snow to school, uphill both ways.

But the expressions of concern about a decline in undergraduate education that we often hear from long-time university faculty members cannot be entirely attributed to the rigid-mindedness or rosy recollection of the past that comes with the effluxion of time. Regrettably, there is a goodly supply of data and analysis to show that much of the undergraduate curriculum has undergone both simplification and slimming down over the past few decades. Writing about this in a balanced way is not easy because the waters have already been muddied by much discourse on this issue that has been unnecessarily polarized and ideological.

I decided to try, but to be true to my adherence to the middle ground, it was important to write about the cure as well as about the disease. The resulting piece was entitled "The Long Decline of University Undergraduate Education: Causes and Remedies." It appeared on December 4, 2020, in *Ottawa Life Magazine*.[17] It is my take on the third bin of university problems. What I wrote was as follows:

The Long Decline of University Undergraduate Education: Causes and Remedies

The generation-long decline of most North American universities has been so gradual that informed observers possessed of only a modicum of denial might have been able to believe either that they are witnessing a small cultural shift or, perhaps, the minor setbacks that are the reasonable price of the laudable goal of bringing the benefits of higher education to as many as possible.

They should be excused our opprobrium, because the decline cannot be attributed to a single, obvious cause. It is due to a constellation of forces which are not obviously related either to higher education or to each other, and which evoke quirky unintended consequences.

The most obvious of these unintended consequences is that, except for professional degree programs which must meet standards set by the regulatory bodies of those professions, most programs of undergraduate study have been considerably "dumbed down" in recent years. On top of this, most universities have needed to institute remedial writing programs and workshops for new undergraduates.

There are, of course, other aspects of the decline as well, including issues surrounding academic freedom and free inquiry, overly specific targeting of research funding, and confusion over the purposes of university education, but I have previously written about all of these in this magazine, and those articles are still available on this site (*Ottawa Life Magazine*, Aug 10, 2020, Aug 31, 2020 and Oct 12, 2020).

Why has it been necessary to dumb down the starting point of most undergraduate programs?

Universities do not exist in isolation, so changes in the broader society must, of necessity, impinge upon them. One profound change is that the students entering university are less well prepared for exposure to higher education than they were in the past.

This is due in part to the ideologies which now hold sway with respect to primary and secondary education in North America. A wag might joke that primary and secondary school students are now expected to get their socialization at school and their education at home. This is almost true. There is a huge emphasis in our schools on not harming the delicate psyches of students, so all are advanced and rewarded regardless of the true level of accomplishment. Few or none are held back to repeat a year. The more accomplished recognise that rewards for true excellence are minimal, and that they can get by with less effort. Many are often pleased to coast, or become bored and inattentive.

Furthermore, the current popular tool to combat boredom is the notion that to be interesting all education must be active learning, ie discovery by problem-solving. While there is no doubt that problem-solving and active learning have real uses, the technique has become so pervasive and all-enveloping that almost all of the knowledge that students acquire is expected to come via this route. Almost none is just learned in the traditional fashion, ie from books or by hearing lectures and taking notes. The problem with this is that it took humans a few thousand years to discover all of our current knowledge via the active learning or problem-solving route. Even in well stage-managed situations, our students will never live long enough to get a good bit of it all by experimentation and problem-solving. Hence the coverage must, perforce, be rather thin.

But the slowdown in acquiring knowledge due to using these "modern" learning techniques and the demotivation of good students by an undifferentiating reward system are only part of the story. It is compounded by the profound societal shift from emphasis on collective rights to emphasis on individual rights and a culture of grievance. Teachers in primary and secondary schools now wield very little authority, to the point where they are physically imperilled and deprived of most tools for keeping order in their classes and fostering the flow of work. Some of the changes that brought this situation about were needed, and no-one is advocating a return to an era when a teacher could be cruel or violent with impunity, but as with all swings of the pendulum, it may have gone rather too far before beginning to return to a logical middle ground.

All this to say that a non-trivial fraction of students leaving high school and expecting to attend a university cannot write a coherent paragraph, make a logical argument, carry out basic mathematical tasks, or analyze data, and are woefully unaware of the underpinnings of world culture.

Universities recognize that many bright and capable entrants have been let down by these preparatory systems, and have tried to remediate these lacunae with special classes which are, in effect, an accelerated version of what should have been done for those students during the decade before. But the quick fix is never going to be as good as doing it better in the first instance.

The universities, however, can not blame all the dumbing down of undergraduate programs on the systems of pre-university educational preparation. The universities themselves are partly responsible. Yes, the starting point of an undergraduate program may now be lower, but that's not the whole story. From that point forward, the material coverage is thinner than it once was, and the slope is flatter.

Why has there been a decline in the quantity of material to which undergraduates are exposed?

Surprisingly, a major reason for the flattened up-slope of most university undergraduate programs is economic. Tuition fees have generally risen faster than inflation and typical student debt levels are remarkably high. Hence, most students need to earn some money while they are at university. It would be fair to say that at one time, for students in an undergraduate programme, study was their full-time job, at least for the two thirds of the year when regular undergraduate programmes were in session. Now, however, the need of so many to hold part-time jobs during the Fall and Winter while studying has made full-time university attendance into something less than the student's full-time job. Universities, seeing looming non-completion rates, have done the only thing they could do in response: they flattened the slope, which is to say they reduced the amounts of materials to be read, of essays to be written, and of hours of study needed to keep abreast of any given course, because to fail to do so would be just to leave behind a cohort of folk who needed to engage in gainful employment during the Fall and Winter terms.

But the economic driver is not the only one responsible for the flatter slope of most undergraduate programs. Another is simply that many university students shouldn't be there, will benefit little from their time there, and could have been happier and more fulfilled doing something else. In adapting to that group, the universities slow down learning for the serious ones.

This is a controversial statement, and easily misinterpreted, so I state *a priori* that there are still substantial numbers of capable North American young (and not so young) people who would benefit greatly from a university education, but who, for a variety of reasons, cannot attend, and there is no doubt that there continue to be issues of socioeconomic stratification related to tertiary education that remain to be resolved.

But on the other hand, there are vast numbers of students at university who ought not to be there and are wasting our time and theirs, and a fair bit of their parent's money. There are three big cultural reasons for this.

Why are there so many university students who should be doing something else?

The first reason is that, for many young people, the rite of passage of going away to university, of being away from parental supervision during that critical period of young adulthood, and of partying for four years in an environment of great freedom is a life objective in and of itself, with the educational aspect being entirely secondary. During the recent admissions scandals in the US, some of the children of prominent folk who were exposed as having gained admission by dubious means were very candid about their purely social reasons for wanting to go to those universities. Frankly, there is far too much going away to school, partly fostered by the notion that there are great universities, usually at some distance, that one must try to get in to.

The fact is, at the undergraduate level, one can get a perfectly good education at most universities. A case can be made, indeed, that there are actually no great universities. Universities are built one programme at a time, and there are many great university programmes. The universities we have come to think of as great may well have a higher ratio of great programmes than the others. But be assured that almost all universities have some great undergraduate programs, and even the so-called "great" universities have a few utterly weak undergraduate programmes. The majority of serious students who live in urban centres could save vast resources by doing a good undergraduate degree while living at home, using the resultant decrease in economic pressure to treat the study as the full-time occupation, and then using the good result thereof to get into a good graduate programme.

The second reason is that, as a society, we have somewhat lost the idea of the dignity of labour, which was a key touchstone of the old left. What is "respectable" now is to go to university after high school. Lesser tertiary education institutions are often viewed as the place for those who couldn't qualify for university. Trades, even brainy ones, are viewed as second best, despite all the data that they may provide better incomes and may make a more substantial contribution to the society as a whole. Frankly, I would rate a good cabinetmaker, machinist, technologist or chef over a bad sociologist any day of the week. We have become too snobbish to respect and honour honest skilled work.

The third reason for the presence in universities of a certain number of undergraduates who will benefit little, and are just being "stored" there is essentially political, especially in Canada, where there are virtually no private universities, and all universities are heavily supported by the upper two levels of government. The political reason is that they keep a lot of the children of the influential middle and upper middle classes off the unemployment rolls, and thereby make the governments look good in terms of their economic policies. Thus, most government funding for universities uses a funding formula based on numbers of students, with some variation in the values of individual programs. The universities, therefore, can only make ends meet by continuing to grow enrollment, which suits the political aims of their paymasters exquisitely, but does not do much for their standards, their class sizes, or the ideals of a university.

How has this eroded the university ideal?

Universities "store" most of these less well-suited students by creating cafeteria-style programs without a coherent core, where the majority of courses are a jumble of unrelated electives, and persist in calling such education a "liberal education." A real liberal education is hugely valuable, and specialization, if desired, need not occur early, but an unplanned four-year incoherent salad of introductory courses is unhelpful. This greatly misrepresents what a liberal education can and should be. *(Note: A more comprehensive discussion of liberal education can be found in section 3.2 above).*

The universities then try to steer the more capable students into more goal-directed programs. Such programs, including professional ones, often have maintained a better standard because of the pressures of accreditation by outside professional bodies, but that leaves the universities with a huge dilemma. Their flagship programs have become the ones which are targeted towards preparation for specialized jobs. They have staked their reputations on becoming high-class trade schools.

Can aspects of the decline be halted, and perhaps reversed?

There is no single magic bullet that will address this farrago of challenges that our universities face. And where the root causes lie outside the universities, the ameliorations they can achieve by their own action are, of necessity, partial. But there are first steps that could blunt the decline and set the stage for further progress.

To their credit, in most universities, the teaching techniques used are better, on average, than they were a generation or two ago. This is due to two factors. The first is the prevalence of teaching assessments by students and by peers, and the use of these assessments in promotion and tenure processes. The second is that today most institutions actually try to give some modest instruction to their graduate students, teaching assistants and part-time teachers on effective teaching methods. In times past, this was often not the case. The older approach was that a person studied and researched until they got an advanced degree, and then, either as graduate students or as young faculty, were assumed to be able to teach by simply emulating their own profs. They were then paid to commit pedagogy on an unsuspecting public without actually preparing them to do so. Thankfully, that era is largely passed. Even the hiring process for new faculty usually involves giving some sort of demonstration of one's lecturing skills.

And for many of the problems and failures discussed above, the remedies are implicit in the descriptions of the pathologies. There are, however, some as yet unmentioned steps which could be taken to address the twin issues of high cost and decline in level and content of undergraduate programs. I use the term "twin" since, as we have already seen, the high cost and the resulting need for many to earn substantially while studying has been one factor in the thinning out of the degree content.

Before the Covid-19 pandemic, the cost of most undergraduate programs was partly driven by the reliance by the majority of universities on an unrelieved pre-Gutenberg model of instruction. By that I mean seating students in front of a lecturer to take notes as if the printing press had not yet been invented. Yes, I do understand that the professor may indeed refer to texts and there may be an official course text and prescribed readings, but physically sitting in the classroom has remained the expected norm for undergraduate students. And I do recognize that it is part of the social experience and is an aspect of the cultural going-away-to-university entitlement.

But over the past 20 years, the improvement in the delivery of on-line and distance-delivery courses is stunning. The residential universities at first sneered at these developments and then grudgingly adopted them for their part-time students (which they largely viewed as second-class students). That was already starting to change when the Covid-19 pandemic forced a huge shift to on-line learning. And while there have been teething problems, what is striking is how quickly the institutions have adapted when driven by absolute necessity.

For undergraduate programs which are not highly specialized or in regulated professions, one can easily imagine a future in which a significant fraction of students could get a first rate education by attending their local university for those courses that the local one, however small, does well, and filling in the gaps with on-line offerings from wherever they are excellent, transferring all credits to one of the institutions they are using and getting their degree with good courses, logically selected, at a fair price, while living at home.

Universities could also improve the degree quality by moving a bit away from the somewhat overdone cafeteria-style approach to the jumble of courses leading to some of their less specialized degrees, and shift a bit more towards core curricula, while still allowing for some electives. No one is suggesting the rigidity of the content of a given degree that was typical of the offerings in the 1960s, but the pendulum has swung so far the other way that many degrees look like a flock of introductory courses flying in loose formation, with very few advanced courses enabled by having as prerequisites the successful competition of related introductory and intermediate courses.

Another experiment which might well make university accessible to some who are now excluded would be an alternate path to admission via examination rather than past secondary school or college record. There are hints of this in the way many universities admit mature students, but more is possible.

There is another use of examinations that could dramatically reduce costs for a subset of relatively capable students. Imagine a course for which a detailed course outline and plan is published. Many courses already have this. For those inclined to study and learn independently, a less expensive alternative to taking the whole course might be for the institution to offer a challenge exam for that course which a person could pay to take, and if they succeeded, would then pay a further fee to have the credit for the course recorded. The exam fee and the course credit fee together would be much less than the cost for the whole course, but still enough to appropriately compensate the university, while having the additional benefit of taking some pressure off of class sizes.

None of these small adjustments will make university education cheap, just less expensive. Student loan systems supported by government remain essential, but they have a particular weakness, which is that the looming debt scares off many, particularly from poorer families, and has profound and often unhelpful steering effects both on program choices and on later occupational choices. It is a system which, perhaps unintentionally, drives people away from socially and culturally important disciplines which do not necessarily lead to high compensation. Not all of this steering is bad, because high compensation in an occupation often implies a high demand for and a shortage of such folk in the broader society. But the steering has become all-pervasive, and it risks relegating into obscurity some subjects that society as a whole would be loath to lose. The least disruptive curative for this is an income-contingent student loan repayment scheme. This approach has been tried in some countries, and has merit. Under such a scheme, all student debt would be repaid, but students whose future earnings turn out to be modest will end up paying somewhat less than they borrowed, while students whose subsequent earnings are more substantial will end up paying back somewhat more than they borrowed. Such schemes are rather like the concept of progressive tax rates on income, a widely accepted notion. The amount of the shift of debt from the poorly paid to the better paid is a matter of tuning the income-contingent repayment scheme, but should not be so great as to give anyone a nearly free ride.

Our undergraduate programs could and should be better. And while the repair may take almost as long as the decline, it will likely be more fun.

The weakening of undergraduate education has, in part, been compensated for by modifying graduate programs to correct for the lacunae in the undergraduate programs. This knock-on effect is not widely discussed, as it would imply actually acknowledging the trends in the undergraduate programs.

There are good and bad aspects to this interim remedy of shoving some of the complexities into the higher degree program. On the plus side, universities don't feel compelled to accept vast numbers of graduate students. There is a good economic reason why this is so. In most provinces, the funding formula for universities confers slightly more money on the universities for each new undergraduate student than the student actually costs the university, when you add in their tuition fees as well. Thus, in most Canadian jurisdictions, the universities make a small profit on undergraduate students, especially in the less specialized programs. On the other hand, even though the provinces do give more funding per student for the graduate students than for the undergrads, the overall effect is one where the universities make a slight loss on each additional graduate student they take in. In short, undergraduate programs somewhat subsidize graduate programs. Hence, universities can be somewhat picky about what grad students to accept, and, as a result, most of the ones they accept can cope with the need to catch up on what they didn't get as undergrads.

On the negative side, however, is that this leads to longer completion times for graduate degrees. In some programs, at some institutions, the completion times are ridiculously long, causing a loss of confidence (and sometimes a loss of viability) in the programs.

While many master's degree programs are styled as "professional" master's degrees, the core of graduate degree study at both the master's and doctoral levels remains the research-oriented degree with a thesis. For the degrees requiring a thesis, there is also a substantial cultural difference between the way the universities handle graduate students in the experimental disciplines versus the encyclopedic disciplines. In the experimental disciplines, the costs of the experimental research, and very often the stipend of the student, are paid largely from grants and contracts attracted by the graduate student's supervisor. The supervisor then has a considerable stake in the student's research progress, and, to some extent, the students are apprentices to the supervisor. Progress is closely monitored, and exaggerated completion times are less likely. The projects are carefully vetted, and there is often considerable mentoring.

In the encyclopedic disciplines, the cost of the graduate student's research is usually not borne by the supervisor. Indeed, the principal research tool in the encyclopedic disciplines is the library (and network of libraries), for which the supervisor pays nothing. This has led to a culture in which many supervisors see themselves just as gatekeepers, not mentors. Long completion times or even graduate students failing to complete at all, and abandoning their programs, do not have a negative impact on the scholarly work of the supervisor, who very frequently is engaged in research that has only the most tangential relationship (or none at all) to the projects of their graduate students.

To be fair, there are plenty of faculty supervisors in the humanities, social sciences, and applied social sciences who do a damned fine job of guiding and mentoring their graduate students. But the need to do so is not driven by the physical facts of the research in the same way as it is in the experimental disciplines.

If the decline in undergraduate education could be gradually reversed (and it can), the extra educational burden that the graduate programs have to carry will be correspondingly reduced, so, at least, there is one university problem that is somewhat self-correcting.

Or, at least, it will be, if the climate for carrying out research is good. But that leads us to the exploration of the fourth bin of university problems, which is another odd, well intentioned but problematic threat to the creation of new knowledge by the universities.

3.4 Curiosity, Creativity, and Progress

Research in the experimental scientific disciplines is vastly more expensive than research in the humanities and social sciences. The bulk of Canada's scientific research capacity is situated in our universities. This is not true in all developed countries, but

Canada never generated the sorts of free-standing research centres and institutes that add to capacity in the United States and some European nations, so we are rather more dependent than they are upon university-based capacity.

But capacity is not output. In the developed world over the past 60 years, the scientists in the experimental disciplines have generated a remarkable amount of new knowledge, which in turn has been a crucial spur to what we usually call progress. But what of the enablers? Having the researchers and their labs available to us is great, but that capacity would lie fallow if there were no grants-in-aid to pay for the costs of actually conducting the research.

Those grants-in-aid are a key lever for converting ideas into facts and facts into useful things. But research is a chancy business. It doesn't always work out. In Canada, at the level of government and in the granting agencies, a lot of planning effort has gone into trying to make the granting of research support less chancy. Some of that effort is almost certainly backfiring. To sound the alarm about what may be going wrong in the over-planning of research support allocation, I wrote "Funding Scientific Research: Sometimes Targeted Research Is the Best Approach, but Not Often." It appeared on August 31, 2020, in *Ottawa Life Magazine*.[18] What I wrote was as follows:

Funding Scientific Research: Sometimes Targeted Research Is the Best Approach, but Not Often

The huge concentration of scientific effort to create, verify and supply a vaccine to protect against Covid-19 and towards improved therapeutics for those who fall ill are perfect examples of appropriate targeted research.

Fans of novels or films about crime know that the iconic enablers of a crime are means, motive and opportunity.

Well, the same dicta apply to the effective use of targeted research, in that targeting a specific practical research objective is only effective when there is means (enough money and research capacity), motive (defeating a deadly plague that also wrecks economies is an awfully good motive) and "opportunity." In this case "opportunity" means that the preexisting knowledge base must be sufficient to achieve the goal in a useful time scale. In the case of a vaccine against SARS-CoV-2, the virus that causes Covid-19, the answer was pretty clear-cut, since eight commercially available vaccines for coronaviruses in animals already existed, including one for a beta-coronavirus (SARS-CoV-2 is a beta-coronavirus as well). So, it seems massively likely in this instance that the targeted research effort will succeed, and be a boon to us all.

But there are plenty of examples of targeted research programs that didn't do nearly as well as hoped. Nixon's "War on Cancer" launched in 1971 was largely a flop, though a reasonable amount of good science did come out of it. But it was not an efficient way of getting that amount of good science done. Clearly in 1971, the "opportunity" was lacking, in that the fundamental understanding of cancer mechanisms and the biology behind them was insufficiently advanced to force a fast push to any revolutionary therapeutic breakthrough. The advances in molecular biology of the past 30 years may well now open those doors, but not the science of 1971. Most scientists of 1971 were critical of the rhetoric and funding approach of those targeted research objectives. One senior scientist who expressed skepticism of the Nixon plan was chided by a reporter, who said, "Well, we did set a target of going to the moon, and we got there." The scientist replied, "Yes, but the "War on Cancer" is like hiring Columbus to go to the moon." Given the preexisting knowledge base of 1971, he was right.

Today in Canada, most advanced scientific research is located in the universities. While some funding for university research comes from philanthropic sources and from research contracts with private sector entities, the importance of research grants from government has been paramount in the research successes of the second half of the 20th century and the first bit of the 21st. This is true in both Canada and the USA. In Canada, the three key federal research granting councils are the Natural Sciences and Engineering Research Council (NSERC), the Canadian Institutes for Health Research (CIHR), and the Social Sciences and Humanities Research Council (SSJRC). CIHR was formerly the Medical Research Council (MRC). These three research granting agencies have a total budget of well over $3 billion a year.

But in recent times the laudable pressures for accountability in government have generated a less desirable side effect. Politicians now feel the need to appear to be targeting research money to objectives that government has endorsed, and to reduce funding available to what they call "curiosity-oriented research." This has fueled a huge drive within government to identify the strategic research topics that will play well politically, and to skew granting systems to favour them. This has led, understandably, to a reduction in resources accorded to basic research (derisively termed "curiosity-oriented research" by some), and a boosting of resources to "applied" or "mission-oriented" research. Hence, in recent years the resources of the three granting councils have largely been directed towards targeted objectives.

Furthermore, a non-trivial portion of that applied research is actually closer to development, rather than research on the "R and D" spectrum. And while promising applied research results should be advanced into a development phase, those development resources should not be subtracted from the research pool. Admittedly, Canada has a poor record of exploiting its own discoveries, which more often have reached the market via foreign companies, but the solution to the dearth of development or demonstration phases in Canada is not to steal resources from those allocated to the underlying research, but to foster an industrial strategy that better facilitates tech transfer to actual application.

As politically satisfying as this trend towards strategic targeting and mission-oriented research may be, it has a number of counterproductive aspects. Researchers applying for funding will, of necessity, distort their plan of work to cater to the articulated priorities of the government granting entities, shelving their best ideas for the moment. One must always be mindful that it is the researchers who have the ideas and the striking insights, and one cannot, from the outside, order them to have their insights on a particular topic. The ideas come from them. Consequently, the folk tasked with coming up with the applied thrust areas to be highlighted and supported are always somewhat removed from the front lines of idea generation, since they are either politicians or bureaucrats, though some of the latter group may be former researchers or researchers nearing the end of their careers. They will, of course, hit the occasional home run by promoting something that yields useful results easily, but they do not have as good a track record as the folk who actually submit the applications for research funding.

The myth that applied research has a bigger and faster payoff rate than basic research is not new. Almost half a century ago the United States Air Force conducted a deeply flawed study called "Operation Hindsight" to ascertain what types of research were the most useful. That study concluded that the momentum for critical advances in applied technology was the result almost exclusively of applied research and development. The authors claimed that the technological revolution, and the so-called Revolution in Military Affairs (RMA) owed little or nothing to fundamental, or curiosity-oriented research, which, according to them, normally had no practical use for at least 50 years.

Doubting the conclusions of that study, two great American medical scientists, Julius Comroe and Robert Dripps, conceived and executed one of the first large-scale research studies on the subject of research and discovery itself. Focusing on fields they knew, which were cardiovascular and pulmonary medicine, they undertook to learn what were the real antecedents of the 10 most critical practical advances in cardiovascular and pulmonary medicine of the period 1945–1975, including things we now take for granted, such as heart-lung machines. The international panels of experts that they conscripted to participate in this look back in time eventually identified some 1500 seminal discoveries which led to those ten critical advances, and followed the trail of discovery as far back as Andreas Vesalius, the famous Flemish anatomist who taught at Padua in the 1540s and Hieronymus Fabricius of Padua, who discovered the valves in the veins some 60 years later. They also identified 112 critical enabling discoveries, which they called "nodal points." And that is where it got interesting.

Comroe and Dripps discovered that over 40% of the nodal points were pieces of basic, curiosity-oriented research, and another 20% were discoveries made during applied research projects which had been intended to yield completely different results for application to completely different practical objectives.

Furthermore, they found that the time lag from basic research discovery to the practical application was sometimes very short. In almost 10% of cases it was less than 12 months, and in 20% was less than a decade. Their findings thoroughly debunked "Operation Hindsight."

Their widely disseminated, rigorous report and related writings transformed official attitudes in the United States and Canada in the late 1970s, and was a significant factor leading to about 25 years of massive publicly funded support for fundamental research in both countries.

But today the communications revolution and the new approaches to conducting policy discourse gives the politicians and bureaucrats an incentive to appear to be "buying progress" in a strategically directed fashion. Regrettably, shopping for and buying something that does not yet exist is a tricky business. We will need to learn again that letting the folk with the ideas make the research proposals, and then funding the most convincing will always yield more than ordering people to have ideas on particular topics, especially when that ordering is being done by folk who have not recently had new ideas.

It is not the fault of the universities that their scholars are struggling with the difficulties presented by the need to fit their ideas to the Procrustean bed of politically targeted granting priorities. But it does diminish the capacity of the universities to build the house of intellect and to advance human knowledge. And I would charge that some universities have been too meek in pointing out the short-sightedness of the present trend.

I well recall a related incident in Canada from the 1970s. At one point the official opposition in parliament was having fun with its criticism of the government spending by reading out in the House of Commons the titles (and amounts) of large numbers of government grants for university research projects in the social sciences and humanities which seemed pointless or humorous to them. And I must admit that some of the titles seemed hilarious. But whenever the title touched on a topic that I knew something about, the title seemed very cogent to me, and I could see instantly why it might be important to carry out such a study. At that time the opposition party's health critic in the House of Commons was a friend of mine, and so I phoned him up and told him that while I enjoyed a good laugh as much as the next person, I feared that mirth over the grant titles being read out in the house conveyed more about the lack of knowledge of the members of parliament than it did about any silly or wasteful government expenditure. The readings of the humorous titles stopped immediately.

The people who govern us are not expected to know what is at the leading edge of every discipline. And they only make themselves look silly when they pretend to do so. Research is a risk activity. We can reduce that risk by vetting requests for funding very carefully to eliminate poorly thought out or unrealistic proposals, or proposals by researchers with poor track records. But we cannot reduce that risk by telling the innovators what ideas they should have.

Consequently, while a certain quantum of targeted research is clearly a damned good idea (like stopping a pandemic), using that approach for almost all of ongoing research funding is not. Universities need to band together to tell our political masters exactly that.

It will not be easy to persuade the leaders of our universities to unite to challenge the current government orthodoxy about how to aim the research funding managed by the major federal granting councils. A degree of solidarity among senior university figures will be needed to resist the decline in funding for basic research and the rise of targeted research.

Such solidarity is rarely achieved among that group. As a university principal for almost a decade, and a VP for some 13 years before that, I experienced the difficulty in achieving consensus in such a group. It's a bit like getting the EU to agree to do something. The principals and presidents are all rather bright, but, in terms of resolve, they cover the whole spectrum from shockingly timid to disturbingly obdurate. Some have unconsciously bought into the defeatist notion that they exist as referees, not as leaders, and that they should step to the sidelines during any crossfire between researchers and the granting councils.

A middle ground approach that might be useful to mitigate the worst effects of the over-planning of research priorities and desired outcomes might be to insist that the guidance given to the research community by the planners in government and the granting councils be of a more general nature. Surely "strategic priorities for research" could be broader and less prescriptive, leaving adequate room for a reasonable amount of support for the truly new ideas that the politicos and bureaucrats have not thought of.

CHAPTER IV

Global Conflicts, Tensions, and Risks

4.1 Terrorism

Before 2006, I had not written on international topics, except to touch on them tangentially in a monograph on Canadian defence policy that I wrote in 1963 and which, to my great surprise, sold almost 5,000 copies. It was the terrorist attacks upon the United States on September 11, 2001, that got me reflecting upon the missing middle ground in some parts of the discourse about international arena. When US President George W. Bush declared his "war on terror," the public commentary included plenty of drum-beating from both extremes, with one extreme declaring that such a campaign was utter nonsense and perhaps racist, while the other extreme, at the hawkish end of the spectrum, was calling for extreme action against nation states that might have harboured terrorists, wittingly or otherwise.

The press had a field day ridiculing Bush and went about interrogating various prominent figures on the international stage about whether they thought the idea was ridiculous. Only one of them made a remark that resonated with me as worthy of research. That person was Ehud Barak, who had, only months before, ended a brief (20-month) term as prime minister of Israel. LGen (ret'd) Ehud Barak is a brilliant man who had a distinguished 35-year career as a soldier and who is highly educated in the sciences. He was the last prime minister of Israel from a centre-left party, until the new interim arrangement in July 2022. The more than two decades since he left office have seen very right-wing governments there.

When a reporter stuck a microphone under his nose and asked whether it was even possible to have a "war on terror," Barak shrugged and, in an offhand way, observed, "Well, piracy was pretty much got rid of, wasn't it?" It was a throwaway line, but hugely perceptive, because it clearly addressed the question as to whether a technique of conflict could be expunged, with international cooperation, as opposed to merely defeating the forces of a known opponent.

That was a busy time for me, and it was somewhat later that I began to actively research the comparison. My research persuaded me that the comparison was apt and that an international campaign against many aspects of terrorism was indeed possible, but that the techniques required might be rather different than those primarily used by the US government. And the long war against piracy did hold some clues.

With my research essentially completed, I used the material as my closing keynote address to the 7th Canadian Conference on Ethical Leadership, held at the Royal Military College of Canada, November 28–29, 2006, and sponsored by the Canadian Forces Leadership Institute, the Defence Ethics Program, the Canadian Defence Academy, and RMC. The theme of the Conference was "Ethical Behaviour in an Environment of Chaos and Complexity."

By that date President Bush was well into his version of a war on terror, but the jury was still out on whether it was to good effect.

My address then became an article in the magazine *Queen's Quarterly*, in the spring 2007 edition.[19] It was well received nationally, and the *Canadian Military Journal* sought permission to republish it in their summer 2007 issue.[20]

The version from *Queen's Quarterly* follows:

Is a War on Terror Possible?

Lessons from the Long War against Piracy

The developed world of the 21st century would like to put terrorism behind it. But is it possible to suppress a form of aggression that has been common for centuries? Perhaps. From earliest times to 1790 piracy was a constant and intense scourge, but by 1850 it was a minor sideshow, and so it remains. Why did the anti-piracy efforts of four centuries prior to 1790 fail, and why did the Long War of six decades against piracy then succeed? Does it yield lessons for the struggle to come, and should those lessons cause us to act differently than the developed world has recently? Almost certainly.

While this paper is entitled "Is a War on Terror Possible?," it is certainly not my intention to address Mr. Bush's war on terror, except perhaps tangentially, and I'd also prefer to sidestep a host of technical issues. I am indeed aware that the lawyers tell us that, technically, you cannot have a war against a technique or activity, but only against a definable human opponent, and the use of the term "War" in this regard is a sort of hyperbolic rhetorical flourish, where the proper terminology would probably be "campaign to reduce or eliminate." In the United States and elsewhere, it's a common way of making something vivid, like Nixon's "War on Cancer" or the perpetually unsuccessful "War on Drugs."

Furthermore, I don't propose to fret overly about the fact that there is not a generally agreed upon international definition of terrorism. And again, the lawyers often object to the term "terrorism" being applied to acts perpetrated or sanctioned by states, as they often view such acts as "war crimes," and yet we speak easily of states and proto-states which sponsor, harbour or assist terrorists. For the time being, I'm prepared to live with a fairly broad-brush definition which has three features: (i) it does not restrict the perpetrators to non-state actors, (ii) it is an action directed against non-combatants, and (iii) it has a "political" purpose (using that term very broadly). For convenience, I'll accept the definition used by Kofi Annan in his address to the Madrid Summit on 10 March 2005, which is:

> "Any action constitutes terrorism if it is intended to cause death or serious bodily harm to civilians or non-combatants with the purpose of intimidating a population or compelling a government or an international organization to do or abstain from doing any act."

It's my view that there is at least one good historical analogy to a "War on Terror," and that analogy is probably worth studying for lessons learned which could be applied to the design of a potentially successful war on terror. I am referring to the long war against piracy, which by the early 1850s was essentially fully successful.

Piracy and terrorism have certain common features. Piracy was directed at civilians or non-combatants, with the intent to do harm. It was for a long time sanctioned by certain governments and used as a form of irregular warfare (and its practitioners called privateers rather than pirates). Consequently, many nation states acted as safe havens for pirates. A handful of such states became, at various points, pretty much pirate states, in that piracy was the defining activity of the state. Many of its practitioners engaged in both government sanctioned and unsanctioned forms in the course of their careers. Even the unsanctioned forms had their political uses for some states. In the early days of opposing it, some of those nominally opposed were two-faced about it.

Pirates operated very much like modern terrorists, in that their weapons were the low-end, somewhat improvised version of the current weapons systems of the states and peoples upon whom they were preying. They were not creators of new technology, but merely daring, unorthodox, and (by the standards of the day) unprincipled employers of the readily available low-end technology of their day. They acquired their capabilities by purchase, or often by theft from their opponents, trading up like the "red paper clip" guy on the Internet. They rarely sought to acquire the heavier ships of their day, as those were too slow for the tactics they had developed, which usually involved speed, surprise and a disinclination to stand and fight against conventional naval or land forces unless it could not be avoided. Today's terrorist organizations and cells arm themselves and function similarly.

But a point was finally reached when, for the developed world, a confluence of four factors made piracy an entirely unacceptable activity and provoked a final, intense campaign to expunge it.

1. By the end of the eighteenth century, privateers operating under letters of marque or letters of reprisal had ceased to be a useful device for increasing the military capability of developed states. After 1790, few such letters were issued, and the very last ones in 1827.

2. Piracy interfered with international trade, and
    international trade had become vastly more central
    to the economic health of the entire population of
    the countries of the developed world than it had
    previously been.
3. More people from a wider range of classes were
    travelling by sea, so the perception of the risk of harm
    by pirates was more widespread and hence there was
    more pressure to remove the risk.
4. Perhaps most importantly (strangely), were human
    rights issues. Piracy was intimately connected to
    the slave trade. Often, or even usually, victims of
    piracy became slaves. Ultimately, laws declared the
    movement of slaves by sea to be a form of piracy. So,
    the growing anti-slavery ideology also became an anti-
    piracy ideology, and added a huge moral fervour to the
    campaign to expunge piracy.

Within three generations, piracy went from being a semi-
accepted form of irregular warfare and an activity viewed as
unsavoury but likely always to exist at the edges of society, to
being gone. Of course, not completely gone, but so entirely
marginalized that it's always a shock when it occurs. Other than
in the Straits of Malacca and the coasts of failed states, it's almost
unheard of. There is no longer an established international
pirate culture, a sort of diffuse criminal enterprise and network
of misfits and thugs, some with political objectives but others
just outlaws. It's gone. So far gone that flying the Jolly Roger
is merely a tasteless joke, and dressing up in mock pirate gear a
suitable activity for children on Halloween.

It is possible that terrorism is today at the point of its
history where piracy was in about 1800. Terrorism is not new.

In its most horrible form, it is genocide and ethnic cleansing, and has existed for thousands of years. Politically motivated terrorist acts by individuals and small groups are also not new, with a rash of it in the late 19th and early 20th century being noteworthy, including the act which touched off the First World War. Developed states have supported it. Even some actions by partisans supported by the Allies in the Second World War fall into the Annan definition, and, as C.P. Snow set out so clearly in the Godkin Lectures at Harvard in 1960 (later published as "Science and Government"), the advice that F.A. Lindemann (Lord Cherwell) gave Churchill and the War Cabinet which led to the Allied bombing campaign was an express targeting of working-class housing, not military targets. Nor was countervailing advice by Sir Henry Tizard and P.M.S. Blackett based upon moral considerations, but merely on what we now know were more accurate estimates of effectiveness and a concern about diverting effort from certain other important activities. Arguably, some American tactics in Vietnam were terrorism, and a reliance during a good part of the Cold War on city-killer nuclear and thermonuclear weapons could also be held to be a planned use of state-sanctioned terrorism.

But that may now have changed. The end of the Cold War in 1989 marks to some extent the end of the bargain with the devil, in which we accepted these methods in the huddling together of Westphalian states in the two great alliances by which the world had squared off into two technologically advanced but implacably opposed camps. The bargain had not only implied the acceptance of "terrorism" but also, to create a system of international security, had accepted an extreme version of the sacrosanct nature of the Nation State, so that almost nothing, not even genocide, could justify intervening in one. But since then, a rise in emphasis on human rights has begun to harden attitudes towards states or non-state actors who intentionally harm non-combatants.

At the same time, technology has reinforced the possibility of avoiding or reducing gratuitous harm to non-combatants, even in serious conflict. It is fashionable to be sceptical of the efficacy of precision guided munitions (PGM's), but the absence of perfection does *not* mean that they don't work. PGM's can and do dramatically reduce the harm to non-combatants in theatres of conflict. This makes it easier to separate incidents of intentional acts against non-combatants or a cavalier disregard for the safety of non-combatants from genuinely unintended collateral harm.

So, a case could be made that 1989 represents the same watershed date for an end of state endorsement of terrorism that 1790 would represent for state endorsement of piracy. A few less powerful states still support terrorism. And until the late 1820s a few less powerful states still licensed privateers. If the analogy holds, and a war on terror is now feasible, that "long war" ought to take until 2050.

How was the anti-piracy "long war" of sixty years won? And what lessons can be learned from it and applied to the design of a "War on Terror" which has at least some chance of success?

There were sporadic attempts to beat down piracy long before the sixty years that I have characterized as the "War Against Piracy." There are good reasons why these earlier efforts did not have long lasting effects, even though they sometimes contained elements which later were quite effective when used in a coordinated fashion during the early nineteenth century.

The first major effort to defeat the Barbary pirates was in 1390, when the Genoese enlisted the help of England and France. The English commander was Henry of Lancaster, later Henry IV. The two-month siege was not fully effective and resulted in a negotiated peace of short effect. The situation worsened after 1492 when many of the Moors who had become refugees when forced out of Spain became pirates. But there was also an internationalization of the pirates of North Africa, with many European renegades having major roles. The two Barbarossas were Greek, but Sardinians, Corsicans, Calabrians and even the odd Venetian, Hungarian and Albanian, as well as Englishmen, Danes and others figured prominently. Until 1570, the Barbarossas and their successors were nominally local sovereigns under the Ottoman sultan in Constantinople. Between 1533 and 1544, the second Barbarossa, Khair al-Din, was admiral of the Turkish fleet of Sultan Sulieman I, and twice defeated Admiral Andrea Doria.

The 16th century saw only minimal developments which presaged future policy changes. Henry VIII of England and Louis XII of France concluded an anti-piracy treaty, agreeing to suppress piracy by their own subjects and to keep their own coasts clear of it. Over two decades later, in 1536, Henry VIII passed the first Piracy Act which created a Vice-Admiral of the Coast.

The 17th century saw little progress in the Mediterranean. It has been estimated that in 1634 there were in Algiers alone 25,000 Christian slaves, largely being victims of piracy, and another 8,000 who had converted to Islam following capture. The expeditions against the North African pirates during this period were half-hearted, except for the great raid led by Robert Blake, ordered by Cromwell. It suited various states to have the pirates of Algiers, Tunis and Tripoli prey upon the shipping of other states.

And while the 17th century was also part of the golden age for buccaneers in the New World, as it drew to a close there were interesting hints of things to come. The first was the concept of co-opting the saner amongst the pirates. The story of the famous Welsh pirate leader Henry Morgan is an example. By 1671 his outrageous exploits, condoned by the Governor of Jamaica, Thomas Modyford, provoked an English reaction. A new governor was sent to arrest Modyford and Morgan. But while Modyford was confined in the Tower of London on his return, Morgan agreed to change sides, was knighted and sent back as Lieutenant-Governor of Jamaica in 1675 with a brief to suppress piracy. From then until his death in 1688 (including two years when he was Acting Governor) he was moderately effective in that role, resulting in a substantial decline in piracy in the region. The second development was another Piracy Act that created Admiralty courts in North America and the West Indies, so that long lags would not exist between arrest and trial. Until then, the costs of sending prisoners and witnesses back to England had frequently caused the charges to be dropped.

But by the last years of the 18th century, the world was primed to stamp out piracy. Letters of Marque or Letters of Reprisal were no longer being issued. Privateering was dead. Admittedly, it had a modest rebirth during the war between Brazil and Argentina which lasted from 1825 to 1827, when both sides issued many such letters. In doing so they did indeed create a new pirate class that went rogue for a couple of years after that war ended, but who by 1829 were beaten down. The end of privateering meant no more ships and bases functioning as officially sanctioned schools for those who would later go rogue and strike out on their own.

It had also long been recognized that the slave trade and piracy were intertwined. There were many reasons. First, slaves were amongst the most valuable cargoes to steal. Secondly, captured crews or passengers could be sold as slaves anyhow.

Thirdly, early in the 19th century the slave trade became illegal in stages. Outlaw seafarers engaged in one criminal activity were naturally the ones to gravitate to another illegal maritime activity. In 1807 Britain made its slave trade illegal. In 1808 the importation of slaves to the US became illegal and trade in slaves was deemed piracy. This law was not enforced for many decades thereafter, but was on the books. At the Congress of Vienna, Lord Castlereagh persuaded the four major slave trading nations, France, Holland, Spain and Portugal, to accept abolition of the trade in principle. In 1824, Britain passed an Act which declared that a British subject "who upon the high seas carries away any person as a slave..." is guilty of piracy. Long before, in 1721 an Act had extended rules related to piracy to those who traded with pirates.

The stage was set for a major effort on piracy. Even the young republic in North America became involved. After 1785 the newly independent United States also found itself paying tribute to the pirates in the Med, but by 1798 the American consul in Tunis, Mr. Eaton wrote advising resistance. The Dey of Algiers offered America "protection" in exchange for a frigate. The Bey of Tunis wanted something too, as did Morocco. After a symbolic act by the Yusuf of Tripoli (cutting down the flagstaff at the US Consulate on May 14, 1801), the US lashed out, generating their heroic stories about Preble and Decatur, but with no real effect on the pirates.

In August 1816 a huge British operation led by Lord Exmouth against the great pirate base at Algiers had a bit more impact. It was provoked by failed negotiations with the Dey of Algiers over the release of Christian slaves. The fleet took 818 casualties, 128 of them fatal, but released 1642 slaves.

Then in 1824 a British blockade and threat of long-range bombardment again brought the Dey onside (26 July) and on

Oct 24 he accepted a British offer to mediate with Sardinia as well. Shortly thereafter the British squadron got the Bey of Tunis to agree not to allow the sale of Christian slaves. By 1828 Tangiers was blockaded, and in 1830 the French, in frustration, occupied Algiers and thence much of North Africa.

But the end of the pirate states of North Africa was not the end of piracy. From 1808 to 1848 the Royal Navy was able, with huge effort, to liberate only about one eighth of the slaves being shipped from Africa to Brazil. In 1848 some 60,000 slaves were landed in Brazil, despite an 1845 British decision to allow the Royal Navy to capture Brazilian slavers even when they were empty. In 1849 Palmerston extended this to Brazilian waters, and in 1850 to entering Brazilian ports for this purpose. The key, however, was the revival of parties *in* Brazil opposed to the slave trade, and hence the decision in July 1850 of a new Brazilian government to enforce its own 1826 treaty against the slave trade. In 1852 only 800 slaves were imported. Force projection without effective diplomacy and politics had failed. Force projection with effective diplomacy and politics had succeeded.

The same lessons were learned over Cuba. There were no successes of any permanent nature over the Cuban pirates by the US or the British, despite many raids, till the mid 1820s when the Spanish authorities began to cooperate. Interestingly, this was the first occasion of really strong British-US cooperation, two generations after the Revolutionary war.

By the late 1820s, even Greek pirate activity was exceedingly low, and in North America the 1832–5 saga of Baltimore clipper ship "Panda," captured eventually in Africa by the British brig HMS Curlew, was the last gasp, except for the slavers. They persisted, and in 1859 15,000 slaves were still landed in the US. In 1861 the American steamer "Mohican" captured the slaver "Erie" with 937 slaves aboard. The captain, Nathaniel Gordon was tried for piracy and hanged in Portland, Maine on 8 March 1862. He was the last to be brought to justice in the United States in this manner for slave trading.

In the Far East the chronology was only slightly later. In the 1840s, Chinese pirate admirals had 500-ton junks with up to 18 guns, some 18 pounders, and crews of nearly 100. Between 1843 and 1851 British warships captured or destroyed almost 150 junks and earned head money for 7500 pirates. In September and October of 1849, the great raids of the pirate Shap-ng-tsai brought him up against Captain Sir John Dalrymple Hay. 58 of Shap-ng-tsai's 64 junks were destroyed and he lost 1700 men. No British were lost. Shap-ng-tsai's deputy was captured, but the pirate admiral himself retired into a Chinese civil service post. While piracy in that region took a further quarter century to fully suppress, with careful British, Dutch and other allied cooperation, 1849 was the watershed point.

Some observers have mused that technology killed piracy. It did not. It would have eventually, with the coming of iron ships and rapid communications. But British statesman Richard Cobden declared piracy dead in 1849, eleven years before the iron hulled battleship HMS Warrior was launched. Piracy grew up during the age of fighting sail and died before its technological context did.

The Long War on Piracy took three generations. It worked where earlier efforts had failed because:

1. The developed nations stopped using piracy as a convenience themselves.
2. It was a multilateral effort grounded in a shared ideological conclusion that piracy had to be rooted out, and citizens as well as their rulers shared this vision.

3. Force projection alone was not effective, but force projection accompanied by intensive diplomacy, co-option and even bribery did work.

4. Laws were important, but laws that governments chose not to enforce were unhelpful.

These lessons may be applicable to the design of a war on terror. It should not surprise us that American moves away from multilateralism have been counterproductive. Multilateralism is awkward. It involves constant negotiation and compromise. It is slow. But it is critical to closing off safe havens. Nor should it be a surprise that America's greatest success to date in its war on terror was its very effective bribing or co-opting of Libya to go out of the terror business. Libya renounced weapons of mass destruction on Dec 21, 2003 and has taken all reasonable steps not to be a safe haven for terrorists. While implied force was certainly a factor, it was not in the end the critical factor.

A war on terror is not a military exercise. It is a political, diplomatic, economic and social exercise in which military force must always be available and occasionally used.

There are those who argue that it's different this time, because the majority of terror incidents today are related to a revolutionary movement within Islam, a movement unlikely to respond to the subtleties of the proposed approach. This is a point worth considering. There is no doubt that there is a fierce struggle underway for the soul of Islam, and that struggle must be resolved within Islam. We on the outside, in Dar al Harb, are not mere bystanders, but we are also not central to the issues at stake. We will need to fight a holding action to prevent that struggle from ruining our lives, and will need to do so until the community of Islam has been able to resolve this internal conflict.

This revolutionary movement deeply believes in a return to an imagined short Golden Age, the 29 years after the death of the Prophet, from 632 to 661, which is the period of the reign of the *rashidun*, the four righteous caliphs, Abu Bakr, Omar, Uthman and Ali. It is a movement distinct from customary Islamic orthodoxy, which had learned to live with political structures, and it is a movement which is useful to certain unprincipled men within Dar al Islam. It espouses certain values that most of us on the outside see as anti-human, and it is these striking and extreme postures which in the end may cause it to fail and may cause other more adaptable theologies within Islam to prevail. There are differing views as to the origins of this movement. Some believe that it has been implicitly present all along. Most Americans seem to believe that it is a child of the austere Sunni branch of the followers of Muhammad ibn Abd al-Wahhab, and dates to his alliance with Muhammad ibn Saud in 1744. Others, including me, would tie it more closely to the Muslim Brotherhood founded by Hassan al-Banna in Ismailiyya in 1928. But in fact, it does not matter. No one living today will see the end of that struggle.

But terrorism is not central to it. It is the tool of the moment. In the same way that the end of the Cold War and a rising tide of sentiment about rights of individuals has made the developed world very recently decide to put terrorism behind it, it is possible to persuade the remainder of the world, over time, that terror is the wrong tool.

And in doing so, it is important to persuade more than just the rulers of nation states. If the *ulama*, the intellectual and theological leaders within orthodox Islam, were to become convinced that terrorism was an unsuitable and inherently inappropriate tool for believers, even the most radical fundamentalist leaders would start to look for other methods to pursue *jihad*.

And there may be other levers. In the first half of the 19th century, the last straw for piracy was its association with the slave trade, about which a moral outrage was developing. The laws making the two crimes equivalent removed the last shred of sympathy for pirates. And recently, Elie Wiesel and others have been trying to persuade world leaders to reach a formal agreement that suicide terrorism is a form of crime against humanity. Perhaps that linkage could be extended over time, so that *all* terrorist acts might be viewed in law as crimes against humanity. Crimes against humanity not only carry the severest penalties, but over the last 60 years the world has begun to develop a suitable moral outrage about them. Linking the two villainies might well be the modern equivalent of the 19th century legal equivalence between piracy and the slave trade.

The techniques for persuading states and non-state actors that it is time to put terrorism behind us are similar to those multifaceted but muscular techniques that made piracy a minor activity at the margins. The struggle for the soul of Islam may be partly a violent struggle right up to the point that it is resolved, but the unethical and unappealing tactics of terror may be discarded by all protagonists long before the greater questions are resolved. It is to producing the pressures to discard such practices that we must apply ourselves. And the Long War on Piracy points the way.

As an attempt to find the middle ground, I wrote that piece to point out that, while the War on Terror launched by US President Bush may have been excessively focused on the military aspect of such a struggle, a multilateral comprehensive campaign against terrorism is indeed quite feasible, provided that one fully embraces the key dictum of the above piece, which I repeat here:

> A war on terror is not a military exercise. It is a political, diplomatic, economic and social exercise in which military force must always be available and occasionally used.

I am told that this article is still on the recommended reading list for those on the Command and Staff Course at the Canadian Forces College, which is the staff college for the Canadian Armed Forces.

The template that I advocated has not always been the approach used in counterterrorism campaigns in the more than two decades since 911. But, clearly, combatting terrorism is not a "one size fits all" sort of project. And the results of the various anti-terrorism drives have indeed been variable. On the one hand, terrorist networks of non-state actors do appear to have been greatly diminished since 911, and it was the suppression of such networks that I was largely reflecting upon when I wrote those words 15 years ago. But ideologies that endorse the use of terrorism continue to inspire significant numbers of lone-wolf terrorists, though, arguably, there may well be a psychiatric dimension in many of those cases.

Furthermore, if we adhere to the definition of terrorism used in the above piece, which was the one set out by Kofi Annan at the Madrid Summit in 2005, there has been no shortage of terrorism by nation states, including the campaign techniques being used by Russia in 2022 against the civilian population of Ukraine in the course of its war against the government and military of that nation state. Some comment upon that conflict, and on Russia's misperception of itself, can be found some pages hence, in the fourth section of this chapter.

4.2 Looking through a Different Lens

Sometimes, to see the world clearly, we need to see it from a different vantage point. The international arena is complicated, and we have a tendency to rely upon habit and confirmation bias when trying to read its vagaries. Sometimes we need a jolt. Such jolts usually come from an external source, but not always. It is possible for the new vantage point to arise from our own thoughts. After all, we are creatures of widely varied experience. In my case, the jolt came from applying ideas from my earlier disciplines to my newfound interests and concerns.

It has been said that we are all captives of our original education and training. It's not that such formative exposures dictate or constrain *what* things we will think about for the rest of our lives, but they do have a profound influence on *how* we will think about them.

My undergraduate education was in physics. In the summers, I worked in the lab of Dr. Gerry Wrenshall. He was a Saskatchewan farm boy who earned an Ivy League PhD in physics before the Second World War and only discovered that he was diabetic when he got bumped out of RCAF pilot training at the beginning of the war because of his diagnosis. Forced by his own lack of insulin to be interested in glucoregulation, he earned a second PhD in physiology with the co-discoverer of insulin, Dr. Charles Herbert Best, in Toronto. By the time I went to work for him, he was a Full Professor in the Charles H. Best Institute at the University of Toronto.

I stayed on as a graduate student and did an MSc with Gerry and then a PhD with Dr. Geza Hetenyi Jr, who was a professor in the same institute. Geza had fled Hungary at the tail end of the Hungarian Revolution, and even though he had an MD and had been an assistant professor in the medical school at the University of Szeged, after coming to Canada in 1957, he did a physiology PhD with Gerry. So, if you worked with that gang, you worked on endocrine projects with a big emphasis on glucoregulation. My later postdoc at Laval University with Dr. Claude Fortier, CC, focused on the control of the secretion of ACTH and glucocorticoids, so, when I finally became fully gainfully employed as a prof in the Faculty of Medicine at the University of Ottawa in 1971, I was well steeped in all the physiology surrounding the "fight or flight" response.

At the same time, I was getting pretty familiar with geopolitical issues, especially as they related to conflict. My first real publication on those issues was my monograph entitled *See No Evil: A Study of the Chaos in Canadian Defence Policy*. It was published as a thin book in 1963 and sold 5,000 copies, which at the time was considered to be very good for a nonfiction policy-oriented volume. It was the next year (1964) that my name first appeared as co-author on a full-length scientific paper on glucoregulation.[21] It was exciting to be co-author of a paper with Dr. Charles Best, and I believe I am the youngest person who has had that privilege.

So, with both of these works appearing before my 21st birthday, I was already deeply involved in studying both endocrine physiology and the geopolitics of conflict. I had always sensed that there was a connection between them, and that nation states seemed sometimes to imitate the behaviour of various creatures in the natural world. But somehow, it took me another 57 years to commit the idea to paper.

The timing was dictated by two things. The seclusion necessitated by the Covid-19 pandemic gave me more time to write, and the need for Canada to do a bit more strategic thinking had become particularly pressing. The result was "Tigers, Rabbits and Foxes: The Physiology of International Tensions." It was first published on February 24, 2021, in *Ottawa Life Magazine*.[22] I freely admit that it feels a bit like an accidental three-way collision of Aesop's Fables with a physiology text and "The Art of War," attributed to Sun Tzu, but writing it even helped me organize my current thinking about geopolitics. And some others have found it useful too. After all, anything that helps us to make sense of some of the mayhem in the world is useful indeed. What I wrote was as follows:

Tigers, Rabbits, and Foxes: The Physiology of International Tensions

All animals exhibit a fairly similar physiological response to threats. This is widely known as the "fight or flight" response, as elucidated first by Harvard physiologist Walter Bradford Cannon in 1914. Thus, all animals react to stress by sending nerve signals to secrete substantial extra adrenaline from the adrenal medulla into the blood, while at the same time triggering a neuroendocrine cascade resulting in the secretion of lots of ACTH by the pituitary, which in turn triggers the secretion of lots of glucocorticoid by the adrenal cortex. Thus, blood pressure and heart rate go up, alertness increases, and plenty of glucose is pumped into the blood for energy for the muscles.

But that's where the commonality bifurcates. It's not called "fight **OR** flight" for nothing. Clearly, lots of factors go into deciding which it is. For familiar threats, the nature of the animal may give a clue. For powerful creatures like tigers, it may fairly frequently be "fight." But rabbits experiencing the same neuroendocrine response are acknowledged specialists at running away and hiding. Foxes, somewhere in between in their ability to project power, may go either way, depending upon circumstance. The judicious variability in their response may even have led to them being stereotyped as clever.

The complexity of the response is the product of many factors, but both power and character figure prominently in determining the choice.

Some of the same notions can be applied to interactions between and among nation states, because when nation states are stressed by external threats, similar forces are at play. The equivalent of adrenaline release is the flurry of alerting discourse that takes place within any nation state that is exposed to an external stressor. The equivalent to a burst of glucocorticoids is the industrial and organizational gearing up to counter the threat. The recently much discussed Defense Production Act in the US, and similar emergency powers in other nations are examples of national mechanisms analogous to the glucocorticoid spike. Nation states are not organisms, but symbiotic systems. Nonetheless, their initial response to threats can look a lot like Cannon's "flight or fight response." This is still true when they are grouped in herds or packs known as alliances.

Of course, in the international arena, "fight" includes not only the military option, but also other power projection methods using economic and trade tools, as well as diplomatic initiatives and the information environment. Even culture can be weaponized in this day of instant communication. Similarly, "flight" can hardly mean moving your country into a safer neighborhood, except perhaps as pertains to cyber and information operations, but it can mean exaggeratedly conciliatory or submissive behaviors and policies.

The capacity of any nation state to project power, be it military, economic, diplomatic, information or cultural power, may be the largest single factor in determining whether a nation is a tiger, a rabbit, or a fox. But other factors play too. For non-democratic states led by despots, the mindset of the despot and of the associated ruling clique strongly influences the "nature" of the nation state, in terms of the response to threat. For democratic nations, the national narrative, in all its variations, largely sets the character aspect of the response.

Thus, it is no surprise that great powers, like apex predators in nature, may be more willing to "fight" when threatened, as they have the tools to do so. At this moment, the ability of the United States to project power in all categories exceeds that of its next few competitors combined. While this situation may not persist indefinitely, for now, at least, the US is obviously and routinely a tiger, albeit one that is sometimes preoccupied with the rumblings in its own guts.

And the world's least powerful nations are mostly content to be rabbits, trying to stay off the radar screens of all the others.

It is in between the extremes that we find the really interesting cases. The so-called middle powers ought logically to be foxes, if we consider only their ability to project power. But lots of other factors crowd in. What is the effect of living in a bad neighborhood? And, like in the animal kingdom, does a previously unknown or relatively unfamiliar stressor evoke a more cautious response?

History matters. Canada is a middle power that probably should be a typical fox. It acted very much like a yearling tiger in two world wars, and found the experience so troubling and hurtful that in the time since, while handling some conflicts and tensions quite effectively as if it were a fox, it has also spent a great deal of energy at a wide variety of gatherings in the international arena doing rabbit imitations and erroneously calling that soft power. And it has used these performances abroad to burnish its rabbit credentials at home, despite outsiders being doubtful. Some modest harm has come from these well-intentioned antics, because they have led to a degree of underinvestment in the capabilities that a fox ought to have, resulting in some weakness in our basic capabilities of defence, as well as an inadequate degree of self-sufficiency in certain key industrial areas.

From this example and others, we can see that while the analogy to the physiological "fight or flight response" holds pretty well, the elements of national character that partly determine this imagined national phylogeny are vastly more malleable for nation states than they are in the rather hard-wired animal kingdom. To some extent, at least, nation states can decide what species they want to be. Of course, they must stay broadly within the limitations of their ability to project power, or the posturing becomes ridiculous. Thus, we have the example of North Korea, a rabbit wearing a tiger skin vest as an unpersuasive disguise, and holding a live grenade in its teeth. It could do quite a bit of damage, but not without making itself into hassenpfeffer. Hence in all probability it can still be expected to act largely like a rabbit.

These somewhat lighthearted caricatures of nation states highlight the above-mentioned key divergence from the animal kingdom analogy. Children's stories notwithstanding, animals cannot significantly change their power or their nature, except on a Darwinian time scale. But nation states can, to some modest degree. They can, with considerable effort, change somewhat their ability to project power. The factors that limit the range of such possible change include size, wealth, population and geography. But, within those limits, the governments of nation states can make choices that either increase or diminish economic, military or cultural power.

The second parameter, the nature or character of the nation state, is also adjustable, and perhaps rather more so than power. As noted above, history matters. But national narratives do change. The things that nation states and their peoples deem important are major drivers. For developed states, where most folk are adequately clothed, fed and housed, ideology is a non-trivial driver. To no-one's very great surprise, nation states often do what they think they ought to do. We should be more interested in why they think they ought to do so.

External factors exert considerable influence on national stances. Australia and Canada have striking similarities, in culture, language, size, history, and the process of national evolution. But Australia lives in a less good neighborhood than Canada. It shares no border with an allied tiger that is obliged to help it out *in extremis.* An unfriendly tiger not too far from it has been a bit aggressive towards it of late. It is a fox with distant friends and closer enemies. The response of the Australian fox has been to muscle up a bit. It routinely invests at least 2% of its GDP in defence, compared to Canada's 1.3%. It is taking further precautions against economic penetration. Australia feels a bit on its own. Indeed, not quite as much as it did during the period of initial Japanese successes in the Second World War, but enough to adjust its stance.

From this and other examples, we can see that when a fox lives in a bad neighborhood, it can make choices to become a somewhat tougher fox. Or perhaps a hybrid fox with some armadillo-like armor or extra tricks to discourage other foxes and slightly shopworn tigers. This is achieved in part by adjusting the national narrative. In a democracy, this is largely by using public debate to shift consensus. In dictatorships it can happen by imperial fiat and propaganda.

No nation state that is a fox facing an external threat, however toughened by good decisions about resource allocation and narrative, can feel entirely comfortable going it alone.

In the natural world, protective packs or herds are invariably of the same species, but, in the international arena, alliances, coalitions and consortia of nation states usually encompass many species.

Tigers rather like alliances, coalitions and consortia, provided that they are allowed to lead them, because such aggregations not only reinforce them against challengers, but they also more widely distribute the costs of the response to threats.

Rabbits are often inclined to eschew alliances in order to keep a low profile, though commercial consortia are more favoured. Some rabbits, however, who live in bad neighborhoods, or who share borders with foxes or tigers, may join alliances and coalitions for the usual reasons of self-preservation.

Foxes are the ones that most need alliances, coalitions and consortia, because without them every fox spends too much effort and treasure looking out for unfriendly tigers and the nastier foxes.

Big alliances like NATO invariably contain a senior tiger, the odd geriatric enfeebled tiger, plenty of foxes, and the occasional rabbit, sloth or vulture. And don't pretend that you don't know which states fit which descriptors.

At this point, you may well ask, is the author having too much fun? Is the comparison of the behavior of nation states to the behavior of animals just a pleasant diversion, or does it actually hold lessons for us? For those of us who reflect only infrequently on geopolitics, it is probably the latter.

Returning for a moment to the animal kingdom, it is evident that the physiological response to threats has evolved to encompass the notion of, "Si vis pacem, para bellum." That is why, in nature, the majority of aggressive gestures are intended not to initiate a fight, but to prevent one.

Once a threat is sensed, displays of strength or of a willingness to stand one's ground do ward off aggressors. That sounds rather like much of the discourse in the international arena as well.

So, what are the most useful lessons that fox-like nation states wishing to prosper in peace can glean from the endocrine-driven responses of the relatively hard-wired natural world? Given the somewhat malleable phylogeny of nation-states, are there empirical guidelines? I can guess at a list of notional recommendations.

1. Do not pretend to be something that you are not. Or at least not exaggeratedly so. If you do, it will muck up your resource allocation decisions, and you'll be found out anyhow.
2. Don't lie to yourself. All your decisions are too visible for it not to be spotted.
3. Within your nature, take all reasonable steps to maximize your clout. In a democracy, the need to inform, persuade, and obtain the consent of the people will ensure that you don't go outside the reasonable limits of change.
4. Help out your allies and friends when they need it. They may reciprocate when you need it. Eschew the traditional platitudinous gestures that might best be described as "all assistance short of actual help," except as provided for in recommendation 6 below.
5. Take steps to build national confidence in the ability of the nation state and its allies to resist inappropriate external pressures, whether they be threats of direct physical or cyber engagement, economic and trade related threats, or attempts at cultural domination.

6. Participate generously in a wide range of bona-fide tension-reducing international multilateral organizations, even if one harbours doubts about their efficacy. It is the one form of virtue-signalling in the international arena that is actually respectable and can strengthen your case for help from allies.

7. Take special care when dealing with another fox that has been infected by any noxious non-state actor. Some nation states have thought they could host such entities in a form of symbiosis, or at worst, commensalism. It normally doesn't work out well, with Afghanistan at the turn of the millennium being a prime example. Commensalism quickly becomes parasitism. A fox infested with parasites is unpredictable.

If we then wished to apply these recommendations to Canada, what should we be doing to give them effect? Within the limits of reasonableness, what steps should the Canadian fox take to be better prepared to address external threats, be they physical, economic or cultural threats?

The most obvious first step would be to actually implement our long-standing notional commitment to spend 2% of GDP on defence. Within our alliances we have actually agreed that it is the appropriate steady-state level of peacetime expenditure, but we just haven't done it. We are still at 1.3% of GDP. This not only makes us weak defenders of our own sovereignty, and limited contributors to the coalitions that we enter into, but also makes some of our allies a bit cynical about us, which has the potential to be risky if and when we need their help. And since, as a relatively peaceable fox, we are inclined to project physical force abroad only in cooperation with established allies in pursuit of widely agreed-upon necessary action, we might become rather more indispensable to them if we developed some very high expertise in some niche areas of defence, without, of course, giving up a general overall competence. Such niche specializations could make us more highly prized in alliance or coalition initiatives. To be fair, some of this has been done, but only very modestly, because the current constrained defence budget just barely keeps the Canadian Armed Forces ticking over.

Economic hardening is relatively straightforward, but it too has some costs. Strategic diversification of trading partners is an oft-touted and laudable goal, but more honoured in the breach than the observance, because it entails some costs. Nonetheless, it remains the best way to still take advantage of the efficiencies that flow from using international supply chains and fully participating in global trade without taking undue risk. But we also must identify a suite of strategically important goods and capabilities for which some Canadian capacity needs to be maintained in the event of a crisis or supply disruption. In the past I have co-authored reports to help the government identify expendable materiel related to defence for which we need an on-shore back-up supply chain. But the Covid-19 pandemic has certainly taught us and our politicians that other things, like vaccines, PPE, and other medical supplies and equipment may also not always be readily available from global supply chains, and that it would be vastly better to be able to develop and produce such things in a jurisdiction over which we have some control, even if it somewhat increases the costs of key supplies.

External cultural threats are primarily information operations, both cyber and conventional. There are costs to countering them too, though they are less substantial than for physical or economic threats. Occasionally the cost is in terms of marshalling the political courage to identify an information operation and subject it to suitable public calumny. And sometimes there is a financial cost of spurning commercial suitors that are information operations in disguise. Canada's relationship with China, for example, has been known to stumble into both these areas.

All the above-listed measures have costs. Up till now, it has been considered politically dangerous to subject the Canadian people to these costs, so political leaders have paid only lip service to the concepts. Emergency supplies expired, vaccine production capacity declined, and defence recapitalization and icebreaker production programs got postponed, all because the politicians believed that the voters wanted very high standards in thriftiness, as well as infinitely slow acquisition processes to absolutely guarantee probity. And yes, the voters do want thrift and probity. But, news flash, those same voters also pay willingly for insurance on their houses, cars, and lives, in the hope that they will never have to collect. If the national government does not do the same, it has failed in its first purpose. The first purpose of a government is to protect the lives and the safety of its citizens and of the state. Fail in that, and no other duty of government has meaning. A smart fox would buy the insurance.

Yes, I admit that the comparison to the animal kingdom was quirky. But the lessons are genuine. And it is perhaps worth reflecting upon the fact that animals, with much smaller brains than us humans, mostly don't make the same range of mistakes in their interactions with other animals that many countries do in their postures and actions toward other nation states.

That got me wondering about some of the more recent situations affecting Canada that seemingly could have been handled better. The most obvious example has been our odd suite of relationships and interactions with China in the last few years. We haven't handled that file especially well, but then again, neither has China. So why have two nations, a fairly sophisticated fox and an emerging, ambitious but fairly brainy tiger, made such a mess of their relations? That is the problem tackled in the next section.

4.3 Unnecessarily Clueless in Both Directions

I remain fairly confident that there is a middle ground available in our relations with China. As I note a few pages ahead, I believe that careful, guarded cooperation with China is possible in some limited areas that are not security-related, once we have fully internalized that China's actions derive from a heady mixture of ambition and fear, and not just ambition alone.

But in the recent past, we've had a great deal of friction with China, and, while that may be an inevitable consequence of China's attempts to extend its influence, a surprising amount of it is because China has blundered badly in its relations with Canada and Canada has blundered (but by no means to the same extent) in its relations with China. So why the cluelessness? To answer this question, I wrote a piece entitled "Canada and China: Neither Seems to Get What Makes the Other Tick." It was first published on May 12, 2021, in *Ottawa Life Magazine*.[23] What I wrote was as follows:

Canada and China: Neither Seems to Get What Makes the Other Tick

Relations between Canada and China are currently rather strained, in part because of the long-running court proceedings over the US request to Canada to extradite Meng Wanzhou, a senior executive of Huawei and the daughter of its founder, to which the response of China was, among other things, to arrest and hold hostage (with a small fig leaf of ersatz legal process) two semi-prominent Canadians who were, at the time, in China. The rest of the response of China has been a few arbitrary unfounded trade restrictions and endless symbolic bloviation.

The wider context, however, is that China has been doing some muscle-flexing, in terms of arms buildup, the extensive use of aid diplomacy in Asia and Africa, and an aggressive enforcement of its unique interpretation of its territorial rights in the South China Sea, carried out in a fashion that departs so far from UNCLOS (the United Nations Convention on the Law of the Sea) that one could imagine that China had never read it, despite the fact that it has signed and ratified that convention.

These actions, and others, have given rise to a narrative amongst the US and its allies that China today is confident and ambitious, and has set a course for itself to become a regional hegemon, a peer competitor, and the most prominent world power. There is a growing literature on the competition and confrontation of the two giants, much of it characterizing it as "a new cold war," along with plenty of speculation about the risk of real war. Some US analysts have opined that China's military buildup signals, among other things, a likely attempt to use military force to reintegrate Taiwan into China within six years.

While I assume that this simplistic interpretation of Chinese intent has some elements of truth in it, it seems unlikely to be very predictive, as it flies in the face of some of the eternal verities of the drivers of tensions in the international arena. And one of these verities is that aggressive gesturing in international relations by states that have some ability to project power often derives more from their fears than it does from their ambitions. Furthermore, manoeuvers in the international arena, especially symbolic ones, often owe more to domestic political needs that to actual objectives abroad. (While this article focusses on China, this truism may be even more central to understanding various foreign moves by Putin's Russia.)

In the case of China, it may well be useful to understand what its greatest fears are, in order to understand, predict, and counter its aggressive gestures. But, on the whole, Canadians reflect little on what scares the daylights out of President Xi and his inner circle of Han autocrats that help him to rule China. In the next section of this article, I will explore four of those existential fears. The first three are very much still in play, while the fourth, as we shall see, has been considerably alleviated by events of the past three decades.

After that, I will explore some aspects of China's naiveté about how Canada works.

Fear #1: Fracture

Viewing China from afar, as we and most of our allies do, we are inclined to miss the fine structure. We accept at face value the Chinese narrative that China is a single unified nation state, and has been for a very long time. The Han autocrats would like to believe it too, but in their nightmares they do not. They are terrified of ethnic division and possible fracture. They still bemoan the loss of Mongolia, which they only officially acknowledged in 1946. This primal fear of resurgent ethnic differences and regional desires to be relieved, in whole or in part, of the heavy hand of Beijing seems to crop up in all of our intelligence feeds, and all the interviews with military defectors of any prominence. It has been a central driver in the long-standing campaign by China to eradicate or trivialize the Tibetan culture.

The pressure against the Uygurs of Xinjang is another example. Despite being one of China's 55 recognized ethnic minorities, the Uygurs, who constitute about 43% of the population of Xinjang, are under horrific pressure. Since 2015 roughly 10% of all Uygurs have been detained in internment camps, with the apparent goal of ensuring adherence to the national ideology. The Chinese authorities maintain that it is an attempt to curb terrorism and Islamic extremism, citing at least nine non-trivial incidents in the 25 years from 1990–2015. The extent of the vast Chinese over-reaction underscores Han fears of ethnic division leading to fracture.

Hong Kong is another setting in which even modest autonomy hugely alarmed the Praetorian Guard in Beijing, because if it persisted, others might think they had a chance too. So, Hong Kong is now being so tightly controlled from the centre that political differences will be of a cosmetic nature only.

Which brings us to Taiwan. The People's Republic of China has had no de-facto control of Taiwan in living memory. The history of Taiwan insisting that it is part of China owes as much to the frustrated ambitions and lurid fictions of the Nationalists under Chiang Kai-shek after 1949 as it does to the history of the People's Republic. But be that as it may, both China and Taiwan still maintain that Taiwan is (sort of) a part of China, even if separately governed. Thus the "expectation" on the part of China that they will, in due course, be reunited.

There is one school of thought, however, that views China's increased military posturing vis-à-vis Taiwan not as a precursor of a military assault on Taiwan, but as something else entirely. The analysts of that school are convinced that China really doesn't want a costly war, even a fairly short one, because it would probably exacerbate existential fear #2 (see below). Rather they see the sabre-rattling, especially in the light of China's increased capabilities resulting from its military buildup, as a technique to guarantee that Taiwan does not take the risky step of declaring itself to be an independent nation state, even though it functions as one. In short, no declaration of independence, no attack. In recent years, independence-oriented political parties have done well in Taiwan, and China's great fear is that a declaration of separate nationhood by Taiwan would have a domino effect, triggering fracture movements on the mainland. There have at various times been hints from China that a declaration of complete independence might even justify the use of nuclear weapons against Taiwan.

In the international arena, however, it is always a mistake to be too transparent about one's nightmares. It gives your opponents a lever. A symbolic act that is someone else's nightmare is easily weaponized. Should a third party recognize Taiwan as a nation state, or even threaten to do so, without Taiwan declaring itself one, no good could come to China from attacking Taiwan as a response. Such precipitous action would merely impose huge costs upon China and unify China's opponents. This leaves China uncomfortably vulnerable to being tormented from abroad on this issue.

Fear #2: Economic Catastrophe, Unrest and Revolt

In the light of China's great economic successes of the past three decades, why would fears of a near-doomsday-like tsunami of economic downturn and social unrest even be conjured up by a neurotic pessimist, let alone by well-entrenched technocratic autocrats? The answers lie in demography and the natural life cycle of totalitarian states.

The leaders of China are rightly proud of the economic advances of recent decades. In fact, they rely on their economic successes for two important things: the acquiescence of the governed and international prestige and influence. But sustaining that economic performance may be tricky, and any failure can be smoothed over for just so long by issuing statistics which are not well anchored in fact.

It has become commonplace to comment that China's long adherence (recently eased) to a one-child policy would eventually create an age distribution in the nation that would predict future economic catastrophe when a smallish number of working age folk would need to support an enlarged geriatric population. The failure of Japan in this regard, which was the downstream effect of a sustained attempt to limit population growth during the second half of the 20th century, is often cited. The over-65 population of Japan today approaches 30%, and there are four over-65's for every five 25–54's.

But to be fair, the age distribution of the population of China is nowhere near as extreme as that of Japan. In fact, it is only modestly different from that of Canada. But danger still lurks, because of two key differences when projecting future ratios of workers to retired in the China/Canada comparison.

The first key difference relates to the invention of the ultrasound machine. When Japan was at its most active in preventing population increase by encouraging abortion, prenatal determination of the sex of the fetus was relatively rare. But by the time China was fully engaged in enforcing its one-child policy, the availability of ultrasound to determine fetal sex was widespread. The preference for male offspring appears to have resulted in widespread sex-selection abortion. Consequently, the skewing of sex ratios at birth was considerably greater in China than in the earlier similar population-control campaigns in Japan. Today in China, for the population under the age of 25, there is a ratio imbalance that represents a shortage of about 30 million women. This does not bode well for future birth rates. The natural sex ratio at birth is slightly tilted towards males anyhow, but the tilt in that ratio in China for the under-25's is three times what it is in Canada, so it is logical to assume that some exogenous non-biological factor was at play.

Furthermore, official data on fertility in China shows that the average couple produces 1.8 offspring, well under the 2.1 steady-state replacement rate. That being said, many scientists believe that to be a contrived figure, with the real rate being about to 1.5. Admittedly, the Canadian rate is only slightly higher, but there is one further huge adjuster of labour force growth and age distribution in Canada, and that is immigration. In Canada, we typically admit enough immigrants each year to equal about 0.8% of the population, and about 82% of immigrants to Canada are under 40 years of age. This fully counterbalances the fertility deficit. China, on the other hand, has an immigration rate of effectively zero. It grants fewer than 2000 permanent residence permits per year. Consequently, Canada will not be beggared by demography 25 years hence, but China might be.

The fear of a looming truncation of the economic miracle is exacerbated in China by the realization that only increasing prosperity keeps two other factors from inducing unrest. Those two factors are inherent in the governance system, and they are extreme economic disparity and rampant endemic corruption. Absent steadily improving incomes, these features can lead to turmoil. Hence the episodic highly publicized campaigns against corruption, which, to be fair, do suppress a portion of some of the coarsest forms of corruption. But, in totalitarian states, corruption, in the form of undue exercise of influence, and compensation thereof, is inherent. It is the only way to get things done, and, absent any grass roots democratic process to "throw the bums out" at regular intervals, such governing structures eventually age out.

In democratic states, governments also get long in the tooth, and show it in irritating, sometimes trivial, ways that eventually anger the electorate, who then replace them. That, in fact, is the main driver for alternating governments in Canada, where the political spectrum (from a world perspective) is surprisingly narrow, so normally policy doesn't change very much, just the folk churning it out do.

In China, absent such mechanisms, and given the massive inherent cost of state control of activities and people, any failure of prosperity risks creating unrest of the sort that drives controlling structures towards counter-measures that can inadvertently trigger regime change by internal coup initiated by frustrated reform elements within the power structure. Or worse yet, if the stimulus is sufficient, real revolution can begin, from the far edges of the power structure. In the lexicon of nightmares, what this one lacks in immediacy, it makes up for in frightfulness.

Fear #3: Foreign Interference

The 110 years from 1839 to 1949 were traumatic for China. Weakness of the institutions of the state, internal divisions, conflict, revolts and civil wars, territorial fluidity with some territorial losses, plus pressure from and interference by technologically more advanced Western nations gave China an inexpressibly difficult time, to say nothing of eight years of war with Japan overlapping with an ongoing civil war. While the narrative that China's long agony was the product of both direct and indirect foreign interference is certainly not the whole story, there is no doubt that the history of China from the first Opium War until the Kuomintang, which had been heavily backed by the US, decamped to Taiwan in 1949 has a profound psychological legacy. And that legacy is the visceral sense amongst the leadership that most problems somehow stem from foreign interference.

Two consequences of this understandable preoccupation remain evident in the stances of China today. The first is a considerable preoccupation with defence of the homeland. A reaction amplified by that preoccupation is explored below in Fear #4.

The second consequence of that legacy is difficulty with the concept of compromise in the international arena. China is quite open to negotiate international agreements of a win-win sort, but any agreement that is a compromise, or partial win only, in order to get the acquiescence of another nation to some arrangement always feels like a return to foreign interference. When this occurs, the US and its allies often read it as China's arrogance. But in part it is a reflex reaction against historic traumas from an era that ended only 72 years ago.

Fear #4: Weakness due to technology lag

The fourth fear is one which has, at this point, largely been assuaged. It is a fear that blossomed over four days in February of 1991. Prior to that date, China had built a powerful conventional army and air force to defend the homeland, using the best technologies of the 1960's and 1970's. It was a large force, well-equipped by the standards of the day, and exercised regularly.

On Feb 24, 1991, an American-led coalition relying mostly on American military assets, launched its coordinated attack against Iraqi forces that had invaded Kuwait (and a bit of Saudi Arabia). The Iraqi forces were extensive, well equipped and well trained, and looked a great deal like the armed forces that China had built. They had been damaged by 42 days of aerial attacks, but it is what happened in the 100 hours starting on Feb 24 that most shocked China.

The American and allied forces used in that assault in 1991 would not be considered especially high tech by today's standards, but they were very high tech for 1991. When these forces met the very capable old-style army, navy and air force of Iraq, what happened was rather like a science fiction novel about parallel universes. The two forces passed through one another as if they were on different planes. Yes, they actually saw one another from time to time, but the perspectives from the two sides were completely different. When each had finished passing through the other, one was intact and the other had, for all practical purposes, ceased to exist.

It was an epiphany for the rulers of China. The reaction was something like, "Damn, we got it all wrong, and now we're almost defenceless." Frantic modernization ensued, enabled in part by a now thirty-year long campaign of espionage (industrial and otherwise) and theft or appropriation of intellectual property. One of the largest irritants still today in China's relations with the rest of the developed world is its ongoing rather cavalier treatment of intellectual property rights. While some observers persist in attributing a failure to honour such rights to the ideological views of communism with respect to private ownership of property, intellectual or otherwise, I suspect that, now that China has almost closed the tech gap, there may be a few more nods in the direction of international norms in this area.

The Sum of All Fears:

It would be enormously helpful to us to be reminded of these fears when interpreting China's stance on any given issue. It will help us to avoid the simplistic interpretations that imply that no cooperation is possible. Careful, guarded cooperation is possible, once we have fully internalized that China's actions derive from a heady mixture of ambition and fear, and not just ambition alone. And we must always be mindful that foreign policy moves, symbolic and otherwise, are always related to domestic politics as well. Such reflections also help us to identify the most powerful levers available to us. For example, in our dealings with China, any admonition we utter about the treatment of regional minorities in China is just another bit of "foreign interference" to be ignored, but threatening to increase the status we ascribe to Taiwan, or actually doing so, that's near the top of China's nightmare list.

China's mistakes in its relations with Canada

If we sometimes fail to understand China, the reverse is also true. The press in Canada has amused itself by pointing out to China that, in Canada, political interference in the court system can easily get you kicked out of office or voted out of office. True enough, but in extradition matters we do have a tradition of ministerial discretion, though it is never exercised until after the courts are done with their work. However, if China is looking for a favourable exercise of ministerial discretion, i.e., deciding not to extradite Meng Wanzhou, in the slightly unlikely event that the US extradition request is upheld by the court late in 2021, China has gone about setting the stage for such a courtesy in the most spectacularly unproductive way. It has sought to slightly bully the Government of Canada into complying with their wish by engaging in hostage diplomacy and heavy-handed trade decisions, as noted in the first paragraph of this article.

Clearly, China missed the course on Canadian Politics 101. News flash: Canada has a minority government. It is a minority government that has just about run as long as a minority government usually can manage, and there will likely be an election later in 2021. Furthermore, it is a minority government of a centrist party that lost any actual driving ideology decades ago, unless adherence to polls counts as an ideology. So, between now and the next election, the key thing that matters to the government is to be popular with Canadians. They need to get that few extra votes a few months hence. Hence, for the coming months, leadership in Canada is going to look a lot like followership. Whatever the mood of the public is perceived to be, that will be the stance of the government, right up to election day. Consequently, if China wanted the Government of Canada to do a particular thing under the present conditions, the only way to ensure that would be to make sure that China is popular with the Canadian people. But right now, the people of Canada are thoroughly irked with China, and becoming more so every day, thanks to poor decisions in Beijing, guaranteeing that our government will be loath to do China any favours. A cleverer tactic for Beijing would be to release the two Michaels (using whatever fig leaf gives them slight cover, like expulsion), and to suddenly find that some of their concerns about Canadian products were unfounded. A few weeks thereafter, Beijing's favourability rating with the Canadian public would have improved enough to give any Minister of Global Affairs adequate cover, should an exercise of ministerial discretion be useful some time in the fall, when a decision on the extradition by the court is possible.

Put simply, pissing off Canadians has never been a good way to get them to help you. It's not in our cultural DNA. Nation states that have land borders with powerful opponents are often accustomed to making some concessions in the face of intimidation. Canada, with a rather large wet spot on either side of it, and a big long-standing ally to the south, has had a long tradition of thinking itself immune to such mafia-like tactics. True, oceans are no longer the protection they once were. But our mindset persists. So, it might work better for China in its relations with us to do what works, instead of what comes naturally.

Some time after the publication of this essay, the extradition case against Meng Wanzhou was resolved in her favour, which had always been the likeliest outcome. Then, after a brief interval, the two Michaels were repatriated to Canada, of course with no admission that their detention had been a quid pro quo. But China's reputation among the Canadian people has not seen much of a recovery, validating my hypothesis about how China's mistakes would play with Canadian public opinion.

Furthermore, US rhetoric on China continues to harden, and China's relations with Australia have not really improved following the change of government in Australia, even though some improvement had been expected. There are other facts that also trouble China's elite and suggest that China may have reached its apogee in some respects. For example, this is the year that the population of India surpasses that of China. The "one child policy" chickens have definitely come home to roost, but they are not laying very many eggs.

The Chinese desire for more influence is also drawing more fire than might otherwise have been the case because of Russia's war against Ukraine. One might have expected that Russia's adventurism would distract world attention from China's increasingly aggressive stances. But quite the opposite has happened. The strategy experts in many of the liberal democracies, having noted the (official) warmth of the relationship between President Xi and President Putin, are actually becoming increasingly vocal about preparing to counter China, not only in economic and diplomatic matters but militarily as well. President Biden's unequivocal assurance that the United States would assist in the defence of Taiwan against an armed incursion was particularly bad news for China, as it confirmed the hardening of attitudes toward China in the United States, and further confirmed that such a shift had taken place in both main political parties in the United States.

China desperately needs a reset with the English-speaking democracies. If China is smart enough to offer one, it should not be automatically rejected but rather should be explored "with safety valves." By that I mean that some trade and other agreements are indeed possible provided that (a) no involvement of Chinese enterprises in work involving the security architecture of other states should be accepted, (b) China must not become the sole or dominant supplier of goods that could become critical in certain classes of emergencies, (c) a hard line must be taken against Chinese industrial espionage, (d) China must respect intellectual property rights, and (e) a rapid, unambiguous, and enforceable dispute resolution system would have to be a part of any negotiated reset. The WTO dispute resolution mechanism has none of these three features.

All that being said, if Canada and some of its allies have failed to understand what makes China tick, it could be said that we also have some misunderstandings about some other states that worry us. But in a couple of those cases, it's not that we don't understand what makes them tick. It's that we don't understand what makes them *fail* to tick. And that is the subject of the next section of this chapter.

4.4 When Unequals Pretend to Compete

This section is not expressly about Russia's bizarre attack on Ukraine and about which it is nearly impossible to imagine a middle ground (and certainly not if one subscribes to the notion of the right of self-determination of peoples). Indeed, the reasoning behind Russia's actions is so peculiar that, similar to the example in Section 1.2 of Chapter 1, it seems likely that purveyors of any alleged middle ground have actually stumbled across another example of a false middle ground.

But even though Russia's new war figures to some extent in this section, it is not the centrepiece of the argument being explored. What this section explores is the negative impact upon the foreign policies and postures of two nation states, Russia and Pakistan, because they each have exhibited a lack of realism and candour about their own state of affairs and capability for decades. Using the analogy of Section 4.2 of this chapter, they might be described as largish foxes who go to a party in tiger suits, get drunk, and then start to believe that they really are tigers.

Those of us in the liberal democracies who are close to my age may have contributed to these misunderstandings because of our strong recollections of the Cold War era that ended in 1989 and our tendency to forget that Russia is not the USSR of old. In part, that is because, when the USSR was at its (admittedly odd) zenith, we usually colloquially referred to them as "The Russians" and have forgotten that it was, in those days, a thoroughgoing misnomer.

And as to Pakistan, my generation tends to make a somewhat similar mistake because we remember when Pakistan included what is now Bangladesh, and when Pakistan was halved, its name didn't change.

It seemed to me that some degree of realism about current conflicts and international competitions was needed, not only in our view of both Russia and Pakistan but in their own view of themselves. To that end, I wrote, "Delusions of Adequacy: How Russia and Pakistan Lie to Themselves in Similar Ways." It was first published on April 8, 2022, in *Ottawa Life Magazine*.[24] What I wrote was as follows:

Delusions of Adequacy: How Russia and Pakistan Lie to Themselves in Similar Ways

The ongoing assault on Ukraine by Russia has drawn plenty of comment, with the focus primarily on those aspects that are now apparent at a glance, and are particularly troubling. They are easy to list. The Russian action is evil. Its justification was absurd. Its conduct has been incompetent beyond measure. It is and will continue to be a catastrophe for both nations. The behaviour of Russia, including systematic war crimes, will make it a pariah state for the rest of my life and longer, and the sustained world response will beggar the Russian people for a generation. Ukraine, with somewhat inadequate but clearly useful military assistance from NATO nations, will survive, and it will subsequently receive considerable development assistance from NATO states for its rebuilding.

All this has come about because of one great lie. And it is not the vulgar and noxious lie that Mr. Putin tells, in which he claims that the Ukrainian people and nation do not exist. It is an even bigger lie, and it is one that not only Mr. Putin, but many prominent Russians tell themselves all the time, and actually believe. It is the lie that Russia is a great power, and a peer competitor (or peer opponent) of the United States of America.

Interestingly, it is exactly the same lie that prominent leaders in Pakistan tell themselves about Pakistan being the peer competitor (or peer opponent) of India.

The truth is that the only fact which underpins this fallacious notion, in both cases, is a tally of nuclear weapons, which shows rough parity. Russia and the US have more or less comparable nuclear arsenals, at roughly 4,000 useable warheads each. On a much smaller scale, India and Pakistan each have about 160. But parity in a class of weapon which cannot be used without serious risk of utterly destroying the nation that uses it is hardly a guarantor of success in all the forms of competition that are actually meaningful for human life. An unused but available nuclear arsenal is a useful guarantee against being overrun, but it is always a two-edged sword sort of problem. Having it and not using it very likely guarantees continued existence, but does not automatically confer influence, or even respect. Ask North Korea for details. Furthermore, having it and using it probably moves the needle over into a competition for best ritual suicide.

In every other conceivable measure, Russia and Pakistan are lying to themselves every day. Russia has about 44% of the population of the US, and about 15% of the population of the NATO Alliance. Similarly, Pakistan has about 16% of the population of India, and, in fact, there are slightly more Muslims in India than in Pakistan. (Russia's population is not growing and is already less than 2/3 that of Pakistan).

The GDP of Russia is well under 8% of that of the United States. In fact, in 2021 the GDP of Russia was perhaps two or three percent higher than that of Canada, but given the impact on its GDP of the current war, it is now very likely less than that of Canada. The GDP of Pakistan is just over 10% of that of India.

The GDP per person in Russia is less than 16% of that in the US. The GDP per person in Pakistan is about 61% of that in India. Clearly, people in the US are vastly better off than their counterparts in Russia, and Indians are better off than Pakistanis by a substantial margin.

Then there is the small matter of corruption, and its corrosive effects. The international Perceptions of Corruption Index, a well-regarded and generally unbiased product of Transparency International, uses a rating scale that goes from 100 (corruption free) to zero (corrupt in every conceivable respect). They rate both Russia and Pakistan in the lower, very corrupt range, with scores of 29 and 28 respectively. India scores markedly better, putting it in the middle tier at 40, and the US makes it into the more satisfactory upper tier at 67. (Parenthetically, Canada scores even a bit better, at 74. I assume that our national propensity for apologizing for just about everything probably makes corruption and its necessary coverup a tad impractical.)

In a corrupt state, many institutions are eroded, and both Russia and Pakistan consequently have very weak civil institutions, so that a failure of probity extends into all aspects of life. To be fair, there is perhaps some differentiation between the two states, in a few respects. For example, the erosion of the autonomy of the courts is not quite as extreme in Pakistan as in Russia.

Democracy is also commonly a victim of corruption. The Democracy Index is a complex annual compilation done by the research division of the Economist Group, which also publishes The Economist weekly newspaper. In the most recent tabulation, Russia scored 3.24, and was classed as "Autocratic," versus the US, which scored 7.85, yielding a classification of "Flawed Democracy."

Pakistan scored 4.31, resulting in its classification as a "Hybrid Regime," while India scored 6.91, and was classed as a

"Flawed Democracy." (Canada, interestingly, scored 8.87, and was classed as a "Full Democracy").

Again, to be fair, Russia was, a generation ago, briefly, a sort of flawed democracy, and Pakistan has slipped into the autocratic zone every time the army gets fed up with the government and stages a coup, which has indeed been a recurrent feature of its history.

But both Russia and Pakistan face a huge impediment if they ever wish to recover from being non-democratic states clothed in the fake machinery of a democracy. That impediment is the exaggerated influence of the security and intelligence apparatus in both countries. The ISI in Pakistan and the FSB in Russia have political influence far beyond anything which could be described as a legitimate remit for a security and intelligence agency. There would not be space in this entire magazine to list their overreach. They also tamper hugely in the international arena. By way of example, the ISI created the Taliban so that Afghanistan could become a convenient, impoverished buffer/client state, and the FSB intimidates and assassinates critics at home and abroad. (Parenthetically, these agencies do not seem to grasp the negative consequences to their parent states of their overreach and foreign meddling. Afghanistan now supports groups that are actively subverting Pakistan, and the widespread revulsion of attacks by the FSB on dissenters and opponents has hardened both domestic and foreign opposition to the regime in Russia.)

Using any rational measure, Russia and Pakistan are clearly not even close to being peer competitors of the US and India, respectively. So, what are they? Crudely stated, they might both be described as "banana republics with nuclear weapons." A more courteous terminology might be "corrupt impoverished dictatorships with nuclear weapons." So, while it is important to stop treating them like the peer competitors that they wish they were, but aren't, their true status leads us to ponder an important question: **how does one handle banana republics with nuclear weapons?**

The short answer is, "always carefully, but with variations that depend upon their posture and behavior." In looking for more clarity, we are somewhat lucky, in that we already have some experience along these lines. The pilot study for how to handle such a state is our experience with North Korea. As I have already mentioned, North Korea's nuclear weapons do influence how others deal with that state. On the plus side, no nation state would consider carrying out a "small" military chastisement of a nuclear North Korea, for fear of a nuclear retort. So North Korea is protected by its nuclear capability in that narrow sense. It might be said that the nuclear capability guarantees the existence of the state.

But its nuclear capability does not guarantee its good health. For a start, the creation and maintenance of such a capability is costly, almost beyond measure, especially for an already impoverished kleptocracy. And, in the case of North Korea, international anger at its choices and behaviour guarantees that it will be economically, technologically and socially isolated. The nation, and its citizens will not have access to goods or channels of commerce, and will not share in any of the benefits of globalization of trade. They will be safe, but in a small, unpleasant cage. Their defence is also their imprisonment.

And there is an even greater down-side risk to a state like North Korea maintaining its nuclear capability. In the event that it did become embroiled in an active military confrontation, its nuclear capability might very well convince an opponent that massive first strike was the least bad option. So, while it can not readily be attacked, it must be wary about attacking others, because of the potential for a self-protective overreaction by a more powerful opponent. In short, its nuclear capability is a great deterrent, but a useless weapon.

How much does our understanding of the situation with North Korea inform our possible stances with respect to Russia and Pakistan? While there are some analogous elements, there are also clear differences in both cases.

The key area of international friction for Pakistan is its list of unresolved disagreements with India. Beyond that, while Pakistan clearly has major failings in the area of human rights and does have a dubious record of encouraging terrorism, it is still open to adequate relations with most of the liberal democracies, and it did accept considerable US advice and financial assistance for a comprehensive program to safeguard its stockpile of nuclear weapons and to create a command-and-control system that militates against accidental or rash use. This relegates its territorial disagreements and religious conflicts with India to a sort of chronic manageable slow burn. There is little evidence at this moment of a need to isolate Pakistan in the same way as the world has needed to isolate a chronically confrontational rogue nuclear state like North Korea.

Russia, on the other hand, is much more problematic. After the end of the Cold War and the breakup of the Soviet Union, Russia had appeared to settle into a pattern of simply being a mendacious nuclear-armed kleptocracy with an exaggerated sense of self-importance.

This exaggerated sense of self-importance is also somewhat amplified by the historical accident of the timing of the creation of the United Nations in 1945. On the heels of the Allied victory against the Axis Powers in the Second World War, this new international forum, created to replace the League of Nations, was designed to accord five of the most prominent victorious states a whip hand when it came to crises of peace and security. Thus, the five permanent members of the Security Council of the UN were each accorded veto power over resolutions of the Security Council. The five permanent members were the US, Britain, France, China and the USSR.

Following the dissolution of the USSR, Russia insisted that it was the continuing state for the purposes of the USSR's membership in the UN and its permanent membership on the Security Council, and while the UN has tacitly acquiesced to that notion thus far, it has never been tested before any adjudicative body. This contrasts with the extensive process that was used when it was determined that the Peoples Republic of China should take over the membership and the permanent seat on the Security Council that had been allocated to China, which culminated with the passage of resolution 2758 of the General Assembly of the UN in 1971.

Given Russia's actions in Ukraine, there now arises a modest risk that it might be challenged on its right to the USSR's permanent Security Council seat, and might need to re-apply for ordinary membership in the UN. After all, the population of Russia is well under half of the population of all the states that made up the former USSR, despite being the largest single state arising from that dissolution. And, amongst the veto-carrying permanent members of the Security Council, it is already an outlier, being, in economic terms, by far the least consequential, with less than two thirds of the GDP of France.

In early March, 141 nations in the UN General Assembly voted for a resolution demanding that Russia "immediately, completely and unconditionally withdraw all of its military forces from the territory of Ukraine within its internationally recognized borders." Only five of the 193 UN members voted against the resolution. It remains to be seen whether this level of solidarity in the General Assembly can be brought to bear on correcting the egregious error of Russia's membership on the Security Council.

The more recent resolution of the UN General Assembly that suspended Russia from the UN Human Rights Council passed 93 to 24, with 58 abstentions, even after extensive Russian lobbying, in which Russia made it clear that it considered even abstention to be an unfriendly act. So, clearly, Russian diplomatic bullying is less than fully effective now that the world has had a sustained and egregious demonstration of Russia's inflated sense of self, massive incompetence and lack of morals.

That vote is historic, because it makes Russia the first permanent member of the UN Security Council to ever have its membership revoked from any United Nations body.

So perhaps a challenge to its permanent member status on the UN Security Council is not completely out of the question.

Beyond that, the containment of a truculent Russia is somewhat similar to that of North Korea, but cannot be handled in exactly the same way for two reasons, one being its much greater nuclear arsenal and the other being that it has a land border with a number of vulnerable states. The fact that its nuclear arsenal is very large, with a full spectrum of long and short range delivery systems, effectively protects it from any real risk of first strike, and this is a good thing both for Russia and the world. But its extensive land borders with potentially vulnerable states makes the need for the big squeeze even more acute than for North Korea.

That is why the scale and nature of the civil and military aid going to Ukraine needs to be ratcheted up considerably, so that Ukraine can quickly drive out the invaders and can avoid being bogged down in another long-running hot stalemate.

At this point, Russian nuclear posturing and the implied threat of strategic retaliation rings rather hollow.

And that is also why the regime of sanctions against Russia which has been triggered by its attack on Ukraine needs to be made as complete as possible, as soon as possible. It must become so total that it ultimately criminalizes on a near world-wide scale any commerce with Russia that has not been approved by a multinational body set up to review such matters. And it has to remain in place until an extensive list of conditions has been met. That list includes withdrawal from Ukraine, multi-year payment of reparations to Ukraine, trial and punishment of those individual perpetrators of war crimes who can be identified, and agreement to a long-term, gradual reduction in Russian nuclear capabilities, internationally verified, in exchange for very firm security guarantees solemnized by treaties.

It is to be hoped that such stages might be expedited, so that Russia and Russians could look forward in due course to economic and social progress. But the history of Russian duplicity does not automatically encourage one to imagine a rapid transition to legitimacy. If this sounds like it might involve keeping much of the pressure on for a couple of decades, well, if it is needed, so be it. Eventually, the world will be the better for it and, hopefully, the new Russia that emerges will be the better for it.

In the meantime, let us have a thought about the two nations that Russia and Pakistan imagined, incorrectly, that they were peer competitors of: the US and India, respectively. Despite their size, economic clout and defence preparation, they both need to be cautious about the risk of hubris. In recent years, both have experienced a decline in political health characterized by a decline in tolerance of and civility towards domestic political opponents, and an overall decline in respect for differences of opinion. It would be both ironic and a great shame if they accidentally began to adopt some of the unlovely features of the aspirants who thought they were their peers, but were not.

As I write this, in the summer of 2022, we cannot know the final disposition of the war that Russia has unleashed upon Ukraine. But it remains highly likely that, over time, the Russian people will come to understand how an outdated imperial ideology and an unaccountable system of government combined to do vast unnecessary harm not only to a neighbouring state but to Russia itself. And then there will be a reconning. We can hope that the mindset of the new Russia that will emerge from that reconning will be more realistic and less inclined to lie to itself.

As for Pakistan, a true reconciliation with India may have to wait for an easing of the jingoistic nationalism and religious exclusionism so prominent today in both Islamabad and New Delhi and a recognition of the shared elements of culture. Given how similar spoken Hindi and Urdu are, the opportunities for communication and understanding remain substantial. The gradual normalization of relations between Pakistan and Bangladesh represents an encouraging signal.

Unsurprisingly, for many nation states, an inability to progress can be due in part to an inability to let go of resentments stemming from long-past conflicts. But the opposite is sometimes possible. In the next section, I shall deal with a case where a nearly impossible level of effort during a tragic conflict was the making of a modern, mostly happy nation.

4.5 A Terrible Time, but a Transformation for Canada

Why would something written about the First World War contribute anything to finding and defending the middle ground today?

Strangely, for Canada, the First World War is still an ever-present cultural driver and one that still evokes some polarization. In some, it evokes only disgust at the pointless harm and loss, while others still see it as a just cause, heroically met. But for Canada, there is a middle ground, because from a terrible thing came the shape of the modern country we know today. About a decade ago, I became involved in a project to restore to Canadian memory the key moment in that evolution, the struggle for Hill 70.

The First World War was an unimaginable tragedy. And with the hindsight of a century, it is widely seen as having been avoidable. This causes many to feel that the slaughter and sacrifice were purposeless, and while this may indeed have been the case for various engagements, it is clearly not so for the Battle of Hill 70.

The war ended with the Armistice of November 11, 1918, but had the German forces been just a bit less exhausted and depleted, the typical winter pause, which would have begun in December, would have allowed the Germans to rest and refit, and the war might have gone on until mid-1919. Many thousands more would have died.

Hill 70 likely prevented this lengthening of the war. The victory of the Canadian Corps at Hill 70 caused horrific German losses, which likely exceeded 20,000. Five German divisions ceased to exist as coherent formations, divisions that could then not be used by Germany at Passchendaele. Furthermore, Hill 70 was never subsequently lost, so the Allies maintained oversight of the entire Douai plain for the rest of the war.

When LGen Currie, in his disagreement with Gen Horne, was given a free hand to capture Hill 70, and won the day so convincingly, it resulted thereafter in the Canadian Corps being viewed by all as more like an allied army and not just another British corps. It was a key inflection point in the Canadian shift to independence.

Unlike the United States, which fought a war of independence against Britain, Canada became autonomous by fighting alongside the mother country. The battle of Hill 70 and Lens, during August 15–25, 1917, was the instant when that looming outcome became inevitable. In 1931 the Statute of Westminster formalized for a number of Dominions what had been for Canada a practical reality by the end of the First World War.

All Canadians know about the Fathers of Confederation, who made the Dominion of Canada internally self-governing. But the Fathers of Confederation are not the fathers of the country called Canada. They are the grandfathers of Canada. The Fathers of Canada are those who fought for Canada at Hill 70.

I have the privilege of being the Vice-Chair and Director of Research of the Hill 70 Memorial. To explain its significance to Canadians, I wrote an essay entitled "Hill 70 in Context," which appeared in the magazine *Queen's Quarterly*, in the spring 2018 edition.[25] What I wrote was as follows:

Victory at Hill 70 in Context:
The Road from Colony to Ally and Towards a Canadian Way of War

The recently dedicated Hill 70 Memorial at Loos-en Gohelle, in France is the first major Canadian war memorial built on a foreign battlefield in the 81 years since the completion of the Vimy Memorial. Its construction, and, indeed, the entire Hill 70 Memorial Project has been carried out without a cent of government funding, by a Kingston-based group chaired by Mark Hutchings.

Most Canadians alive today had never heard of Hill 70 until recently. The Canadian decision after the Great War to centralize Canadian commemoration by building the extraordinary and moving monument at Vimy Ridge had, as an unintended consequence, the near disappearance from memory of another transformative event for Canada.

The Hill 70 Memorial project aims to insure a good understanding of the battle and its significance. The striking Memorial in France is for commemoration, while the definitive history of the battle, Capturing Hill 70 (UBC Press, edited by Doug Delaney and Serge Durflinger), has become a best-seller. Packages of interesting teaching materials were sent to every Canadian high school.

This essay is not a detailed battle history, but describes how Hill 70 was indeed transformative, and dissects where it fits in the maelstrom of events of First World War. The Great War compressed into under 52 months a massive wave of some of the most rapid political and technological change ever seen. And Canada rode the crest of that double wave. But Canadian culture came into play too.

Though most Canadians believe that the BNA Act created a country in 1867, it only provided for internal self-government of the colony of Canada. In the 47 years from Confederation to 1914, no country had an embassy in Canada, nor did Canada have any representatives abroad, except for a High Commissioner to the UK (1880), and an Agent in France (1882), both with limited duties and limited access to information. If Canada wished to communicate with a nation state, the Governor General would write to the Colonial Office in London, who would forward the communication to the Foreign Office, who in turn would move the question to the British Embassy in the country of interest.

On 4 August 1914, the day that Britain declared war on Germany, Sir George Perley was appointed Acting High Commissioner from Canada to London. But Sir George was not allowed to see correspondence between the Governor General and the Colonial Office.

At the outbreak of the war, Canada declared war on no-one. Britain did it for all of the Empire. Canada merely got to decide how it would react to being at war.

The first commander of the Canadian Corps was Lt Gen Edwin Alderson, a British officer appointed by Britain after consultation with Canada. He was reprimanded early in the war by the War Office in London for responding directly to questions from Ottawa. He was reminded that all communications with Canada were to be passed through the War Office. Thus, early in the war, Canada was seen merely as a source of manpower for the British Army.

When war broke out, Canada's population was seven and a half million. Some 680,000 went into uniform, about 625,000 of them into Canadian uniform, and about a half a million went to Europe. About 66,000 died and 172,000 were injured or fell gravely ill during operations.

But in 1919 Canada had a seat at the negotiations for the Treaty of Versailles and a seat in the League of Nations. Effectively, Canada was a nation state, and somehow four and a half years had done what 47 earlier years had not. Canada had acted like a nation, and so came out of the Great War as a nation.

Canada's war of independence was the First World War, the so-called Great War. Unlike the Americans, our war of independence was not fought against the entity from which we became independent, but alongside it. We started the war as a colony and ended it as an ally.

The autonomy came gradually. Political efforts by Borden and his ministers were important, but the real lever for that autonomy came from the performance of the Canadian Corps and its first Canadian commander.

In Canada students are taught variously that complete independence from Britain was achieved by the Statute of Westminster (1931) or by the patriation of the Constitution (1982). But no-one is really so naïve. Paperwork never leads events, it follows them, to solemnize what is already empirical fact.

Canadians learn about the Battle of Vimy Ridge, 9–12 April 1917, the first action in which all four divisions of the Corps fought together. At the time the Corps was commanded by Lt Gen Julian Byng, a British General who in June was promoted to command the British 3rd Army. In the 1920s, he was Governor General of Canada.

His senior division commander, Maj Gen Arthur Currie, had considerable input into the planning for Vimy, informed by his study of the French defence of Verdun. Because of meticulous planning and rehearsing, recent technological advances, and good leadership, the Canadian Corps succeeded where, in 1915, French troops had twice failed, and suffered about 150,000 casualties. During a period with little other good news, the Canadian Corps victory got tremendous attention. It has since rightly taken on iconic significance for Canadians; it changed Canadian attitudes profoundly and set the stage for what was to come. But it was not uniquely Canadian, nor under Canadian control. Of the 170,000 men involved in the allied attack on Vimy Ridge that day, only about 97,000 were Canadian. In some ways, it was not a Canadian battle, but a British battle with high Canadian content and some Canadian planning.

But exactly two months after the start of the assault on Vimy Ridge, a Canadian, Sir Arthur Currie was promoted to Lt Gen and given command of the Canadian Corps. On 7 July 1917, when Currie had been corps commander for 28 days, he received orders from Gen Horne, commander of the 1st British Army, of which the Canadian Corps was a part, to attack the small industrial city of Lens, somewhat north of Vimy. Currie objected. In the ensuing exchanges, Field Marshal Haig and Gen Byng both agreed with Currie's reasoning, and counselled a rethink.

Why had Currie balked? For good reason. Canadian generals were more inclined than British generals to do their own reconnaissance. Perhaps that was a residuum of the class system. Indeed, the casualty rates for Canadian general officers in the corps were higher than for the corps as a whole (42% vs 37%), partly as a result of this. Currie had done his own recce of Lens and considered it a killing ground, as it was an open book to the German artillery observers on the hill to the northwest. From that hill, the German gunners could see the entire Douai Plain, the flat coal-mining area east of Vimy Ridge. Currie made clear that he would prefer to attack and capture the high ground first.

Currie's view prevailed. Three days later, on 10 July, after a meeting of commanders in his HQ, Horne issued revised orders to his army.

It begins, "As a result of discussion with the GOC Canadian Corps, and of the allotment of additional artillery to the 1st Army, the Army Commander has decided to amend the objectives laid down for the Canadian Corps." I have perused lots of army-level orders from the Great War, and not seen another which begins with such a personalized phrase. It is almost certainly formal British understatement (or "Britspeak") for "You can't imagine how irked the GOC Canadian Corps was with the previous version, but this should calm him."

The new orders moved Currie a bit further north along the front, and essentially turned that section of the front over to Currie. Paragraph 3 reads, "The adjustments detailed above will place the whole of the operations for the capture of Lens in the hands of the GOC Canadian Corps, and his immediate main objective will be the capture of the high ground NW of the town." It is the first mention in army-level orders of high ground subsequently known as Hill 70.

Between 15 and 20 August, the Canadian Corps battled five German divisions and took and held Hill 70. The attack cost the Corps some 3,500 casualties, and the clever and innovative defence against days of large scale counter-attacks, which constituted 21 distinct counter attacks, cost another nearly 2,300 casualties. But the Canadians held, and some German sources place German casualties above 20,000. The five German divisions virtually ceased to exist as coherent formations. The action at Hill 70 had been intended to weaken the forces available to the Germans for Passchendaele and it clearly achieved that aim.

I have focussed upon the capture and holding of Hill 70, and not the subsequent only partially successful attempt to invest Lens. Generally, Canadians think of the two actions together, covering Aug 15–25, 1917, as both are addressed in Horne's order of 10 July, and juxtaposed in Nicholson's official history. But the Lens phase was hastily planned, and the plan never fully developed. As it happens, it was probably an unnecessary action, as the requisite damage to the German units which the British had hoped to interdict from reinforcing Passchendaele was achieved in the earlier Hill 70 phase. And the Germans remaining in Lens could never be secure or at ease, with the Canadians holding Hill 70 and being able to see and hit targets within Lens at will.

It had been a hard fight; six Canadians received the VC for their actions at Hill 70, versus four at Vimy Ridge.

The successful battle for Hill 70 was the watershed. After that Currie had new status. He was viewed as having superb judgement. Army commanders treated him carefully (Horne, 1st Army, and Rawlinson, 4th Army). Suddenly the Canadian Corps had become a national allied army, and not just another unit of the British Army.

The Canadian Corps under Currie was doing very well indeed, and began to differentiate itself from a typical British corps. It always had one advantage over a British corps, and that was the lack of churning. A British corps was an ephemeral sort of thing, with divisions being switched frequently from corps to corps. Reorganization, a new group of commanders to deal with, and a rapidly changing order of battle were constant. The Canadian corps, thanks to Borden's and Currie's insistence, stayed together, and relationships and expectations stabilized.

Later the Corps carried some of its own reinforcements with it, and it had always had a consistent support organization. But the Canadian differentiation was driven as well by three other factors, which I am tempted to ascribe to both the slightly different nature of Canadian society and the unusual backgrounds of the leaders of the Canadian Corps.

First, in the Canadian Corps, there was always a tendency to accord junior leaders more responsibility than might be expected, and hence to delegate further down the chain of command than others might.

Secondly, the avoidance of unnecessary casualties assumed greater importance in the Canadian Corps than it seemed to amongst our allies.

And thirdly, the Canadians were avid adopters of new technologies, at a time when new gizmos and techniques were appearing with great frequency.

It is common to ascribe at least the first two of these to the fact that early 20th century Canada was dramatically less class-ridden than early 20th century Britain, and the Canadian existence still embodied a fair bit of can-do pioneering spirit and a stronger tendency to look out for one another in harsh settings. All true, indeed. But something additional was also at work.

Most of the general officers of the Canadian Corps had not been lifelong full-time soldiers.

This did two things. First, they knew they were not as completely steeped in military lore as their regular force British counterparts, and so they were very open to learning new stuff.

Secondly, they brought quite a bit from their other careers. Of the general officers in Currie's Corps, two had been career journalists, four had been lawyers (one of whom, BGen Griesbach, had been mayor of Edmonton), and two were trained scientists and engineers. One, Andrew McNaughton, had been Assistant Professor of Mechanical Engineering at McGill, and the other, Charles Hamilton Mitchell, became Dean of Engineering at U of T immediately after demobilization.

A majority of the leaders of the Corps were gunners, and it's often said that the First World War, for Canada, was a gunner's war. But one must remember that in the late 19th century, the artillery were the intellectuals of the profession of arms, as they represented and used the high science of the era. In those years, after the publication of Maxwell's Equations, but before the rise of atomic science, many learned people felt that science was nearly complete, with just a bit of polishing left to do, and that the macro world it described was "the end of science." And the gunners used all that macro science.

The dismal facts of 1914 forced rapid technological change. 1914 was worse than anything ever portrayed in film.

The tactics were little different than the mid-19th century. There was no fire and movement, no lateral trench-clearing raids, but the machine-gun existed. 1915 saw new tactics and 1916 saw new technologies, including the tank. Even the concept of using wire cutters in trench raids for stealth, rather than using artillery to cut wire was an innovation, coming from the 25th battalion of the 5th brigade in Jan 1916.

By 1917, the set-piece attack had been nearly perfected. Improved barrel wear algorithms and better standardization of shells meant being on target without registration. Better fusing meant the artillery did often cut the wire. Scientific skills were brought to the design of the rolling barrage and the back barrage, including the first use of large numbers of machine guns in barrage work. Counter-battery fire was perfected, with important Canadian advances in sound location of opposing batteries, using wave-form matching from an arc of microphones. The Canadians knew of flash spotting as well, but used it less. In the Corps counter-battery office, led by Andrew McNaughton, the projects were the beginning of operations research. At Vimy, 83% of the 212 heavy guns in the German batteries opposing the Canadian positions were put out of action early by extensive counter-battery fire buried in the rolling barrage.

Other innovations were things like careful repeated rehearsals for attacks, using similar terrain. There were new systems of giving orders, so everyone down to the rank of corporal understood their objectives and those of the people or units about them.

Hill 70 saw elements of all-arms battle. Wireless communication from aircraft-borne observers allowed the artillery to target German troops massing for counter attacks, by hitting them in their assembly areas. Hence the horrific

German losses in the counterattack phase of Hill 70. At last, the artillery forward observer was not limited by the tallest tree he could climb, and the gunners now had eyes beyond the horizon.

In the months that followed, Currie differentiated the Canadians even more. In January 1918 he refused triangulation of Canadian divisions, and in doing so refused personal promotion to Army commander. At that time, British divisions had moved to a structure which included three brigades, each with three somewhat understrength battalions (6–700 infantry each), hence the 3x3, or "triangulation."

Currie believed that triangulation could cause pointless casualties, and preferred to fight divisions at full strength. He kept the infantry in the Canadian divisions at three brigades, each with four battalions of infantry. These were over-strength battalions too, at about 1100 men each, as each carried 100 of their own reserves. He kept the Canadians as a corps rather than an army, eschewing the complexity of having two corps HQ and an army HQ. But the Canadian Corps was by then larger and more powerful than most British armies, and each of the four Canadian divisions was equal to at least 1.7 British divisions. In 1918, Haig started adding to the impact of the 156,000 strong Canadian Corps by placing additional British divisions under Currie as well.

In the spring of 1918, when the Canadians had been held out of the line during the attempted German breakout, the Canadians began experimenting with the development of open warfare doctrine. While still based upon the building block of the set-piece battle, it envisioned rolling battles designed in steps, a series of set-pieces, each separately planned, each separated by 4–6 hours, like a ponderously walking giant. By Amiens, it worked just that way, with the 3rd Division halting at noon on 8 August, and the 4th driving straight through it in the next step. The guns moved up to five times a day, without registration. At Amiens, Currie used many tanks as ammunition and water carriers, and the CIF (Brutinel's Force) used the parallel road on the right hinge of the battle, between the Canadians and the French, to run their trucks armed with 6" Newton mortars and heavy machine guns. That had been Currie's addition to Gen Rawlinson's plan. In a new all-arms twist, at Amiens low-flying coordinated aircraft were used to make noise to mask the noise of the tanks, delaying considerably the German realization that tanks were advancing upon them.

By then, the Corps had become quite different. By 1918, a Canadian division had one automatic weapon for every 13 men, vs one for every 61 men in a British division. A Canadian division had about 13,000 infantry and 3,000 engineering troops, vs about 5,400 infantry and 650 engineers for a British division. Curry disliked exhausting the infantry to terraform the battlefield. And the Canadian Corps had 100 more trucks than any British corps. Every Canadian division had 66 bridge-building experts. There were the beginnings of a distinct Canadian way of war. Move fast. Do the impossible. Build six bridges in one night, and three more the next day. At the Canal du Nord, the Germans overreacted, estimating that they were facing 12 Canadian divisions, not 4, and moved all available reinforcements in that sector to oppose them. Frequently, during the weeks of the difficult and hard-fought pursuit towards Cambrai and then towards Valenciennes and Mons, the Canadians would outrun the units on their flank, would have to widen their front, and slow down.

In the last 96 days of the war, known as the "100 days," the Canadian Corps engaged and defeated 47 German divisions, one more than the 46 divisions defeated by 650,000 Americans in the Meuse-Argonne Campaign. But the Canadians took half the casualties of the Americans, using twice the number of artillery shells. Currie's slogan was "Pay the price of victory in shells, not men."

They were inventing as they went. New Canadian doctrine on open warfare, issued early in the 100 Days, included "Employment of Mobile Corps Troops," issued 19 Sept, and "The Policy as to the Command of Artillery Units during Offensive Operations," issued 20 Sept.

But Hill 70 had been a watershed point in both Canadian autonomy and Canadian military differentiation. The important decision taken during 7–10 July 1917 to focus Canadian effort on Hill 70 was crucial. But Currie's bold choice to question an order that was not in Canada's interest would have had little ongoing impact if his judgement hadn't been vindicated by the events of August 15–20, 1917, when the Canadians, under his command, won the battle for Hill 70.

They were not alone. The Australian Corps had engaged and defeated 37 German divisions. Thus two "colonial" corps representing less than 10% of allied forces on the Western Front had put paid to half the German units on the Western Front.

The successes of the Canadian Corps, particularly those under Canadian command, beginning with Hill 70 and culminating with the Battle of Amiens and the subsequent "100 days," achieved great recognition for Canada and greatly enhanced Borden's role at Versailles.

While, at the end of the Great War, there was something of a Canadian way of war, did it persist? In some ways the differentiation was ephemeral, in that the Canadians were "early adopters" of techniques and technology which were starting to penetrate elsewhere as well, and which in due course were adopted by most armed forces in the developed world. But traces of those early differences remain today.

For example, compared to American or British forces, Canadian officers and senior NCMs today usually have responsibilities roughly equivalent to those carried by folk one-half to one rank higher amongst our allies. And comparing to other NATO allies, especially the more recent members, the disparity is often greater than one rank. Others may talk about the strategic corporal, but we have them.

Concomitantly, we have a flatter income distribution across the rank structure than other nations. And our NCM's are somewhat older, with lots more education and life experience.

This differentiation from other militaries has been a godsend for us now that technology has dramatically increased the power of relatively small forces. But it would not have been surprising to leaders of the Canadian Corps from Hill 70 onwards.

While it is interesting to observe that there are still effects of the Great War on the Canadian Armed Forces, the bigger story is, of course, the effect on the country as a whole and, indeed, even on the speed with which it actually became a country. There is little doubt that Canada would have eventually become independent. After all, the other dominions of the UK have also now gained independence. But the First World War (often called the Great War), and especially battles like Vimy Ridge and Hill 70, certainly hastened that process and shaped the character and attitudes of Canada. My contextualizing the battle of Hill 70 may be useful as a contribution to the debate about whether it was a necessary war for Canada, but it barely touches on the changes that the war wrought on Canada. A quite interesting account of Canada in the aftermath of the war, focusing on those changes, is a book entitled

A Time Such as There Never Was Before: Canada After the Great War by historian and diplomat Dr. Alan Bowker. It is a relatively recent (2014) volume that is still available. Alan and I have been close friends since our time as undergraduates at the University of Toronto in the early 1960s, and we have had plenty of opportunities to exchange thoughts on the making and governing of Canada.

There is still a kind of historic sadness about our losses in the First World War. As Dr. Bowker notes in his book, it is why the bell and clock tower sitting on the central axis of the Centre Block of the Canadian parliament buildings in Ottawa is called the Peace Tower, when it had been planned as the Victory Tower.

Wars today remain a risk and a concern for the liberal democracies, but the most probable and most frightening global risks to life and limb may be from disease rather than war. And while we may have stumbled, half-blind, into the First World War, expecting it to be over in four months, there is some evidence that we are equally lacking in prescience about other risks. Some simple steps to reduce those risks are the subject of the final section of Chapter 4.

4.6 One Mistake We Don't Need to Make

The Covid-19 pandemic is possibly the most consequential event of the 21st century so far. It is caused by the SARS-CoV-2 virus. The origin of that virus remains unclear, but the debate over its origin has not remained scientific but has also become political and highly polarizing.

Thus, it has become something of a tenet of faith on the right, particularly in the United States, that the virus was released as a result of a lab leak at the Wuhan Institute of Virology, in Wuhan, China, while an opposing view, often strongly held in more progressive circles, is that it arose in nature, passing from a bat to an intermediate animal host, to humans, probably in the so-called "wet market" in Wuhan. That, too, would result in some opprobrium for China as well, since "wet markets," where all manner of live creatures, mostly from the wild, are sold to the public for food, are supposed to be illegal.

There is a profound lack of hard evidence, so either remains plausible. (What is not plausible are occasional claims by Chinese authorities that it came from abroad and was mailed into China by some malevolent party.)

The political polarization is pointless because the answer isn't important. It doesn't matter where the virus came from because of the very fact that either is possible. Fact #1: Wet markets are dangerous and must be expunged. Fact #2: Levels 3 and 4 biosafety research labs have a long record of being dangerous too, and there is something that needs to be done about them. The issue is not about blaming one or the other. It is about fixing both. Or rather, banning one and fixing the other. And the fix is not especially complex. It just costs a bit. That is why we needed both a bit of history and a bit of logic to move this issue out of politics and back to science. Back to the middle ground. To that end, I wrote, "Risks from Biocontainment Labs: A Puzzling Lack of Realism about Human Fallibility Prevails." It was first published on January 25, 2022, in *Ottawa Life Magazine*.[26] What I wrote was as follows:

Risks from Biocontainment Labs: A Puzzling Lack of Realism about Human Fallibility Prevails

We will never know whether SARS-CoV-2, the virus that causes Covid-19, began to spread in Wuhan in late 2019 because of a lab leak. Was there some small handling mistake with a sample in the collection of coronaviruses being studied at the Wuhan

Institute of Virology, or did the virus pass naturally from bats to some other host, and thence to humans without having been collected, moved, stored and possibly subjected to some study? But even if the Covid-19 pandemic did begin with a lab leak, it would only be the most recent in a long line of failures in biocontainment by laboratories across the globe.

Indeed, the world's scientific community has, for generations, been of two minds about whether certain types of laboratory work on dangerous human pathogens was a good or bad idea. When modern techniques of genetic manipulation first became available, there was a period when the international scientific community agreed upon and instituted a moratorium on certain types of experiments on such pathogens. The arguments against the work focussed on the risks of failure of biocontainment, while the arguments in favour focussed on the need to carry out such work in order to be able to design and produce cures and preventatives for such diseases, and whatever new forms they mutated to.

After a time, the moratorium was lifted. Those who had wanted it lifted had argued, with some cogency, that (a) not everyone was honouring the moratorium anyhow, (b) in certain quarters work on unethical bioweapons would continue in secret and could not be regulated, and (c) there was, by then, a generally agreed upon classification of levels and practices of biocontainment, and, if appropriate standards could be maintained, the benefits of the knowledge gained outweighed the risks of leaks.

But historically, there have been plenty of leaks. More on that below, but first, a bit of formalism on biocontainment jargon.

The classification of biocontainment levels for laboratories has, for the most part, settled on four generally accepted levels of procedures and precautions. In Canada these are termed

Containment Levels, or CL, and in the United States they are called Bio-Safety Levels, or BSL. The highest level is CL-4, which is the same as BSL-4. We hear more use of the term BSL because the US nomenclature dominates the airwaves, so I shall use that terminology, except when referring specifically to Canada.

BSL-1 and 2 are fairly easily accomplished, and most labs have no problem meeting that standard. But BSL-3 and BSL-4 are much more stringent. Historically, most coronavirus work was at BSL-3, while BSL-4 was mostly the province of the really scary pathogens like the highly lethal hemolytic viruses, such as Ebola and Marburg. Perhaps today, out of increased caution, some pathogens formerly worked on at the BSL-3 level may now be studied using BSL-4 containment protocols.

The same classification system for containment exists for animal pathogens, and, in some cases, plant pathogens, and there are many BSL-3 and 4 labs in the world that do not work on any human pathogens at all, but are focussed on preventing, curing or understanding animal and plant diseases.

Canada has only a single CL-4 lab at this time, the Canadian Science Centre for Human and Animal Health, in Winnipeg. But there are Level 4 labs in at least 23 countries, and, while the exact number of such labs that exist is not precisely known, it probably approaches 100. There are, as well, a few thousand Level 3 labs in the world.

And humans are fallible. Mistakes are made. Leaks occur. All modern deaths from Smallpox, for example, have been caused by lab leaks, notably three outbreaks in the UK (1966, 1972 and 1978). Anthrax deaths in Russia were a lab leak, and Marburg escaped from a lab in Germany in 1967 and one in Russia in 1990. It is also pretty clear that the H1N1 influenza strain that caused the 1977 pandemic was a lab-leaked strain.

SARS has escaped from labs in Singapore, Taiwan and China. Ebola escaped from labs in the UK (1976) and Russia (2004–5). A prion disease escaped from a French lab in 2019. And in the US, in 2009, an associate professor at the University of Chicago was killed by a lab leak of the bacterium Yersinia Pestis, the same pathogen that was known as the Plague in Europe, which, in the six years 1347–53, killed more than a third of the population of Europe.

And large numbers of leaks with little widespread consequence have occurred, which had the effect of dulling the scientific community's sense of concern for the problem.

Consequently, to expect that even the most stringent containment protocols are an absolute defence against human error all the time is the height of folly, of course.

How often do we hear the expression, "To err is human"? If it were possible to train professionals to always be error-free, at least when their own lives or livelihoods were at stake, we would never hear of commercial aircraft crashes that were due to pilot error. Or ship collisions at sea. Or sponges being left inside surgical patients, for that matter. Yet the dangerously arrogant assumption that, somehow, the operation of biocontainment-rated labs is the unique exception is widely prevalent. That stance reflects a complete lack of realism about human fallibility.

But, for the world's Level 3 and Level 4 laboratories, there is a simple way to dramatically reduce the chance that the inevitable but rare error will result in an epidemic or pandemic. And, by not thinking the matter through, we've dropped the ball on that simple safeguard.

The vast majority of Level 3 and Level 4 biocontainment facilities are in cities. For the ones associated with centres of higher learning (which is nearly half of them), they were built to be essentially co-located with their universities. The people who do the experiments in them live their lives in those cities, go home to their families in those cities every night, go to parties, and shop on the weekends. Bad idea.

The logical concept for a Level 3 or 4 lab ought to be to place it in a less populated space, even though it could be near a city. But it would need to be more than just a lab building. It would have to be a self-contained campus, so that there would be living quarters as well, plus all basic services. Those carrying out the work there, when finished with their direct experimental work with the pathogens, would move from their working living quarters to an on-site quarantine living facility for a prescribed period before returning to their homes, their home university, and their normal lives. So would folks whose tasks required them to come in contact with the researchers actively engaged in the experiments or quarantined.

As a former medical research scientist myself, I know that the number of days in a year that I actually carried out my experiments was small compared to the great swaths of time spent designing and preparing for the experiments, analyzing data, writing grant applications and papers, and even building equipment. Consequently, the disruption to the life of a researcher to take this extra precaution during the period of actual manipulation of the pathogens is unlikely to be extreme.

Now, I'm sure that the rejoinder to my suggestion will be that the academic bio-scientists who would do such experiments could never be induced to work in such a dislocating environment, and wouldn't hear of having to go off-site from their home universities to carry out certain experiments. But that is a small matter of cultural adjustment. After all, their colleagues who are archeologists go to digs in remote locations. Oceanographers go to sea (even the ones that get seasick). And while automation does help in some cases, some of their astronomer colleagues still go to observatories in Hawaii, or in the Atacama Desert of Chile. The historians go to remote archives. The wildlife biologists go, well, into the wild, from time to time. The glaciologists have an even worse time, because they go to damned cold places.

But, when it comes to biocontainment, to avoid the extra inconvenience and extra cost of the extra layer of protection that I am suggesting, the scientific and regulatory community is exposing the entire human race to an unacceptable and conceivably terminal risk. The assumption that they can always be perfect flies in the face of all other human experience. How can they always be error-free when no other group is? And, indeed, how can they be error-free when their own colleagues and predecessors have failed on that score so many times before? I used the expression "dangerously arrogant" earlier in this piece, and I wonder if perhaps that may be an understatement.

I started this piece with a reference to SARS-CoV-2. While we do not know that a lab error played a role in unleashing it upon us, the majority of experts maintain an open mind on that question and do not rule it out. But the disease it causes is not a particularly effective people-killer, having so far done in, by official counts, only about 6–7 million people, though the actual figure is likely to be vastly higher. But the cost to humankind of the spread thus far of this single pathogen is so much vaster than any cost of doing a dramatically better job of laboratory biocontainment that it is rather like comparing the weight of an elephant to that of a bee.

However, the political cost of appearing to "waste" money on an over-cautious approach to biocontainment is certainly one driver behind our failure to do it better. Humans routinely do a bad job of preparing for very unlikely but very consequential events. We've all heard variations on the notion that, when faced with a choice, people and organizations deal with and invest in "urgent" matters at the expense of pushing off to the future the investment in those "important" matters that are not seen as immediate. We have certainly seen this worldwide in the almost universal poor preparation for the current pandemic, despite plenty of learned advice to most governments of developed states to prepare better, and despite government claims that they were prepared (sort of).

So, what can be done to create a climate of greater care in biocontainment? Perhaps a lesson can be drawn from some of the (admittedly imperfect) safeguards around nuclear power generation.

Because of the existence of nuclear and thermonuclear weapons, the word "nuclear" continues to be scary for most folks. It is just over 2/3 of a century since the first full-scale nuclear plant for generating electricity was put into operation (1954). Yes, there have been some mistakes, with all three of the really notable ones due to a combination of slightly silly design and bad operator decisions (in one case exacerbated by a tsunami). The Fukushima evacuation may have caused or accelerated up to 2,300 deaths (not from radiation, but from displacement and chaos), and radiation from Chernobyl, worldwide, may have caused or accelerated up to 60,000 deaths, using the most extreme model. Three Mile Island was expensive, but the most thorough analyses suggest that no lives were lost as a result of the accident. So, those lost from the three aforementioned high profile nuclear accidents total a fraction of one percent of the more than seven million lost due to just the 1977 lab-leak H1N1 pandemic, and, if perchance Covid is eventually to be found to be lab-leak related, it would be a lab leak that will have caused or accelerated the deaths of vastly more millions than the 1977 pandemic before it is done.

Is nuclear power generation inherently safer than studying and modifying dangerous pathogens in BSL-3 and BSL-4 labs? I suspect that it is, but I don't know. But I do know that the world took the concerns about nuclear power generation seriously, which is why an international agency with global reach exists to put pressure on nation states to behave responsibly in their development of such nuclear capabilities. That agency is the IAEA, the International Atomic Energy Agency. It has existed since 1957, and promotes safety in nuclear power generation, discourages nuclear weapon development, and promotes the distribution of isotopes and equipment for cancer therapies to nations that cannot easily afford them. It has 173 member states, including any that we would think of as capable of work on nuclear projects.

The IAEA is imperfect, and its responses have occasionally been criticized as too slow and/or too mild. In part, this is because the agency understands that the only tools it has for applying pressure on any nation state to allow access or to comply with its recommendations are its power to cause embarrassment or loss of face. These tools, however, should not be underestimated. And it did win a Nobel Prize in 2005. Despite its shortcomings, it's a damned sight better than not having it at all.

I would suggest that biocontainment of dangerous pathogens needs the same type of international regulatory and promotional agency of good repute that has brought some order, caution, and standards of practice to nuclear issues for 65 years. And Canada could make some waves by proposing, championing and offering to provide some seed money for such an undertaking. If such an agency existed, getting BSL-3 and BSL-4 labs properly located and isolated would be a doable international task. Additionally, it would be a fine forum for establishing best practices for the limits on gain-of-function studies and other work deemed to have some inherent risk.

If our PM wants a flagship peaceful international project to promote, he could do far worse than the creation of the International Agency for Monitoring Biocontainment and Instituting Controls (IAMBIC). He could even get poetic about it. Yes, the acronym is intentional.

Of course, there is the small risk that launching a campaign for the creation of such an agency at this time might be taken by China as a veiled accusation about the origins of Covid, despite the obvious need for such an entity, given the extensive worldwide history of lab leaks. And, as we have seen recently, a hissy fit by the government of China can involve hostage taking. But I think any outrage or strong opposition from that quarter unlikely, because the superb tacticians in Beijing understand that overreaction and self-incrimination look a lot alike.

Unfortunately, the divisive bickering over the origins of Covid-19 has poisoned any rational public discussion of biocontainment lab risks and the mitigation thereof. There seems to be no structured debate about international monitoring of such laboratories or research protocols. It is a clear case of the logical middle ground being swamped by extremism, partisan politics, and juvenile name-calling.

In scientific circles, however, the discourse is more moderate, and ideas such as those outlined above are being discussed, but the portion of the plan involving separate, slightly remote campuses is always discussed in very hushed tones, because, as research institute directors will tell you, they just don't have the financial support to begin to make the changes I have suggested. They fear that they might be forced to stop all work if they are too vocal about risks before the resources for risk mitigation seem likely to become available. It is a classic chicken-and-egg problem: The gatekeepers of public funds must have a clear perception of the current risks before the money for the proposed safety reforms could be allocated, but, on the other hand, the expensive work on risk mitigation must be carried out before there is broad public acknowledgement of the current risks, or the situation could provoke both a politically damaging public scandal and a moratorium on the research work.

In such a situation, there may only be one practical solution: determined gradualism. If a single president of a university with an associated BSL-3 or BSL-4 facility moved ahead with the plan for relocation of the lab and its supporting infrastructure and services, adhering to the suggested self-contained design, the others would feel pressure to follow suit. The best first candidate would be an institution that already owns some undeveloped real estate that is located in a relatively unpopulated setting separate from the principal campus but still fairly accessible. This safety enhancement could then receive widespread praise, generating imitators.

International regulation and an international regulatory agency are less easy to institute. Such a project would require prominent champions from a number of nation states with high-end bioresearch capability. I cannot see a project of this sort succeeding without active endorsement from most of the permanent members of the UN Security Council. Support from the United States plus support from at least one of China and Russia would be needed. That makes such an initiative very unlikely in the near term, given the near-cold-war level tensions between the United States and Russia, and the current chill in relations between the United States and China. But, in the roller-coaster ride of international relations, there may come such a moment. When it does, it must be seized.

The other lesson for us in all this is that common sense about science often has to wait for a lucky moment in politics in order to catch a wave of public support. But science and politics often don't cohabit well. That is the theme of Section 5.1, in Chapter 5, coming up next.

CHAPTER V

Improving the Politics in Democracies

THIS CHAPTER DOES NOT even try to paint a comprehensive picture of efforts to seek out and reinforce the middle ground in the politics of the liberal democracies. That task would be hard to complete in an entire volume, let alone a single chapter.

My goal in this chapter is much more modest and has three facets. The first is to try to explain why certain classes of issues are always handled poorly in democracies and to guess at how this may be ameliorated. The second is to take a tour through various democratic systems, including ours and the one in the United States, to examine structural biases in voting systems. In the third part, and in light of the importance of leaders' debates in modern election campaigns, I examine the reasons behind the shockingly bad quality of the leaders' debates during the 2021 federal election in Canada and suggest some possible correctives.

5.1 About Things that Many Politicians Handle Badly

Politics in the liberal democracies has never been a pristine landscape. While his words are often cited in truncated or slightly altered form, Winston Churchill articulated the balanced case for democracy, with all its mayhem, on November 11, 1947, in the House of Commons, when he said:

> Many forms of Government have been tried, and will be tried in this world of sin and woe. No one pretends that democracy is perfect or all-wise. Indeed, it has been said that democracy is the worst form of Government except all those other forms that have been tried from time to time; but there is the broad feeling in our country that the people should rule, and that public opinion expressed by all constitutional means, should shape, guide, and control the actions of Ministers who are their servants and not their masters.

That being said, there are some things that democracies handle better than others. Legislators usually understand the structures, relationships, and attitudes of civil society and so have a pretty adequate track record when it comes to passing laws that tell us what is acceptable conduct, or how property can be developed or how resources are collected fairly for the expenditures that government makes on our behalf.

But there are broad swaths of human knowledge that are likely to remain a source of puzzlement for the sort of folk who end up as our elected representatives. Some of these zones of legislative cluelessness are gradually becoming rather more central to the issues of the day. The early phase of the Covid pandemic highlighted this fact for me and stimulated my thinking about how badly our democratic governments handle issues in which science, especially new science, plays an important role. In July 2020, many months before any vaccines for Covid were available, I wrote something entitled "Science and Politics: Always a Stormy Marriage." It appeared on July 29, 2020, in *Ottawa Life Magazine*.[27] What I wrote was as follows:

Science and Politics: Always a Stormy Marriage

The global Covid-19 pandemic seems an all-consuming issue these days, but it is by no means the first of a burgeoning new class of public policy issues. In trying to make sense out of the important issues public policy issues today, one must accommodate two important new facts of life.

The first is that, compared to past eras, more of the key issues of public policy don't stay confined regionally. Of course, the current Covid-19 pandemic has underscored that in the most dramatic way, but it's not the only issue that breaks the conventional bounds of geography. Globalization in trade and finance has tied together the economic realities across the entire developed world as never before. Some of the physical threats are also not easily confined geographically or attributed to specific nation states either, from militant jihad, sometimes expressed as terrorism, to the ripple effects from failed and failing states, as exemplified by the piracy concerns extending from East Africa across the Indian Ocean. And regardless of one's take on climate change and the scale of anthropogenic contributions to its rate, it also has no borders, and neither do all the attendant energy issues.

The second new fact of life is that to a greater extent than ever before, political decisions on large-scale issues also rest on an underpinning of complicated and uncertain science, whether that science is biology, medicine, climate science, nuclear engineering, aeronautics, or information technology. But science and politics are uncomfortable travelling companions, and always have been.

Distortions of science by the political process are inevitable, even in the most open and democratic systems, because they are inherently different processes and reach conclusions or decisions by entirely different methodologies. Ideally, in science, there is a process of continuous refinement, building on past established data and facts, with experimentation, confirmation, open verification and civil discourse.

In politics, with all the best will in the world, the competition for media attention and popular support produces tactical exaggeration, incomplete discourse, huge oversimplification, transient effects, short memory, intense partisanship, and convergence only when absolutely necessary, and not always even then. Overlaid on all that are the complications of secrecy, sometimes needed, especially where issues of national defence, security or even general well-being of the state are concerned, and sometimes merely desired by government to avert complexity and embarrassment in the political arena. So it is unsurprising that plenty of lawyers and relatively few scientists end up in parliament, and that the political sphere may unintentionally abuse science for political purposes.

There is another reason why there are so few scientists in the elected legislative bodies of the liberal democracies. That is because, in real democracies, elected office is a contract job which may well last decades, but may also be as short as a few years. Folks coming to politics from the encyclopaedic disciplines like law, political science, or the humanities can return to their former occupations after they leave public office. They might require a modest updating to be fully aware of the latest work in their fields, but can still be effective in returning to their prior lives. Often the activities and issues of their political lives have actually kept them well informed of evolving trends in their former occupations. But those coming from leading edge research in the experimental disciplines can rarely go back. Once they leave the research granting stream, and their original field passes them by, they can almost never catch up again. So few take the risk to go into the contract-work of elected office.

Back in the late 1970s and early 1980s, I led the attempt by a consortium of learned societies to educate Canadian parliamentarians on the need for investment in fundamental research, and in doing that task, I sent two-person interviewing teams of experts once or twice a year to meet with every MP who would consent to such discussions, which usually meant about 70% of the members of the House of Commons. Because the interviewing teams met privately with each MP, discussions were relatively open, and the team members got good insights into how knowledgeable each MP was about scientific issues.

The reports from our interviewing teams included a scoring system for their estimates of how knowledgeable the MPs were. We used a 1–5 scale, with "5" meaning "as knowledgeable as our experts" and "1" meaning "has virtually no comprehension of science or scientific issues." Then we aggregated the data from five years of this process, grouping MPs by their prior occupation. We could then see that on scientific issues, the two best informed and most knowledgeable groups of MPs were (a) the small group of MPs who were physicians, and (b) the MPs who had been farmers. By the numbers, the few physicians had an average score of about 4.5, the few farmers about 4, the large group of lawyers about 2.7, and the self-made business folk about 1.6. Hence it is probably unavoidable that the Canadian polity would show some lack of prescience, some opportunism and some political missteps on science-based issues.

And that's the best of it. Worse yet, history is replete with examples of repressive regimes making bad science serve ideological purposes. Within the past century, Nazi science appalled humanity, while Stalin harnessed the fraudulent work of Trofim Lysenko to create a noxious fable running counter to modern genetics. Nor is this new. The Church's concerns about Galileo and about Copernicus, and two millennia of deference to Aristotle's reasoning at the expense of experimentation, or the stagnation of medicine because of slavish reliance upon Galen, only finally countered in part by William Harvey, are earlier examples of ideology trumping science.

Sometimes the public is fed bad science for a good reason, as during the Second World War, when the biochemically plausible but untrue link between consuming carrots and improving night vision was widely circulated by UK authorities as a security ruse to explain away the success of British night fighters, by then secretly equipped with airborne miniaturized radar, against German bombers. How many of us were brought up being told, "Eat your carrots, it's good for your vision"?

And even "good" governments can have their favourite scientists and their preferred science. In the Godkin Lectures at Harvard in 1960, physicist and writer C. P. Snow detailed the wartime feud in Britain between key science advisors Sir Henry Tizard and Frederick Lindemann (Lord Cherwell). Published as "Science and Government" a year later, his discourse is persuasive about how badly even democratic governments inevitably handle scientific knowledge and opinion on questions of key national interest, especially when secrecy is required. And 60 years on, the US intelligence failures over weapons of mass destruction in Iraq underscored how, in a necessarily secret environment, evidence and opinion link arms so tightly that they are hard to disentangle.

Clearly a good part of the uneasy fit between science and government hinges upon the occasional need for, and the rather more frequent desire for, secrecy by government. China's delays and lack of candour over SARS in 2003, and more recently over Covid-19, and similar temporizing and understating during nuclear accidents by the Soviet Union at the time of Chernobyl, and to a lesser but non-zero extent by Japan over Fukushima Daiichi were doubtless intended in the first instance by those governments to protect them from embarrassment and perhaps to be ameliorative by preventing panic, but objectively did harm by delaying the appropriate full-scale responses.

But inability of most governments to cope with science is not only about delay and under-reaction; political overreactions, while less frequent, do occur as well, especially with anything which sounds scary, whether it is or not. For example, in the nuclear energy field, a venting of a trivial amount of a relatively short lived and weak beta-emitter like tritium is often spun and then reacted to as if it were a near-meltdown.

Canada has no immunity from the science and government conundrum. In the early 1960s the Liberal decision to accept four separate American nuclear weapons systems for use by the RCAF and the Canadian Army under dual key arrangements with the US was justified by quite out-of-date science and strategic thinking that largely had just gone out of fashion in the US at the moment we came on board, but the decision suited us politically for a brief period.

More recently, we had a notable failure in Canada in 2003, when extremely ineffectual, even minimalist, steps at both the federal and Ontario levels during the SARS outbreak underscored the collision between science and politics. I have set out the view elsewhere that Ontario handled that matter more awkwardly and less effectively that any other jurisdiction in the developed world. In some ways, that bad experience with a fairly hard to transmit virus did, however, condition our governments to do a vastly better, but far from perfect job dealing with Covid-19.

Today, other than the centrepiece of the struggle against the Covid-19 pandemic, Canada faces a broad range of near-term questions that are underpinned by the sort of scientific complexities that tend to befuddle governments. Some examples are:

1. How do we counter cyber threats? What legal changes are needed for active cyber defence, as opposed to merely passive measures? What research is critical to keep ahead of those threats?

2. What additional weapons of mass destruction (WMD) proliferation risks are posed by various actors on the world stage? How close is Iran to a nuclear weapon? Is Iranian rhetoric about wiping out Israel to be believed, or, perhaps more cogently, can one justify discounting it, since all other Iranian rhetoric seems to have been acted upon to a degree? Will Iranian devices find their way into the hands of non-state extreme Islamist groups in the same way other Iranian weapons do, and over what time scale? And what about possible transfer to other actors of devices made by Pakistan or North Korea? What are current risks from dirty bombs, chemical and biological weapons, and how are these technologies evolving?

3. To what extent have the early extreme opposing views on rates of climate change converged on a middle ground?

What are the best estimators of time scales for dealing with sovereignty issues in a more open arctic? To what extent and how quickly will climate change issues produce human migrations more extensive than those being seen now, and how will our policies, and our defence and security postures be affected by these instabilities?

4. What other pandemics are on the horizon? What preparations, both scientifically and in the policy and legal domain, do we need to be reasonably prepared for pandemic risks in general?

5. Can we predict the economic patterns to come? How much budget manipulation is needed, and for how long? In terms of risks, is the dismal science able to keep up with the inventive minds of those who package investments in weird forms?

6. Do we have a correct threat taxonomy? Are there substantial threats we have not foreseen? Are we making the usual mistake of extrapolating from only the most recent past, and assuming threats will be similar? On the other hand, have we rigorously extracted all the good lessons we can from the recent past?

Many of these questions will need years of additional study to be answered adequately, and possibly years after that to fully penetrate the political consciousness of the nation. Sometimes that work falls upon those who do not expect it. For example, the process of reforming or simplifying defence procurement or any other technology procurement, and indeed, the entire operation of procurement abuts against these science-based problems every day, with all of the attendant uncertainties inherent therein. It was always thus, when setting out to buy a thing which does not yet exist, but technological intensification now just makes it harder.

Elected governments and legislative assemblies are not especially good at addressing issues that have a time base longer than a couple of electoral cycles, not do they do well with world-girdling issues with a science component. They need to get better at these things, and, in some ways, Covid-19 may have shed a glimmer of light on how that might happen. An encouraging feature of the struggle against Covid-19 is the new emphasis upon and respect for actual expertise. In Canada, the highly visible, credible roles played by provincial and local directors of public health have been notable. And while the news media still dumb down science stories more than they need to, there are many more knowledgeable voices on the public stage than in the past. In the United States, the President backed away from a campaign he had begun against Dr. Anthony Fauci because, if forced to choose, most Americans found the scientist more believable than the politician. A crisis can sometimes diminish the importance of issues of style and appearance and boost the importance of tested, confirmed fact. So, when we come out of the other side of the current crisis, probably some time in 2021, maybe the marriage of science and government will be just a little less stormy than before.

It was, perhaps, a bit optimistic of me to suggest that we would come out of the Covid "crisis" at some point during 2021. But that is, at least in part, a matter of semantics. By late 2021 both my spouse and I had received our third Covid vaccine dose, and while we remained careful, some aspects of life had begun to normalize. Economic activity in 2022 seemed robust, even if some patterns were permanently changed from before. The pandemic has not ended, but it might not still be classed as a crisis, or certainly not "the" crisis, as other matters come to the fore. It has been the cause of a degree of well-tolerated adaptation, and, since the prospect remains for even better vaccines and therapeutics, it could become simply another part of our risk universe.

As I noted in Chapter 2, the democratically elected governments of Canada and its provinces did not (at least initially) handle the developing pandemic ideally. But, as time wore on, they adapted. I spent the first half of my working years as a professor in a faculty of medicine, and, despite what I have written about the poor fit of science and politics, I would give Canada and many of the provinces a reasonably high score for their handling of those parts of the pandemic that lay between mid-summer 2020 and the present. For everything during that period, I would probably give Canada a solid "B." But will we learn from this? Will we avoid the dithering of February to June 2020 the next time? Will we be anticipatory when it comes to onshore production capabilities or to emergency stocks of crucial goods like PPE? Can democratic governments develop real scientific literacy, and can they actually adjust to let the important trump the urgent rather than the reverse? Only time will tell.

This brief glimpse at why many of our political leaders struggle with issues that have a science component causes some voters to wonder how such undeserving folk got elected in the first place. Whenever various of our elected representatives display cluelessness in the face of a crisis, there is an understandable temptation on the part of portions of the public to doubt the legitimacy of the process that placed such individuals in positions of power. But, in the liberal democracies, the slightly unpalatable truth is that, most of the time, elections are true reflections of two things: the rules we have put in place to conduct them and the will of the voters. But the rules we have agreed to put in place for elections may not satisfy everyone's sense of fairness. In the next section I will try to take you on a guided tour of the vagaries of some agreed-upon systems, especially those used in the United States and Canada.

5.2 Electoral Systems: Historical Quirks and Tricky Balancing

Canadians relish comparing their parliamentary system to the electoral system in the United States. It is a mainstay for facile profundity by pundits, monologues and jokes by comedians, and essays by political science students. The tsunami of nonsense being promulgated by conservative American voices about the US presidential election of 2020 is almost enough to evoke snobbery and haughtiness in even the most self-effacing Canadian.

But there have long been critics of established democratic practices in both countries. Many of them have made cogent, reflective cases for bits of electoral reform that might indeed be helpful and that meet both analytical and intuitive tests for fairness. Today in the United States, those more scholarly commentaries are now being swamped by faux reformers who are really just seeking partisan advantage. Especially troubling is the trend of opponents of democracy to allege that they are actually defending democracy with their proposals.

Everyone who engages in debate over democratic forms claims to want a "level playing field." But are they credible? By the beginning of 2021, the growing divergence over what measures would ensure electoral probity and what types of electoral reform would be useful prompted me to try for some sanity on these issues. I wrote a piece entitled "Designs and Democracy: The Politics of Imperfectly Levelled Playing Fields." It appeared on January 11, 2021, in *Ottawa Life Magazine*.[28] What I wrote was as follows:

Designs and Democracy:
The Politics of Imperfectly Levelled Playing Fields

One of the facts of life on the water is that reckless operators of boats are legally responsible for their wake damage. But you have to catch them first.

In the politics of democracies, it's even more of a free-for-all, but sometimes your wake damage does catch up with you. That is why the Trump soap-opera in the US has had such an inglorious final season. And as it winds to a close, we have heard a great deal about the rigging of elections. The fact that Mad King Donald's maunderings are nonsense does not make the subject of election fairness an uninteresting topic.

I take the term "election rigging" to mean the tilting of a playing field that might otherwise be closer to level, as opposed to "election fixing," which would imply a predetermined outcome. Election rigging, in the sense of causing an unlevel playing field, is inherently of two types. One type is legitimate, in that it is above-board and is inherent in the agreed-upon structure of the election process. The second type is illegitimate and seeks to undermine and distort the agreed-upon process. This second, illicit type of rigging is traditionally carried out by unscrupulous regimes that are already in power and are prepared to commit crimes in order to retain power.

Mr. Trump's claim that the US presidential election was illicitly rigged against the incumbent would, if true, make it unique in rigging history. It would have been an election rigged by the folks who weren't in power. Were it true, it would have been so extraordinary as to be worthy of some special prize, probably in physics or thermodynamics.

But the fact that the US election was conducted with scrupulous probity and under intense bipartisan scrutiny does not mean that the playing field was level.

There is nothing mysterious or hidden about the forces which produce legal, long-standing tilts of electoral paying fields in many western liberal democracies. This long-established, structural "rigging" exists to varying degrees in virtually all democratic systems; it arises largely from five factors.

These five factors are: (a) infelicities introduced by geographic representation and its manipulation, (b) limitations on the franchise, (c) the incumbent advantage, (d) the multiplier effect of money, and (e) electoral designs in which a winner may lack a majority of the votes cast.

All these forces were at play in the US federal election of 2020. It is not surprising, given that the US is a collection of federated states, that geographic representation remains important. But the archaic arrangements thereof yield some truly bizarre asymmetries, most of which currently tilt the playing field heavily in favour of the Republican party. By way of example, a vote cast in an election for the US senate, if cast in the very Republican state of Wyoming carries 69 times the weight of a vote cast for the US senate if that voter resides in the very Democratic state of California. And even the presidential election has similar but less extreme biases, in which a vote by a Wyoming resident for a presidential candidate carries 3.8 times the weight of a vote cast by a Californian. A quick perusal of these ratios across all states explains why no Democrat can reasonably expect to win the presidency without garnering at least some 3–4 million votes more than the Republican candidate, but a Republican can very probably win the presidency with 2–3 million votes less than their Democratic opponent.

Furthermore, only two US states do any dividing of their electoral college vote by district, while all the rest use a winner-takes-all approach. That would be roughly equivalent to selecting a Canadian PM by treating each province as a single riding, with the winning party naming all the MPs for that province.

And then there is the incumbent advantage. The person in the highest elected office is always vastly more visible and better known than the leader of the leading opposition party, and this publicity, with name recognition and myriad photo-ops doing good things and giving away money, confers an obvious electoral advantage. Many liberal democracies reduce the incumbent advantage somewhat by separating the roles of head of state and head of government. In a constitutional monarchy, the monarch (or representative thereof) gets the fancy ceremonial roles, and the prime minister gets to be a distinguished spectator. Some republics solve the problem with a ceremonial president who is expected to be relatively apolitical, even if elected, while the prime minister runs the government. This is a bit riskier than the constitutional monarchy approach, because sometimes the connection between the two offices is too close, or one becomes the other, as occurred in Erdogan's constitutional manoeuvre in Turkey.

In the US, where the two top offices are combined, the incumbent advantage has historically been so powerful that, following the presidency of Franklin D. Roosevelt, the 22nd Amendment to the US constitution was passed, mandating a two-term limit for president, which prior to Roosevelt had been customary anyhow. Next month that rule will have been in force for 70 years. Because a sitting president has the huge incumbent advantage of the combined visibility of the two top offices, the effective term of a US president is not really four years. It is effectively eight years, with a four-year off-ramp for those who appear to have severely underperformed.

As to limitations on the franchise, while it is true that conservative forces in the US have been in a century and a half long battle to slow the extension of the franchise for distinctly racist reasons, all the liberal democracies have a long history of struggle for gradual expansion of the franchise. Votes for women, votes for minorities and for aboriginal peoples, and the gradual removal of property and educational requirements for voting have been the standard tale of the evolution of democratic rights in most democratic nations, as well as a gradual reduction in the minimum voting age. This long struggle for expansion of suffrage has often been described as a part of the gradual evolutionary process of monarchies or oligarchies transitioning towards democracy. This is a bit glib, as it neglects realities of the social mores of the 19th century. The case of Belgium is instructive, because Belgium was never anything other than a democracy. It was created as a democracy 190 years ago. For a very long time it had "the plural vote." Voters (male adults) had one vote. If they had a certain level of education, they had a second vote. If they had a certain minimum amount of property, they had a third vote. Thus, Belgian voters of the 19th century each had 1, 2 or 3 votes, depending on how much they knew and how big a stake they had in the system.

The battle in the US to fully extend the franchise to long-disenfranchised minorities is nearing its end. It will be concluded within our lifetimes. But the last gasp of attempted voter suppression by the far right in the US is at the root of Mr. Trump's implausible prevarications about the election, and it will leave a legacy of resentment on both sides that will influence voter alignment for many years to come.

There is even the slight possibility that the present turmoil may signal the beginning of a very rare event in US politics. Roughly every three quarters of a century or so, the party system in the US seems to have a massive convulsion that changes alignments and sometimes even party names. This time there is a modest chance that the Republican party is in its death throes, condemned by demography to perpetual minority status. Its remaining moderates, plus the great bulk of the Democratic party could form a dominant party of the center, and the most strident left democrats may end up as a separate or semi-allied social democratic party. And a big-tent party of the center may be what the US needs in order to champion the structural reforms that could modernize its creaky proto-democracy.

Canadians tend to a bit of smugness now and then. So how level is the playing field in Canada, when compared to our American neighbors? The answer is probably that it is better, but by no means perfect.

One difference in Canada is that it is much harder to tilt the playing field by applying very large doses of money. Political donation limits are low and election expenditures and subsidies are tightly regulated in Canada. Not so in the US in the decade since the "Citizens United v. FEC" decision removed all effective barriers to pouring money into elections by declaring such funding protected by the right to free speech. Many US elections are so awash in money that merely tracking who is buying the influence is impossible. Free speech is a fine thing indeed, but continuous free speech with a megaphone so loud that it drowns out all other voices may not be what the originators of the concept had in mind. And it creates an extraordinary headwind against the rise of any new small party that does not have a billionaire as a patron.

Furthermore, no political party in Canada espouses any interest in any type of voter suppression.

The incumbent advantage in Canada, however, is non-trivial. And the situation may be getting a bit worse. It is understood, of course, that certain high-visibility duties of the head of state are executed by the Governor General (on behalf of Queen Elizabeth, who is the head of state). But there is a grey area, and the current Prime Minister is relatively adept at the platitudinous speech expected on such occasions, and seems to be gradually usurping the Governor General's role except for expressly mandated matters such as the speech from the throne. The visibility of the Governor General is much less than in the past.

The Harper government did make an attempt to reduce the incumbent advantage by passing a parliamentary resolution on fixed election dates. The western Conservatives particularly had long held strongly to the belief that the ability of a sitting PM to decide the timing of an election conferred an undue advantage on the party in power, which could opt to go to the polls when it was experiencing a period of popularity. Unfortunately, the shift to fixed election dates seems to have backfired. A careful examination of the past suggests that, while the ability of the PM to trigger an election at will should have been quite advantageous, it was not, and sitting PMs had guessed wrong with frightening regularity as to optimal election timing. But what the old rule had done was to guarantee short periods of election campaigning, because the date could not be anticipated until the writ was dropped, or perhaps just before, given the power of rumors. The new fixed election date rule has, in effect, greatly lengthened the informal election campaigns that precede the official campaigns, and consequently greatly lengthened the period prior to an election during which the incumbent advantage is thrust in the face of the people.

Canada, like the US, is a large, geographically diverse country, and so the importance of geographic representation is substantial. Furthermore, Westminster-style parliamentary systems stand heavily upon the bedrock of the idea that a local MP known to the community will sort out a whole host of minor administrative problems for individual constituents.

But given the vagaries of geography, it is not possible for all constituencies to contain the same number of electors. Fortunately, Canada is largely free of the very fancy gerrymandering of local electoral boundaries that has been carried out in part of the US with the express intention of disenfranchising certain groups, but nonetheless, we do have considerable variation in constituency population. There are 338 parliamentary constituencies in Canada, and eight of them have fewer than 30,000 voters. However, in four cases that can be explained by the vast territory the MP must cover, as those four seats are Yukon, Nunavut, the Northwest Territories and Labrador. The other four somewhat underpopulated seats are the four in PEI, which is the residuum of the founding constitutional deal. For all of the remaining 330 seats, they each contain 50–100,000 electors. Examining the remaining 330 seats, the greatest disparity by province would be between Saskatchewan and Quebec, with one vote in Saskatchewan having the weight of 1.52 votes in Quebec. Not a completely level playing field, but a far cry from the imbalances in voter weights in the US.

We do, however, have a serious problem of "wasted votes." In a simple first past the post system, if there are more than two candidates the winner in any contest may well have substantially fewer than half the votes cast in that constituency. Thus, it could be argued that the majority are unrepresented. On the whole, such effects tend to average out, but the phenomenon does still rankle with the voters.

There are various known fixes for this, but in some cases the cure is worse than the disease. Proportional representation is often touted as the answer, but its two failings are the elimination or dramatic reduction of geographic representation, and perpetual minority government. Another fix, which actually used to exist in Canada, is enlarged multi-member ridings, so a riding might well end up with its multiple MP's not all being from the same party.

But by far the best solution, especially in the light of automated vote counting, is the single transferable ballot, where electors mark not only their first choice, but, if they wish, may indicate second and third choices, etc. When the count is made, if their first choice is dropped off the bottom of the pack, their second choice then gets counted as if it were a first choice, and so on. So, their voice is still heard, right up to the final two candidates. The winner then always has a majority of sorts. This method has been poorly explained to Canadians, who are usually wary of change, but, frankly, not only is it fairer than what we do now, but in reality, many MP's are already effectively chosen by that method. How so? Well, in seats that you might describe as "safe seats," meaning ones almost always won by the same party, it is the nomination by a vote in the riding association for that leading party that effectively selects the MP. And constituency nomination votes are virtually always carried out using the single transferable ballot method. Arguably, then, something more than half of Canadian MP's are already selected/elected using this method.

And as for the illicit, nefarious sort of election rigging, well, since the coming of cell phone cameras and the internet, it's gotten much harder to accomplish and probably a lot less fun. But it wasn't always easy even in the bad old days. I recall conversations I had in the early 1960s with an acquaintance who was a senior election organizer for the Liberal Party of Canada. He had been given the fairly straightforward task of organizing the party campaign in the 1959 provincial election on Prince Edward Island. It should have been a doddle. The Libs had held PEI since 1935, winning six elections in a row.

Of the 30 seats in the PEI legislature, they had never dropped below 20 during that time, and had 27 seats at dissolution. My interlocutor, on arriving on the island, had asked his local subordinates, "So, what is the price of a vote here?" The response he got back was, "Two bucks and a pint." He thought they meant two bucks and a pint of beer. They meant rum. This misunderstanding engendered so much animus amongst the island's electorate that he blew the election. A tiny shift in votes gave the Progressive Conservative leader Walter Shaw and his running mates 1,631 votes more than Alex Matheson's Liberals; Shaw, who had begun the election campaign with three seats, gained another 19 and became premier with 22 out of 30 seats.

The debate on electoral reform in Canada has not been well conducted. Because it is difficult, in the current political climate, to give even moderately complex explanations, the discourse has been conducted in simplistic sound bites. That is why an easily understood concept like proportional representation gets so much play, despite its unsuitability for Canada. As I noted earlier, it is a recipe for continuous governmental instability. The most obvious example is Israel, where coalitions fall apart with such regularity that it is now heading into its fifth general election in just over three years. But it also is problematic for a country of vast area, where geographical representation and access to one's local MP are important. Israel, after all, is not large; its maximum length is less than the distance from Toronto to Ottawa, and its maximum width is less than Toronto to Coburg, Ontario. The distance in Toronto from the train station to the airport is nearly twice the minimum width of Israel. Thus, geographic representation is much less critical in Israel, and any politician can get to any locus quite quickly.

However, enthusiasts for some form of proportionality often cite the mixed-member proportional system (known as MMP) as a curative for the infelicities of proportional representation. In that variant, many MPs are elected in the current customary fashion and do represent their geographic electoral districts, while an additional group of MPs are elected by the same votes, tallied in a proportional representation fashion, from non-geographic party lists. While it is an adequate compromise that is used in some countries, including Germany and New Zealand, it is unnecessary, given that elections using the single transferable ballot, or, as it is often called, the ranked ballot, are now much easier to conduct because of modern technology. In the past, ranked ballot counting was laborious and lengthy, delaying election results and creating uncertainty. This is no longer true. Furthermore, the ranked ballot forces voters to think about second choices, which has the salutary effect of leading voters to think about the qualities of individual potential representatives, instead of just automatically voting for a particular candidate out of party loyalty.

There is, however, an additional possibility that should be considered, which, when combined with the ranked ballot, could make our elections both more democratic and more interesting without foregoing geographical representation. It has a historical twist. To stick with the historical feel, I will, on occasion, use the older, colloquial term "riding" as a synonym for the more formal "electoral district." In Canada, constituency associations of individual political parties are still widely known as "riding associations." (Contrary to myth, the etymology of the term "riding" has nothing to do with horses.)

Most Canadians think that our current electoral system, the "single member riding" system, with a first-past-the-post single winner from each constituency, is an inheritance from the system used for electing the UK parliament at the time of the passage of the BNA Act of 1867. But that was not the case. When the UK parliament passed that act that made Canada internally self-governing, most British parliamentary constituencies were actually multi-member constituencies. Furthermore, large multi-member ridings with enough voters to justify having multiple MPs existed in many urban parts of Canada for much of our history.

A system of high-population multi-member ridings in urban areas does not do obvious harm to the concept of geographic representation or to the notion that MPs should be of assistance to individual constituents in their dealings with bureaucracy. People would still have easy access to local area MPs, who would not need to travel far to meet constituents.

The Canadian experience with multi-member ridings is extensive. At the federal level, three cities had two-member ridings over a long period, Ottawa (1872–1933), Halifax (1867–1966), and Victoria (1872–1903). One city, Winnipeg, was a 10-member riding from 1920 until 1949 and also used the single transferable ballot. After 1949, for some time Winnipeg was divided into four 3-member ridings, still with the single transferable ballot.

At the provincial level, six provinces had multi-member ridings. BC had some multi-member ridings from 1871 until 1991, Alberta had three ridings in Calgary, Edmonton, and Medicine Hat that at various times returned two, five, six, or seven members. Prior to 1924 these seats were first-past-the-post, with constituents having multiple votes, but from 1924 to 1956 the single transferable vote was used. In Saskatchewan there were multi-member provincial ridings in Saskatoon, Regina, and Moose Jaw from 1920 to 1967, and the constituents had multiple non-transferable votes.

Ontario had a more limited experience, restricted to Toronto. From 1886 to 1890, the entire city was a single multi-member provincial riding, and then, from 1908 to 1914, the four Toronto ridings elected two MLAs each. In New Brunswick, some multi-member provincial ridings existed between 1935 and 1974, and, in PEI, there were dual-member provincial ridings from Confederation until 1996.

Imagine the use of such an approach today, with modern counting devices. The average Canadian single-member federal electoral district currently has a population of about 113,000, of whom about 81,000 are eligible voters. Thus, it would be possible to envision in a city of (say) 565,000 people as a single five-member electoral district. There would be about 400,000 eligible voters.

In such a five-member electoral district, each party would be able to stand five candidates. Each voter could vote for five people and might very well not choose them all from the same party. One could easily imagine a voter who was normally a party stalwart but who might think that one or two of his/her five votes might go to people of known high quality running for other parties. And if one adds the single transferable ballot to the mix, which would give a voter in this imaginary city not only five first choices but five second choices, etcetera, the likelihood of somewhat more voting based upon the perception of the qualities of the candidates, rather than just the name of their party, increases substantially. (Admittedly, such a ballot really needs computer counting so that the local returning officer can remain sane.) I can think of no better way of reinforcing the middle ground than by giving people the choice to not be entirely partisan while still backing their usual favourite.

However, such encouraging possibilities do implicitly raise another question. How will voters know what qualities the various candidates possess? Of course, one can read about the career of the candidate, but that hardly tells the whole story. Of course, the traditional method for sizing up political aspirants was to listen to them speak at length, or debate, and, despite the communications revolution, this is actually becoming more difficult to do, not easier. That conundrum is the subject of the next part of this chapter.

5.3 The Great Need for Real Debate

Voters want and need coherent discussion of the issues of the day. They have a great desire to know the reasoning by which those who govern them are making choices and decisions. Strangely, it is getting harder to have access to such discourse. It is paradoxical that, on the one hand, television and the internet could bring such discourse into almost every home, but it does not. That is because, for the most part, that discourse does not exist in a public setting. The networks purport to provide it, but they do not. Instead, they feed us spectacle, as if we were ancient citizens of Rome, going to watch death in the Colosseum. And not very good spectacle, at that.

The quality of political discourse among Canadian political parties seemed to reach a new nadir during the election campaign of August and September 2021, prior to the federal election, which occurred on September 20, 2021. The excruciating experience of watching the debates among the party leaders prompted me to write "The Spectacularly Awful Leaders' Debates: Causes and a Remedy." It appeared on October 27, 2021, in *Ottawa Life Magazine*.[29] What I wrote was as follows:

The Spectacularly Awful Leaders' Debates: Causes and a Remedy

Now that a discrete interval has passed since our recent federal election, it is an opportune time to try a bit of dispassionate analysis to explain to ourselves why it felt like such a shambles. It launched amidst some controversy over whether it was needed at all, but it seems to me that it didn't entirely become a festival of mutual ox goring until the so-called leaders' debates.

Something very odd has happened to the word "debate," if those leaders' debates are anything to go by. Perhaps it's my inner curmudgeon speaking, but through most of my life, there were two incontrovertible properties of a debate. The first was that all the debaters were expected to speak about the same subject, and the second was that each side had a substantial reserved block of time to elaborate their position (and sometimes more than one block) and a further consolidated block of time for rebuttal. Interruptions by opposing debaters were usually heavily penalized.

The first of the two debates in French had a hint of the original definition of "debate" in its structure, despite the woefully short time blocks. It was conducted with considerable decorum (with only odd exceptions), and the referee (called a "moderator" to mollify the media folk) was respectful, helpful and not especially intrusive. The participants were expected to address the same topics.

By the time we reached the sole English-language debate, the concept had transmogrified itself into an egregious caricature of a sort of demented collective press scrum. The central focus was on the so-called moderator, who peppered each of the leaders with different questions, allowing seconds, rather than minutes, for an answer. It felt more like the interrogation of captured spies than a debate.

But enough about the dubious features of the event. Amongst my usual interlocutors, I have found none who found it edifying. The more interesting questions are, first, what are the causes of that sort of debacle, and, secondly, what can be done to give us something more useful during future elections.

I suspect that there are many causes for what we saw. It is popular to blame the communications revolution and social media for some perceived decline in the attention span of some folk. I'm not entirely certain that attention spans have declined. People still develop intense interests that evoke sustained concentration on a single subject. But some other causes are fairly obvious. Some portions of the press and media have, over the last two generations, become hugely narcissistic. They have gone from reporting the news to thinking that they are the news, and reporting incessantly on themselves.

Again, perhaps it is the curmudgeon in me that makes me think that journalists were better forty years ago. Given the critical importance of free speech and a free press in guaranteeing democracy, I am relieved that there still are a non-trivial number of exceptional, well-informed and perceptive journalists. But many are not. A significant slice of the fourth estate is neither literate nor numerate, and do us the huge discourtesy of assuming we aren't either. They are wrong; large swaths of the voting public in Canada are well-educated and somewhat reflective.

Compounding that is the perceived broadcast need to compress complex issues into 10–30 second soundbites. I say "perceived" because it isn't necessarily true. Newsmagazine shows that take 20–60 minutes on a single issue remain hugely popular.

But if some in the media give new depth to the word "shallow," are leading politicians similarly limited? Admittedly, some politicians and their media advisors have bought into the "soundbite" myth. The result is scenes of political leaders spouting snappy "talking points" and catch phrases, instead of marshalling evidence and outlining their logic. But that doesn't mean that they are all incapable of serious, reasoned debate.

I've known many Canadian politicians, including 3 PMs, 7 party leaders who did not become PM and dozens of members of parliament or senators who were cabinet ministers, and certainly more than half are or were genuinely impressive in private.

So just imagine an election debate in which unelected journalists didn't participate, and didn't interrupt our representatives every 30 or 60 seconds. Imagine candidates debating each other in long enough blocks to be coherent, and on subjects which *they* think we might wish to hear about before we judge their fitness to govern. After decades of watching news anchors and reporters tampering with debates under the guise of being moderators, contemplate the possibility of political discourse not pushed through microcephalic filter of some ill-educated stage prop of a newsreader.

We might get political discourse appropriate for a free people, and I have no doubt that a critical portion of the swing vote would have the knowledge, powers of reasoning, and attention span to assess it properly.

So how can the trend be reversed? Is it possible to get from where we are now to a more civil and substance-oriented debate? Perhaps.

Ironically, the Covid pandemic may just have begun a series of cultural changes that may make such debate more possible. Two important changes in our culture are the public's wariness of crowded in-person events, and an increasing familiarity with on-line events, some of which are interactive. Neither of these trends is likely to be a transient.

This could somewhat reduce the attraction and utility of "whistle-stop" campaigning across the country by party leaders and put more emphasis on broadcast or internet-based events, of which there would logically be more of them and longer ones. That opens the door to a much more extensive series of debates, and that is the crucial key to making them better.

More debates means that each one can cover a single topic, or at least a narrowly defined group of topics. More debates also means that not every leader needs to be in every debate.

Some debates might even be in the traditional format of only two sides in the debate. Furthermore, an extended series of debates provides an opportunity to appropriately scale the participation of party leaders whose parties have not achieved official party status in the House of Commons. Leaders of parties below the official party cut-off could be invited to participate in perhaps one or two debates in each official language, and all the others could be invited to many more, though not to every one.

Such a framework would lend itself well to a format that gives individual debaters non-trivial blocks of time, and would push the leaders to make more detailed arguments, and to marshal facts and data to support their stances. It might also allow for two-person teams, especially when the topic of the debate is one that falls primarily within a single cabinet portfolio. Imagine a debate, for example, on health policy issues, with the sitting PM and the Minister of Health on one side, and the leader of an opposition party, plus that party's health critic (or shadow minister, if you prefer the older term) as the participants in a four-person traditional debate. Or, with a couple of opposition parties, that would be six speakers, with each given a couple of opportunities to speak, which is not impossible for a 90–120 minute event.

This approach, with three or four major parties, implies quite a number of debates. But if these debates, rather than whistle-stop rallies, become the central features of the campaigns, that is not an insurmountable problem. The whistle-stop rallies are just a form of targeted advertising, and such advertising can be done without traipsing the leader across the country from riding to riding, (which, as a modern apparent sin, dramatically increases the leader's carbon footprint). Plus, it is an opportunity for each party to raise the public profile of some of their more local senior MP's, by giving them some ambulatory public exposure roles during the campaign. For those aspiring to cabinet roles, or who already hold them, this is a great opportunity, and also helps to move us away from the drift to cult of personality politics which has been plaguing the US and some European nations.

I suspect that the real impediments to making such a debate series the centrepiece of election campaigning is that the idea of it will evoke instant revulsion amongst the spin doctors, professional publicists, and campaign advisor hangers-on which burden every party. They will fear that a certain fraction of them will become redundant. And if they are what is standing between the voters, and real transparency in political discourse, their ranks should indeed be thinned out. Replacing some of them with folk who can actually develop and articulate real policy, rather than catchphrases would be a boon to national mental health.

The television broadcast networks as well may not look warmly upon such a significant series of disruptions to their normal broadcast schedule, in which case they may need to be reminded of the effects of the communications revolution, including the existence of the internet and the many other platforms over which such programming could be distributed widely, and in real time.

But you may well ask, "Given the opportunity, can the leaders actually debate effectively?" It is very likely that they can. Of the six party leaders during our recent election, four had trained and worked as lawyers, so they certainly had considerable exposure to the debating which is fundamental to our legal system, with its teachings and methodologies. And of the other two, one had been a drama teacher, so even if he could not prepare a solid debate argument from scratch, he could certainly simulate one quite well, if handed a decent script. The remaining leader was a well-educated individual with a long history of successful entrepreneurship in the entertainment industry, so he likely could cope too.

The role of the moderator thus becomes essentially that of a referee. After delivering a welcoming announcement outlining the scope and rule set of the debate, the moderator's job should consist of keeping time, discouraging and penalizing interruptions, calling upon debaters when it is their turn, and generally keeping order and decorum. Sort of the equivalent of the speaker of the House of Commons. A key tool for the moderator would need to be a control panel of microphone switches for each participant. Turning off a microphone when debater has gone past the allocated time and not heeded a polite request to wrap up within one sentence is hugely effective for encouraging compliance.

The moderator should not be expected to act as a fact-checker, and should not try to steer the debate content or context. The public, and after-the-fact pundits are the fact checkers, and the politicians should make their own choices of emphasis on the issues, at their own peril.

For our democracy to function properly, real and substantive public debate is essential for making wise choices. And that debating needs to take place in two critical fora. One is in public, so that we can effectively select representatives who will accurately reflect our views and implement our wishes, and the other is in parliament, where the legislation to carry out those wishes is examined, refined and enacted. One forum, parliament, already has a long tradition of orderly debate, and a set of rules largely perfected by Arthur Beauchesne prior to his retirement in 1949. The other forum, the public setting of an election campaign, desperately needs an improved form of orderly, comprehensive explanation and testing of competing ideas.

In short, we need a coherent and substantial series of real debates, not a couple of playground brawls replete with one-line imprecations from the brawlers and chiding remarks from passers by.

Can such a transformation occur, or are the forces of trivialization, superficiality, and sloganeering too imbedded in the cultural changes that have accompanied the communications revolution to allow it? Strangely, on this matter I remain slightly optimistic, because, in this instance, it is the potential debaters themselves who are in the driver's seat. The broadcasters and the commentators need the politicians at least as much as the politicians need them. Thus, if the politicians themselves wish to elevate the discourse, and to make it more substantive, fact-driven, and respectful, it will occur.

How could that come about? At least two things would have to happen. The first is entirely within the gift of the voters themselves. It starts at the grassroots level, in the individual party riding associations. If these associations select candidates who have both the attitude and the intellectual capacity to treat issues as complex problems to be solved carefully, and who are resolved to treat opponents as colleagues with whom one disagrees to a degree, the first big step is taken. The second step is to rein in the publicists and spin doctors who currently exert undue influence in our political discourse. Such people do have useful expertise, but that expertise must be subservient to the broader goal of the proper functioning of the democracy. If we had better people as candidates, they would have both the confidence and the clout to suitably adjust the role of the publicists and the spin doctors.

Impossible, you might say. Surely people seeking power will use whatever techniques are effective and can fit within the rules. But we must remember, we make those rules. In the same way that the Speaker of the House of Commons can discipline the otherwise all-powerful MPs for using inappropriate language, there is no reason why a degree of decorum and respect cannot be maintained outside the House. All that has to happen is that we require it. How do we get to that point? The answer is that a customary practice is built one step at a time. As soon as the most egregious individuals are punished at the polls for their degrading of the political process, the sooner a new spirit will become customary in our political life.

There is a logical cascade that follows from even the beginning of such a process. Better debate leads to better-informed citizens. A better-informed citizenry leads to better and more substantive discussion of all aspects of public policy. That, in turn, would very likely lead to improvements in public policy. That is the subject of the next chapter.

CHAPTER VI

Thinking About
Public Policy

PUBLIC POLICY IS NOT just the ongoing manifestation of the detritus of past politics. Yes, it is, in part, the outcome of the complex web of choices that we have made, through our elected leaders, to address issues in our society. But it also includes a vast array of regulation and tactical or operational decisions, often not specified in legislation but put in place by invisible bureaucrats to reflect their own interpretation of the political intent.

It is constantly under revision, and the facts or reasoning behind much of it are not always known to the public. This lack of transparency can leave confusion in its wake, so it is no great surprise that large numbers of our fellow citizens are uncertain about why our nation does a whole range of things in certain ways and whether they work well or not.

In this chapter, I shall try to tackle four non-trivial issues of public policy that are notorious for being poorly understood and for generating extreme divergence of opinion in a society that is not greatly given to such divergence. The four areas of public policy are (a) the taxation of capital gains, (b) the provision of health care, (c) the defence of Canada, and (d) the Canadian approach to nuclear power generation.

6.1 Replacing a Bad Compromise with a Better Compromise

Unlike the aficionados of the dismal science, I don't spend much time thinking about taxation. Of course, I pay my taxes, and, in a certain way, I am happy to do so. I certainly recognize all the benefits and services that I receive from all four levels of government and tend to think that it's not a bad bargain. So, anything that I would write about taxes is not prompted by any personal peeve about our system of taxation.

Most of my exposure to any question of tax policy has been from listening to friends. Some of those friends come to the subject as (occasionally irate) taxpayers, but some (I must confess) are, indeed, economists. It is through such friends that my stock of economist jokes has become substantial.

My interest in the Canadian approach to the taxation of capital gains was only aroused because that policy appeared to me to be simply a mechanical interpolation of two completely opposing views. Furthermore, it leaves the holders of each of the two divergent points of view with no joy other than the knowledge that the holders of the opposing view did not get their way either.

Reflecting upon the possibility of a more palatable middle ground, it occurred to me that perhaps all capital gains were not the same. But I also recognized that ease and simplicity of application was a necessity for a useful tax policy. The middle ground version that occurred to me seemed to give a bit of a nod to the theoretical stances of both of the two divergent camps, was revenue neutral, and was easy to administer. I tried it out on some colleagues who are economists, and, to my surprise, they seemed quite positive. No, that's not the lead-in to an economist joke. The piece I wrote about it, entitled "A Fairer Capital Gains Tax," appeared on March 30, 2021, in *Ottawa Life Magazine*.[30] What I wrote was as follows:

A Fairer Capital Gains Tax

For the most part. our tax system does not arouse great passions amongst Canadians. We generally accept that there should be personal income taxes and consumption taxes and corporation taxes, and we argue dutifully about what the rates, brackets, and exemptions should be, but on the whole, there is a rough consensus on the structure and only modest divergence across the mainstream political spectrum as to the rates. The range of divergence is modest compared to other nations because every caricature has a grain of truth in it, and the old joke about "Why did the Canadian chicken cross the road?" (Answer: to get to the middle) does contain a nugget of truth about the general absence of extremes in most Canadian debate, including debate on tax policy.

However, there is one tax in Canada where the rule we currently live with was a saw-off between two widely held but quite incompatible extreme views. And that tax is the tax on capital gains.

One school held to the view that capital gains was just a form of business income earned by fat cats, and ought to be taxed like the ordinary income of the common folk.

The other school held to the view that most capital gains were earned by the middle class, which was just trying to avoid losing ground to inflation by investing some earnings they had already paid income tax on and were saving for their old age, and that it ought not to be taxed at all.

The odd compromise between the extremes which resulted left us with a complex system in which most capital gains are taxed as if half of the gain was income. But a number of hot button items were exempted. Gains on a principal residence are untaxed. To tax that would be a fatal political mistake that no government is likely to make. You can just imagine legions of homeowners shouting, "But it's the same house it always was! I already paid for it! Why should I pay the government more to be allowed to move?"

Other exemptions were settled on for ease of administration, so, for example, no capital gains tax is charged on items disposed of for less than $1,000.

And charities were given a nod, so that no capital gains are charged upon securities or some designated cultural property gifted to charities.

To be fair, the two extreme camps I mentioned above each have a point. There are almost two separate paradigms of capital gains. Some capital gains are, indeed, made by high flyers who look for big gains, take a few chances with money they can afford to risk, and can end up with gains far exceeding inflation. But most capital gains are made by the middle class just trying to have their later-in-life nest egg keep pace with inflation, and they tend to invest very conservatively, and are often happy just not to lose ground to inflation.

This latter group would argue that, if instead they had put their money into (say) a supply of long-lived canned food, no-one would charge them tax when they later opened a can just because the price of that item had gone up in the stores over the years. The same would be true of pre-purchasing a lifetime supply of socks or firewood. So why, they ask, should they be taxed on protecting their saved wages from inflation? Yes, RRSPs are a partial answer, but even those who have taken full advantage of RRSP room would have great difficulty living on just the RRIF that those RRSPs would eventually be converted to.

The inclusion rate of 50% of capital gain as taxable income is not wildly unfair, and it has been argued that, being less than 100%, it partially addresses the "saving for retirement" argument. But there is one big elephant in the room. The capital gains tax as currently structured is a harmful tax in another way. It damages the national economy because of the "locked-in" effect.

Economists engage in plenty of esoteric debates (insert your favorite economist joke here). But we would still do well to look at some of their more interesting concepts from time to time. One relates to the idea of the efficiency of investment. What on earth is the efficiency of investment? It is the idea that capital does best for the economy when it is free to move from less productive investments to more productive ones. The notion is that each dollar invested in a productive concern is a more efficient booster of economic activity than a dollar invested in a company that is somewhat stagnating.

But the capital gains tax is a huge disincentive for middle class investors to sell a less productive investment in order to redeploy the money into a more productive one. And that is because the tax is only triggered by disposing of an investment. So, imagine someone who has had a long-term investment that has just barely kept pace with inflation. If they sell it, even though it has not performed especially well, they will still pay capital gains tax, which will reduce their net gain to much less than inflation. If it has been a long-held asset, the tax may be quite substantial. They will then have a much smaller pool to reinvest, after adjusting for inflation, than they started with. No surprise, then, that many will hold on to a poorly performing investment that is still making some modest gains, rather than moving their dollars to something expected to do better going forward. This is the "locked-in effect."

The locked in effect is frequently cited by some economists as an argument against any capital gains taxes whatsoever. Such relatively conservative voices justify their stance by pointing out that the capital gains tax is not a major source of revenue for the Government of Canada. Only about 2.3% of all income tax collected is capital gains tax. And only about 1.1% of all federal government revenue comes from the taxation of capital gains.

But given the costs of the social safety net during the pandemic, no federal government will be keen on abandoning a non-trivial income source. And abandoning a capital gains tax entirely could be seen as pandering to the so-called fat cats. It might also draw too much capital out of the lending market.

But I would suggest that there is a way to minimize the locked-in effect while preserving the revenue stream for government and the integrity of the tax system. It is simple, it relies on data already available, and has an inherent logic that makes sense to both factions of the capital gains tax debate.

So, what are those data already available? Well, first there are the facts already known about any individual capital gain, which are essentially the answers to four simple questions: when did you buy it, how much did it cost you, when did you sell it, and how much did you get for it? And one other fact is needed, which is the official Government of Canada inflation number for the period you held the asset. This is a well-known parameter, currently used to index tax brackets and CPP pensions, among other things.

My simple proposal, therefore, is as follows: for every capital gain on a non-exempt asset, the portion of that gain equal to the official inflation during the period the asset was held would be exempt from tax. And all gain above the inflation component would be taxed as ordinary income.

This paradigm should satisfy everyone. The cautious middle-class investors making conservative investments to protect assets for their retirement and whose gains only keep pace with inflation would pay no tax on their gains, and the high flyers who did much better than inflation would pay the full tax rate on the portion of their gains that exceeded inflation. Psychologically it satisfies too, because the investor who did much better than inflation probably feels flush enough to bear the taxes.

But it also resolves the greatest part of the "locked-in effect," as most investments that an economist would class as "inefficient" likely have not done better than inflation. The investor who wishes to dispose of those investments to invest in something more "efficient" would pay no tax to make the transfer. So, there would be no impediment to seeking a more efficient use of the capital.

Furthermore, rudimentary modelling of this approach suggests that initially it does not reduce the amount of capital gains tax collected. Exempting the basic inflationary gain and taxing the additional gain as regular income should produce at least as much tax revenue from capital gains as the current one-size-fits-all inclusion rate that decrees than half of all capital gain is taxed as income. Some simulations suggest it would actually yield more revenue than at present, which, if true, could open the door to an inclusion rate somewhere between 50% and 100% for the gains above inflation, while remaining revenue neutral. But it apportions the tax more fairly, virtually eliminates the locked-in effect, and thereby stimulates the economy.

Such a modified capital gains tax is also amenable to the same kind of aggregating of realized gains and losses that is currently used to simplify tax returns. Under the existing system, all realized gains are added together, from which the taxpayer then subtracts all realized capital losses for the year. It is the aggregated resulting net gain that is currently subject to the 50% inclusion rate.

Under my proposed new system, all realized gains above the amounts exempted by the inflation calculation could be aggregated, and then reduced by any aggregated outright capital losses. The net remainder would be taxed as regular income (or at whatever new inclusion rate is decided upon).

There is, however, one related idea that is clearly "a bridge too far." A colleague asked me whether I would advocate that, to be consistent, any realized gain less than inflation should create a deductible "virtual loss," being the difference between that paltry gain and the one which would have countered inflation. I would be strongly opposed to allowing such a deduction, as it would be tantamount to having the government guarantee return rates on private investments. That would seem to be profoundly unwise both politically and economically, and would work against efficiency in capital deployment.

But the simple device of exempting inflationary gain and taxing the gain above that as income also has the further advantage of relieving government of the constant pressure to invent new minor measures to protect savings. The rather limited Tax Free Savings Account (TFSA) springs to mind as a classic example of a minimalist band-aid solution that pays lip service to the problem without solving it.

And lastly, the overarching political and social benefit of my plan is that it fixes the one part of the system about which Canadians are really not "middle of the road," but are divided by a wide gulf, with each camp obdurate and unimpressed by the soulless compromise of the current rule. As we have seen in our neighbor to the south, a too great political divergence can lead to dangerous polarization where each side is utterly tone deaf to the other. The rule change which I propose would give each camp a component of the system that accurately reflects their social and economic outlooks. "One size fits all" doesn't work for shoes. It doesn't work for investments. And it doesn't work for taxation of both gradual (inflation-like) and rapid capital gains.

One would hope that any Canadian government might be intrigued by such a reform, because, in addition to being fair and being somewhat satisfying to the two disparate ideological notions mentioned above, it holds the prospect of (a) somewhat increased government revenues, and (b) more efficient allocation of capital, and hence better overall economic performance. I would expect that the most noticeable pushback would come from the civil servants who would need to implement the change, but, given the power of modern computing, even that may not be a substantial issue.

I find the solution satisfying because I always prefer a middle ground position to have its own distinct rationale, rather than just being an arbitrary point lying between ideological extremes.

But, not being content to comment just upon how the government raises its money, I'm also inclined to be mildly irked from time to time by how it chooses what to spend it on. As I've noted before, it is difficult to persuade governments to spend money either to prevent somewhat unlikely disasters or to fix a problem that takes longer than one election cycle to show real improvement. The next section of this chapter deals with a pair of issues that have both of these politically problematic features.

6.2 The Cheapskate's Route to Lack of Resilience

If you aren't ill, you don't need health care. If you have no enemies, you don't need armed forces or intelligence services. If you are not targeted by hackers, you don't need cyber-security. If your house is not on fire, you don't need a fire department or fire insurance. The fact that you don't need these things on any given day is not evidence that you don't need them at all, and to assume you won't need these things at some point is folly. Furthermore, when you need them, you actually want them to work.

As individuals, we understand these matters well. We keep some resources aside for emergencies. We know where the extra set of car keys are kept. We carry an umbrella or put on a raincoat if it looks like rain. We pay our insurance premiums.

As a country, however, we don't do these sorts of things as well as we should. It's not that we don't do them at all, but, during periods when we aren't using these emergency capabilities, we are inclined to let them run down. There are understandable political reasons why this occurs, but it's still a very bad idea. Recent events, including the Covid-19 pandemic, a land war in Europe, and increased sabre-rattling by China have highlighted areas in which we are less resilient than we easily could be. That is what prompted me to write "Memo to Canada: Pay Your Insurance Premiums." It appeared on March 15, 2022, in *Ottawa Life Magazine*.[31] What I wrote was as follows:

Memo to Canada: Pay Your Insurance Premiums

Most Canadians are pretty prudent. They pay the insurance premiums on their homes and their cars. If they have dependents, they probably buy life insurance. It is a logical risk mitigation strategy. However, the country that is Canada has consistently failed to purchase high quality insurance on the whole enterprise that is Canada, in a host of domains, including health care, defence, intelligence, and a long list of fragile supply chains. There are good reasons why this happens, but there are also ways to change the political culture and the dominant narrative so that it happens considerably less often.

Preparing for rare but serious crises always looks a bit wasteful when those crises are not occurring, and politics in the liberal democracies stresses the short term. Furthermore, any appearance of "waste," even if that waste is the intentional price paid for robustness, is often spun by political opponents as evidence of incompetence and/or corruption. Indeed, if a given expenditure can't be shown to have been beneficial in the ordinary course of events within the current election cycle, or, at worst, two election cycles, it doesn't contribute very much to political capital. When this essential truth is coupled to the normal human inclination to let the urgent displace the important in the competition for our attention, the stage is set for a range of tragedies.

The Covid pandemic has certainly reminded us of weaknesses in many systems. First of all, we had very little surge capacity in our health care system. That has been the case for a long time. During 2001–2002 I chaired a study for the Department of National Defence on asymmetric threat, and wrote a fair bit of the final report. One issue we examined in that study was the absence of sufficient surge capacity in health care. Back then I had joked that the City of Toronto had enough surge capacity to handle a serious double bus crash, but not a great deal more. Today Canada has far fewer hospital active treatment beds per capita than most developed countries, and ranks at the bottom of the OECD countries in this regard. Furthermore, and probably at least as problematic, we have no real system of paid "reserve" health care staff who can be used to augment regular staff on short notice. To be fair, the decline over the years in active treatment beds has been partly due to the advances in medicine. Many procedures that formerly required hospital stays are now so improved that they can be carried out on an outpatient basis. But every improvement in techniques resulted in a decline of capacity, as we bumped our way along the lowest edge of what was adequate in normal times. Hence the chronic long waiting times that Canadians normally experience for a variety of surgeries and treatments.

This absence of surge capacity in health care made the management of the Covid pandemic much harder. The initial lockdowns and constraints were, of course, desperately needed to prevent unnecessary illness and death in the waiting period before we had excellent vaccines, and would have been imperative even if greater surge capacity had been available. But the reason why there was a dire need for significant restrictive measures in the year since the spring of 2021, during those waves of the pandemic that occurred *after* the widespread availability of the vaccines, was primarily to spread out the expected hospitalizations over a longer period, in order to reduce the risk of overwhelming a health care system with no surge capacity to speak of. It will eventually be interesting (and sobering) to see studies on how many Canadians died during the current pandemic because of delays that the pandemic caused in treatment for conditions unrelated to Covid.

The health care system is not unique in its lack of robustness. During the last thirty years, the idea of doing everything more economically by reducing costs with "just in time" delivery of goods and services has infected the whole society. That trick, which seems to have originated with the Japanese auto industry, became the Holy Grail for cost reduction in a whole range of endeavours. Of course, everyone loves a bargain. But, while tailoring every process for minimum inventory and minimum unused capacity may make it very price competitive, it also makes it vulnerable to shocks. Shocks like being far back in the queue for supplies that come from abroad, especially when they come from places that are not our allies. No, that's not an argument for bringing all supply chains onshore, at huge cost. But it is a legitimate argument for a judicious mixture of onshoring, "friendshoring," and diversifying by having multiple suppliers, even if it costs somewhat more.

It is a basic fact that if you want robustness and resilience, it costs more. Most societies understand, for example, that armed forces are not especially economical. Their costs, particularly in capital requirements, often provoke astonishment and ridicule. But any large organization that is supposed to continue to function well in conditions of chaos and complexity cannot be economical in the usual sense of that term. It can be effective, and may even be seen as efficient, but never "economical."

Canada has a long history of neglecting its armed forces until the very moment they are sorely needed. That was the defining narrative of Canada's military preparedness in the early days of both World Wars. And, regrettably, it is somewhat the situation we find ourselves in today, as we watch the Russian invasion of Ukraine grind inexorably towards an ugly stalemate steeped in human suffering, with uncertainty about what actions we may eventually need to take to defend our own sovereignty or uphold our international obligations.

There are others far better equipped than I am to set out in detail the capabilities that the Canadian Armed Forces need, but currently lack, and to elaborate upon the increased resources needed to carry out such a reinvigoration and modernization. Two recent articles by two long-time friends are a good starting point: the first is a CGAI piece on March 3 by Hugh Segal,[32] and the second is an article in this magazine on March 11 by LGen (ret'd) Michel Maisonneuve.[33]

But there is plenty of evidence that our government does not take the need for robust armed forces very seriously. We only pay lip service to our agreed-upon NATO commitment to spend at least 2% of our GDP on defence; we are still below 1.4%.

Successive governments seem to have assumed that there is little political mileage in doing a good job of paying that particular insurance premium, and have telegraphed that opinion in many other ways as well. For example, one only has to look at the arthritic, never-ending procurement process for pretty much anything military, be it ships, planes, vehicles or even the pistols carried by into combat by our army officers. The first thing that one notices is that the whole procurement system is intensely focussed on the spin-off economic benefits to Canada. The process is predicated upon the elaborate falsehood that the regional economic benefits that the Crown will insist upon do not increase the cost of the project or product. Since these benefits are routinely negotiated after a given bid is tentatively selected, all bids are padded heavily in the first instance, as the suppliers who are bidding know they will be beaten up severely after being selected by being subsequently dragooned into doing much of the manufacturing of the product in some slightly economically disadvantaged part of Canada, regardless of the extent to which that change will increase their costs. To be crude about it, procurement of equipment for the Canadian Armed Forces routinely functions as an elaborate subsidy program for political campaigning by pouring government dollars into marginal ridings, with the possible side effect of getting some equipment for the armed forces eventually.

A dramatically more forthright approach would be to give the department responsible for regional economic development its own budget. Then, after a bid for equipment has been accepted on its merits for both price and capability, the department responsible for regional economic development can use a portion of its budget as an additional inducement to persuade the winning bidder to locate some or all of its manufacturing in Canada (and perhaps in specific parts of Canada) in exchange for the extra payment. Such a division of negotiating responsibility and costing would have positive effects. There would be transparency about the true price of the economic offsets, and we would no longer fear that extraneous factors other than suitability, sustainability, and affordability influenced the selection.

Of course, security of supply is enhanced if the product is made in Canada, but concern about the fragility of supply chains is an issue that relates primarily to the mostly rapidly expended supplies that need to be replenished often, not to capital equipment that is replaced only every couple of generations. Once we've got the capital equipment, we've got it for its entire service life, especially if we purchase the related intellectual property at the time of initial acquisition, giving us complete control of all maintenance and upgrades.

The other great nonsense in defence procurement is our insistence upon long, drawn-out competitive bidding processes for everything, under the assumption that competitive bidding is the only way to guarantee probity. Competitive bidding in Canada works very well for routine goods. But it only works well for specialized military equipment in huge markets like the USA, where there are enormously robust industrial players. In Canada, most of our local defence industry players that we hope will bid on complex defence equipment contracts are fairly weak, so making them fight one another to get contracts is a bit like making two drunks fight, meaning that both are likely to fall down. When faced with real emergencies, we ought not to do that. As we learned during the Second World War, it makes more sense to force the Canadian industrial players to cooperate with one another, rather than compete. In emergencies, of course, it is also entirely legitimate to sole source for rapid effect, as we did for the C-17's that we desperately needed during our involvement in Afghanistan, and which have turned out to be enormously useful.

But however desirable it might be to have adequate surge capacity in health care, or adequate armed forces, or robust supply chains, or better cyber safety, how do we get there when the political process that we are all inured to rewards cheapness and fragility, and denigrates any politician who actually seeks robustness as an irresponsible and wasteful steward of the public purse? How do we change the narrative in a way that encourages the country to pay its insurance premiums as readily as its individual citizens do?

In a way, we may be lucky in our misfortune. The Covid pandemic and Russia's war against Ukraine are sufficiently grave crises that they will not soon be forgotten, and may therefore act as signposts for how we treat certain issues of public policy for a good long while, perhaps a generation or even a bit longer. The "Oh, that will never happen" factor has been removed, and that memory will persist for a considerable time. The narrative has already begun to change.

So, what discourse will keep up the momentum for reform, so that it can be carried out well before the next crisis? We must remember that the needed robustness and resilience has a great similarity to a parachute: when you actually need one, it's rather too late to go out and order it. And when you need it, you really need it.

It might be a useful addition to the revised narrative to point out that the extra dollars spent on robustness may yield some modest cost reductions elsewhere, even if the rare but grave emergencies for which the robustness was put in place never occur.

There are examples in health care of savings to society as a side effect of increasing hospital capacities, staffing levels, and throughput. The reduction or near elimination of waiting times for a variety of surgeries and treatments would have the effect of returning large numbers of people to the workforce sooner, earning wages and paying taxes. And we know that shortened waiting times prevent many conditions from becoming more severe and requiring even more expensive and extensive treatment later.

Interestingly, some of the surge capacity needed for robustness in health care already exists, but can't be used, due to the bizarre mismatch between how most physicians are compensated and how hospitals are funded. In Canada most physicians, except for full time clinical faculty in the 17 medical schools, are compensated on a fee-for-service basis. The more they work, the more they can earn. But hospitals are on fixed budgets, so that when they experience financial constraints, their only method of cutting expenses is to do less, which often means fewer hours of use of operating rooms or expensive diagnostic equipment, because this reduces their expenses for nursing and other staff and for some supplies. This often results in some of the most expensive capital facilities in the world getting used as little as five shifts a week (40 hours), out of an upper limit of 21 shifts.

I know many hospital-based clinicians who complain bitterly that they get only two or three clinics a week, when they would rather do considerably more. This mismatch in the two funding methodologies means that, in many settings, we do not have a lack of physicians, just a lack of physicians' services. And those fancy machines that can't be used for patients the other 128 hours of the week? Well, in some jurisdictions they do get used, but for extra income from veterinary service providers. In some places you can get an MRI or CT scan for your dog or cat right away, but your mother may have to wait weeks.

Increased robustness of the Canadian Armed Forces can also have a few side benefits that can justify a narrative about how the extra costs for robustness will have some modest return, even when threats to Canada are minimal. Improved search and rescue capability is one desirable effect, as is increased utility of the Canadian Armed Forces during internal natural disasters, which one must admit are not all that rare. And while bringing the CAF up to a reasonable strength for a country of our size implies a non-trivial increase in the numbers of those who serve, all those new members will be employed, pay taxes, and will be learning skills, many of which are technical, analytical or management skills transferable to their civilian lives and jobs when they leave the armed forces.

So, the only way to change the political climate that currently prevents us from having robustness and resilience in key areas is to consciously decide to do so.

A collective resolve not to attack political opponents for capacity-building in the key areas would go a long way. There will never be a dearth of things to squabble over in the political arena, so a multiparty understanding about some shared objectives in these critical areas would not materially hamper lively political competition. And such a resolve might actually restore some respectability to political discourse in this country, which at this point is in somewhat short supply.

   After all, the first duty of government is the safety and security
of its citizens. Fail in this, and no other role of government has
meaning. We should pay the insurance premiums.

In the five months since I wrote that piece, I have heard
absolutely no public discussion of any of the specific suggestions
therein. Defence procurement is still a bizarre compendium of
pseudo-competition, infinite process, and an intense focus on the
centrality of regional economic benefits. Improved health-care
capacity is further away than ever, captive forever of the perennial
federal-provincial bickering over the dollars for health care, while
staff numbers continue to shrink for a host of reasons, ranging
from discouragement and exhaustion related to the Covid
pandemic to poor pay and working conditions. An ongoing lack
of training positions guarantees that the situation will not be
reversed quickly.

   It is interesting to note that health economists tell us that the
very long wait times for many medical acts in most provinces are
due to only a very small steady-state lack of capacity. As counter-
intuitive as that may sound, it is logical. Health economists have
shown that making people wait a long time for a treatment does
not ultimately reduce the demand on the system by more than
something like 4–5 per cent. It's not like a long waiting line at
Burger King, where you can just decide to go elsewhere or home.
If you are in a waiting line for a medical act, there are only three
ways to get out of that line before you get to the head of the line.
The first way is to die, and that is so embarrassing for the system
that it will usually rush you to the front of the line to avoid the bad
PR. So only a handful of patients outright die because of delay.

   The second way to get out of the line without consuming a
medical act is to get better on your own, just by waiting. This does
indeed happen and is responsible for much of that 4–5 per cent

compressibility of demand. And the third way to get out of the line is to go abroad for treatment at your own expense. This is somewhat unusual and probably accounts for only a per cent or so of that few per cent compressibility of demand.

Does all that mean that if we just had 5 per cent more capacity, there would be no waiting lines? Well, yes and no. If we had 5 per cent more steady-state capacity, waiting lines would start to shrink slowly, and eventually there would be no waiting lines, but it doesn't promptly solve the long waiting lines that we've built up now, some of which are many months or even years. So, a politician who takes steps to increase capacity by a bit more than 5 per cent will not see the waiting lines shrink very much before the next election. And therein lies the problem. Political credit for any bold move is needed quickly, not a decade hence. So, how do we get rid of the current backlog? There are only two ways. One might have to look to a combination of both. The two ways are (a) a huge one-time expenditure to get a significant part of the backlog attended to promptly elsewhere (i.e., across the border in the United States) and (b) trying for much more than a 5 per cent increase in capacity, with a view to dialing some of it back later, keeping it just ticking over as "reserve capacity."

While the latter is likely more politically palatable, some of the former might be wise because a system already exists in most provinces to approve government-funded out-of-province treatment in those cases where a given treatment is not readily available in-province. A temporary expansion of the criteria for these out-of-province authorizations, to encompass unacceptable wait times, would be fairly easy to justify politically. Furthermore, the regulations of the Canada Health Act already set out target maximum wait times for many procedures.

In the section above, I characterized the funding of robustness and "surge capacity" in health care and in defence as a form of insurance premium. These are not the only areas of public policy where we should be looking at a somewhat longer time horizon than is typical and preparing for rare but awkward challenges. Thus, there may be some other areas of national policy where we haven't been keeping up with our premium payments. In the next section of this chapter, I will address some myths about one such area.

6.3 Facts Are More Useful Than Myths

There is a considerable movement across much of the developed world that seeks to reduce reliance upon the combustion of coal, oil, and gas for energy because of concerns that the resultant rise in atmospheric concentration of carbon dioxide (CO_2), which now somewhat exceeds 0.4 per cent, is contributing to warming the earth's climate. While no-one can yet know precisely what portion of recent warming is anthropogenic, and, of that, what portion is due to atmospheric CO_2, clearly it would be unwise to wait for more precision before taking some action. Consequently, it is entirely reasonable to reduce the burning of such fuels, for that reason and a whole host of other fairly immediate reasons as well (see Chapter 1, Section 1.3).

But the environmental movement, which was very much a scientific movement a couple of generations ago, has by this point taken on some of the trappings and aspects of a religious movement. As a result, there are some fractures into factions, with the rationale for such ruptures sometimes mired in ideology and sometimes in myth.

It is widely understood that humankind does need sources of energy to live and thrive, to grow food, to make things, to stay warm (or cool), and to move about. Disagreements among self-styled environmentalists about what constitutes "green" behaviour and what sources of energy are acceptable have led to some of the fractures. Some see a legitimate cascade of carbonaceous fuels, with coal being the worst, oil in the middle, and gas the least harmful. Others see them all as anathema. Some even view the entire level of economic activity in the developed world as a sort of capitalist conspiracy. But the vast majority would like to be logical and scientific, if only they could.

One of the major fracture lines in the movement toward "clean" energy is whether there is a role for nuclear fission as a source of power generation. One faction says never, and another says yes, under the right conditions. The recent move by the European Union to add nuclear power to its list of acceptable "green" sources of energy is interesting.

In Canada, this debate over nuclear power is profoundly skewed by extraordinary misconceptions about the technology involved. From what I can tell, most Canadian opponents of nuclear power suffer from two great difficulties. First, they've been scared out of their wits by the word "nuclear" itself. It conjures up for them the images of mushroom clouds over Hiroshima and Nagasaki. This is the same reason why the entirely safe and radiation-free medical imaging process originally known as Nuclear Magnetic Resonance had to be renamed Magnetic Resonance Imaging, or MRI.

The second difficulty that the opponents of nuclear power in Canada suffer from is that they've been colonized. "Colonized by whom?," you might indeed ask. Well, mostly by the Americans, but to a lesser degree by the rest of the world, because, when it comes to nuclear power, Canada does it differently than almost anybody else, but most of the public gets its limited knowledge about such things from international sources, almost all of which are using US or European light-water moderated nuclear power generating technology. So, almost everything the anti-nuclear faction in Canada thinks it knows is wrong.

Nuclear power is not perfect. But it does have a role. There is a middle ground on this issue, and to explain where that middle ground lies in Canada, I wrote "Canadian Nuclear Power: Different from the Others." It appeared on February 2, 2021, in *Ottawa Life Magazine*.[34] What I wrote was as follows:

Canadian Nuclear Power: Different from the Others

Most of the public discussion and debate in Canada on the subject of nuclear power generation contributes little to our understanding. The two sides rarely engage in real interaction, and most published discourse is flaccid, incoherent and largely fact-free.

On the one hand, while most of the public utterances from experts in the nuclear industry are accurate, they are also vague, lacking in detail and specifics, and often condescending. Yes, we do understand that replacing carbon combustion with nuclear power reduces CO_2 emissions, but talking down to the public on all the other issues and hugely underestimating the ability of the public to understand and evaluate real scientific concepts is not an effective method of debate or persuasion.

On the other hand, many opponents of nuclear power are consumed by paroxysms of fear over the mere mention of the word "nuclear," preventing almost all real discussion, and harmfully splitting the environmental movement into two camps—those who see a role for nuclear power in reducing carbon combustion and its pollution, and those who don't.

Furthermore, even having context to understand this non-debate is not easy, because we are exposed incessantly to opinion and information on nuclear power from "everywhere else," meaning anywhere but Canada. Consequently, only a minority of Canadians are aware that the Canadian approach to nuclear power generation (the CANDU power reactor system) is surprisingly different from that used by the rest of the world, and that these differences have conferred some extraordinary advantages.

But before diving into those complexities, the whole discussion needs some kind of a frame. I have a physics background, and I am comfortable with the Canadian approach to nuclear power generation, but at the same time I appreciate that those who worry about nuclear power basically have four concerns, all of which need to be addressed. Those four concerns are:

(a) fear of exposure to dangerous ionizing radiation in the vicinity of the generating plants,

(b) fear of catastrophic accidents at such plants,

(c) concerns about export of the technology for such plants facilitating the proliferation of nuclear weapons technology, and

(d) concerns about the disposal/storage of spent reactor fuel.

I shall try to address each of these in turn.

Radiation Levels near CANDU power generating stations:
If one were to go and lean against the fence of a CANDU plant, the level of radiation there would indeed be a bit above background. But by how much? The best way to illustrate that is by a comparison. Humans are a bit radioactive, with almost all of it due to the potassium in our bodies. We have rather a lot of potassium in our bodies, as it is important in biology. An average adult would have about 150 g of potassium. Almost all of it is Potassium 39 or Potassium 41, but something more than a hundredth of a percent of it is Potassium 40, a naturally occurring radioactive isotope of potassium with a very long

half-life (about 1.2 billion years). So, if you sleep next to your spouse, you will be exposed to a substantially greater increase in radiation above the natural background level than you would if you spent the same amount of time leaning against that generating station fence. And while we do hear scary stories from time to time about sleeping next to someone, most of the risks seem to be centered upon snoring and stealing the covers. Nothing about Potassium 40.

Risk of Catastrophic Accidents:
It is always possible to have an accident. That being said, CANDU nuclear power generating stations have been generating electrical power since the first one, a prototype plant known as NPD (for Nuclear Power Demonstration) at Rolphton, Ontario, went on line in 1962. In that 59 years, there has not been any event or incident which could be described as an accident. NPD itself operated until 1987. There have been the usual expected occasional malfunctions, but they were addressed in the ways anticipated. There are good reasons why CANDU plants are much less likely than others to have significant accidents, and they will be outlined below.

On the other hand, there have been two non-trivial nuclear reactor accidents in Canada in research reactors. At Chalk River, Canada's first research reactor, known as NRX, which began functioning as a neutron source in 1947, and at the time was the most advanced in the world, had a serious accident in 1952 which caused an ignition of highly flammable hydrogen gas, which exploded. The cleanup took two years, and involved over 1200 people in the cleanup. One cleanup crew leader was Jimmy Carter, later president of the United States. That reactor then went on to operate until 1993. Canada's second research reactor, and our primary source of medical radioisotopes for decades, was NRU, also at Chalk River. It had a less serious accident in 1958, but went on to provide a neutron stream for research, and radioisotopes for hospitals until 2018. Extensive dosimetry associated with these two accidents and their cleanup has led medical scientists to conclude that the radiation exposures experienced by those doing the cleanup were so low that, statistically, it is unlikely that the radiation exposure above background caused even a single serious illness. But a huge amount was learned about reactor and fuel rod design from these experimental reactors. These lessons were incorporated into the currently active full-scale CANDU power generating plants.

What makes these reactors so different from those of all other countries? To answer that requires a brief reprise of some nuclear science. The fissile material that is used as the fuel for power reactors is uranium-235. Uranium exists in nature, but it consists mostly of uranium 238, which does not give off neutrons. Only a small percentage of the uranium, about 0.71% is U-235. That rare isotope is radioactive, with each atom that decays sending off two neutrons. If such a free neutron is captured by another U-235 nucleus, it too can split, producing two more neutrons in turn. This is called a chain reaction. However, in nature, a neutron from a U-235 atom decomposing is travelling too fast to be captured easily by another U-235 nucleus, so to build a reactor that can sustain a chain reaction and produce heat, the core must be suffused with a material to slow the neutrons down. Such material is called a moderator. Three materials have been commonly used for this purpose, being ordinary water (known as light water), graphite (carbon), and heavy water. Heavy water is H_2O where the hydrogen atoms each have a neutron as well as a proton. This double mass hydrogen is called deuterium. Heavy water is completely stable and exists in nature, in that one in every 5000 water molecules contains a deuterium.

Heavy water is vastly better as a moderator than either light water or carbon, but is damned expensive to purify. The US decided to base its power reactor programs upon using light water as a moderator, largely because it is an outgrowth of the US nuclear submarine technology. Most of the world now uses light water as the moderator, though some plants have used carbon. Only Canada uses the expensive heavy water. But the heavy water is so much better in terms of neutron economy that the Canadian reactors can burn uranium in its natural, unenriched form, containing only 0.71% U-235. All the others need to enrich their fuel to somewhere between 2.5–5% U-235. This means that Canadian reactor fuel is much less energy dense than that of other nation's reactors. And it also means that we have had no need up to this point to engage in uranium enrichment (more on that later).

So CANDU reactors use unenriched fuel, with heavy water as a moderator, and have neutron-absorbing control rods inserted into reactor cores from above, with the rods held in place by electromagnets, so should there be an electrical power failure, for example, the electromagnets release, and the neutron-absorbing rods fall downward into the core, shutting down the reaction. A CANDU reactor shuts down in somewhat under one second if it detects a problem. A malfunction that would raise temperatures to problematic levels, with the fuel currently being used, would need more than two seconds to produce problematic temperatures. This is not always the case with the reactors of other nations. Furthermore, Canada has put a huge effort into the development of accident tolerant nuclear fuel.

It is useful to reprise some of the facts behind the world's most notorious and catastrophic nuclear power generating accidents. Chernobyl (1986) was a carbon pile reactor, meaning that carbon was the moderator. Leaving the series of bad decisions leading up to the accident aside, a huge factor in the horrific damage caused was that the overheat caused the moderator to catch fire and burn like a huge fire in a coal mine, or like an oil well fire. This open-air reactor core fire burned for 9 days, releasing considerable airborne radioactive material. Clearly, having a flammable moderator in a reactor that cannot be passively cooled is not a good idea. The UN Scientific Committee on the Effects of Atomic Radiation had concluded that this accident caused something under 100 deaths, but some models suggest that the long-term death toll from residual contamination might actually be 4–16,000.

The other notorious nuclear power generating accident was Fukushima Daiichi (2011). This was a light water moderated enriched uranium reactor designed by General Electric, and built in 1971. It was a design so peculiar that it is amazing that anyone would have undertaken to build it. In addition to a plethora of other design problems, the control rods for the reactor core were inserted from below by pistons driven by compressed air, with that compressed air provided by electrically driven compressors. With any loss of electrical power, the control rods would begin to back out of the core, increasing the chain reaction in the core.

This was already known, as such an incident had occurred once during a refueling. Furthermore, the emergency electric generators for the plant were in the basement. When the tsunami struck, flooding the basement, all electric power was lost, and the chain reaction, far from being shut down, was accelerated by the gradual withdrawal of the control rods. Imagine, if you will, an automobile designed so that the accelerator is always flat to the floor unless the driver constantly pulls on a lever to reduce the throttle. That was, effectively, the design of the reactor system at Fukushima Daiichi. Not a good idea for a car, and not a good idea for a nuclear reactor. The dreadful result is known to all.

The design ideas behind the Canadian approach to nuclear power consciously sidestepped all the issues that have been implicated in accidents in dissimilar systems abroad. It would be a serious mistake to lump all the technologies together in a single assessment.

Concerns about Proliferation of Nuclear Weapons:
For the first half century of nuclear power, it could be argued that the Canadian approach to nuclear power generation, using unenriched uranium, was a bulwark against nuclear weapons proliferation, because a uranium fission nuclear explosive device needs uranium enriched to greater than 90% U-235. Other power generating systems exported by other nations, including the US, using light water as the moderator required enrichment of the fuel to 2.5–5% U-235, so that exporting such technologies meant providing for uranium enrichment as well. To be fair, enriching to 5% U-235 is a rather different task than enriching to greater than 90%, but the proliferation of enrichment technology and capacity was then appropriately considered a weapons proliferation risk.

This anti-proliferation advantage of the CANDU system is less important now than it once was. That is because, as far as enrichment is concerned, the horse is already out of the barn. First, the world now has a surplus of enrichment capacity rather than a dearth, with perhaps 50% more enrichment capacity than is needed. Secondly, the technology for carrying out uranium enrichment has gotten easier and cheaper with the passage of time. The earliest method for it, using gaseous diffusion, was long, complex and hugely energy-hungry. It was in turn supplanted by a method that employs gas centrifuges, a technique well-publicised in all the journalism surrounding the Iran nuclear agreement. The gas centrifuge technique, while using substantially less energy than its predecessor, is still rather energy hungry. But now a new technique using tuned lasers to selective pick U-235 out of the U-238 has reached a state of development that it seems ready for industrial scale use. It is much less energy-hungry, and implies that controlling nuclear proliferation through controlling enrichment is going to be vastly more difficult, if not impossible. There are, of course, other technological choke-points for the development of nuclear weapons, but, increasingly, anti-proliferation efforts will need to be carried out by agreement and verification rather than denial of technology. Denying any nation states the knowledge of the technology for nuclear power generation today does very little to prevent them from developing nuclear weapons if they are so inclined. In some cases, however, where no indigenous source of fissile material exists, denying the raw materials can be effective.

Concerns about the disposal or storage of spent reactor fuel: Canadians may not realize that the great bulk of radioactive waste created in Canada is waste from hospitals. This material is much less radioactive than spent reactor fuel rods, but it really is garbage. This medical waste does go into specialized land fills.

On the other hand, spent fuel rods from reactors are not garbage, but are enormously valuable. They may be the most valuable "waste product" in history. Plans for how to store the fuel rods from Canadian power reactors have been the subject of much public attention over the years. The ideal seems to be to store them, imbedded in glass, in storage facilities in a tunnel in a rocky pluton somewhere in the Canadian shield.

But some portions of the public still seem to have a mental image of leaky metal drums rusting away in some abandoned disposal site for thousands of years, contaminating the ground water. Nothing could be further from the truth. No reasonable person would wish to put such spent rods beyond human reach, because we will almost certainly need them back within decades. Why is that? Well, for a start, those rods still contain about two thirds of the U-235 that they started with when they were fresh. Today it is still somewhat cheaper to go and mine new uranium to get material that contains the naturally occurring 0.71% of U-235. But at some point, the equation will shift, and the 0.45% or more of U-235 that is still in the so-called spent rods will be extracted and re-concentrated so that it too can be burned. No-one ought to wish to put something so useful beyond our reach. And there are other useful isotopes in them as well. So, do we have confidence that we can maintain a tunnel in rock for some decades? Well, we have railway tunnels and mine tunnels that have been maintained for well over a century that are still perfectly serviceable. Establishing a specification and a maintenance standard for such a storage facility is actually very straightforward. And, in due course the "spent" material will be reprocessed, which is an opportunity to reduce the volume we need to store.

Canadians get the idea of recycling. We recycle plastic, metal, glass, paper, and a host of other things, and we have developed a bit of a habit of shaming those who don't recycle. Well, we should similarly expect to recycle reactor fuel as well.

What comes next?

The Government of Canada and some provinces have, of late, expressed an interest in the development of Small Modular Reactors (SMR's). Their notion is that these could be used in off-the grid settings like remote communities, where power is now supplied by burning diesel fuel in generators. Such SMR's could also be used in off-the-grid industrial applications, or added to the grid where needed to replace outdated CO_2 emitting plants. How small is small? They vary, but some are so small that major assemblies like the reactor vessel can be moved by road.

There are many designs contemplated, and some nine designs are at various stages of review or approval by the Canadian regulator, with three being quite far along in that process. The designs vary as to the coolant, fuel and moderator, but all seem to have two key features in common. First, they would all would be capable of cooling down passively on shutdown, obviating risks associated with electric power loss, so all are inherently incapable of a meltdown type of failure. Secondly, they would all have a sealed core which would either remain for the lifetime of the unit or be replaced in its entirety at long intervals, obviating any mechanical refueling issues.

In these features, they have some passing similarities to the last operating federal research reactor, which is the Slowpoke research reactor located at RMC in Kingston. I am very familiar with that reactor, as I was principal of that university from 1999–2008. The RMC Slowpoke was put into operation as a neutron source in the mid-1980s, has been operated ever since, and is due for it's first refueling in 2021. As a source of neutrons, its main use has been to carry out neutron activation analysis of chemical samples, as part of a huge environmental research program aimed at detecting and remediating chemical pollution. Its various features make it so safe that it is the only current reactor I know of that is licenced to run without an operator present.

It remains to be seen whether the small modular concept can fully realize the cost advantages of greatly reduced on-site construction, and standardized components mass produced centrally. It now seems likely that at least two Canadian demonstration projects will be completed during this decade, so that an evaluation can be made.

The future of nuclear power generation in Canada is uncertain. Clearly, amongst the other green technologies it has some obvious advantages, such as constancy. It is not dependent upon weather or time of day. But other technologies are also improving. The recent advances in photovoltaics are impressive. Furthermore, nuclear power must also be viewed as a transitional technology, since the supply of fuel is not infinite, though it is certainly sufficient for a few centuries.

But assuming, as some folks do, that all nuclear power generation is inherently too dangerous to be contemplated is rather like assuming that all dogs are dangerous or that all sports are dangerous. Fortunately, we know enough about dogs and sports to separate pit bulls from poodles and football from ping pong. Learning a bit about Canadian nuclear technology should give us the ability to discriminate in that area as well. Then we can ascertain rationally what fraction of our power we want to get from that source.

I make no secret about being in favour of nuclear power. However, by no means is it the end of the quest for better sources of energy. While I recognize the strides that have been made in wind power, I remain convinced that it is a dead end, given its unpredictability, the low energy density of its use of space, its harm to various life-forms, and its high cost. I am much more impressed with the gradual progress in photovoltaics, which continue to improve and which can now be viewed as more predictable, given that the newer versions generate moderate amounts of power even on cloudy days.

But much more encouraging is the dramatic progress in recent years toward fusion power, which promises to be clean, with no radioactive spent fuels and unlimited feedstock for fuel (water). Yes, I am familiar with the customary cynical observation that fusion power is just 25 years away and always will be. But the orders of magnitude improvements recently in the duration of sustained controlled fusion reactions convince me that the cynics are wrong and that it will be viable.

I also remain convinced that the currents caused by the tides can be tapped. There are a number of such experimental power-generating projects already in place. In coastal areas around the globe, tidal rips (which is what strong tidal currents are called) are more than speedy enough to drive substantial "undersea windmills," and such mills have three significant potential advantages over atmospheric windmills. First, the tides are predictable for a thousand years at the press of a button. Second, water is much denser than air, so moving water contains much more energy per unit of volume than moving air. And, lastly, along any coast, the tidal rips do not all peak at the same time, and may even be hours apart, so using multiple loci blends the timing of the supply. In most locations, tidal rips peak four times a day, implying that any tidal rip turbine might provide useful output for a predictable 8–12 hours every day, with different loci peaking at different times. With proper planning of the locations, this can result in a reliable, continuous supply.

There are interesting historic reasons why we are so late-to-task with extracting power from tidal currents. Humans have, at this point, more than two hundred years of experience and research on using small amounts of water with high pressure heads for power.

Water wheels in fast streams and at waterfalls powered mills in the 18th and 19th centuries, leading to hydropower generation of electricity starting in the early 20th century. But we are a couple of centuries behind in studying how to get power from great masses of water with low-pressure heads, like the tidal rips. But it will come.

Readers will notice that I have not mentioned extracting tidal power by damming estuaries to create "conventional" episodic hydropower-type generation, using water height differences across the dam to drive turbines. While this has been done, and does work, it may be sufficiently harmful to local environments of the estuary and its marine species that its disadvantages may outweigh its benefits.

Society does need power to thrive. The only way to have civilization while using less of it is to have fewer humans. While most current models of human population growth show a plateauing of the world population late in the current century, no-one is expecting much of a decline. So, the fraction of the environmental movement that simply advocates using less power is, in fact, a quasi-religious movement to "go back to a simpler time," which, for much of the world, is code for going back to a much harder time with much shorter lifespans. Not the first choice for most people.

Thus, not infrequently, proposers of radical changes to public policy are, in fact, intending to remake society as a whole. Public policy, with its careful parsing of rules and conventions, is merely a governance-oriented way of describing a society, whether extant or wished-for. Thus, the "back to a simpler time" faction of the environmental movement will never be at peace with the more moderate mainstream environmentalists, because the moderate mainstream group wants a society very similar to what we now have in the developed world, but which operates in a cleaner and more easily sustainable fashion than at present, while the more radical "back to the past" faction is a cult of well-off first world types who have very little concern for the death sentences they are effectively passing upon those large swaths of humanity still trying to rise out of conditions of poverty, pestilence, and risk.

To me, the more moderate environmentalists are another example of a thoughtful middle ground, to be preferred over the extremes. By rejecting deindustrialization on the one hand and yet requiring that the most polluting practices be modified as adequate technologies become available, even at some increased cost, on the other hand, they set a course that the vast majority can feel at ease with, once it is adequately verified and explained.

Public policy does reflect society, and, while its intricacies are a sort of description of society (albeit written in the language of the bureaucrats), there are more interesting, more direct, and sometimes more insightful lenses through which to view our society.

In the next chapter, the focus is on our society, with some of its attitudes, expectations, and quirks.

CHAPTER VII

Canadian Society—A Bit of Introspection

A SINGLE CHAPTER COULD NEVER be an adequate description of our society, and this chapter does not purport to try. But understanding our own society has always been an exercise in assembling and examining a surprising range of bits and pieces. The full picture is a riotous jumble of facts, impressions, traditions, assumptions, and expectations.

In this chapter the proffered introspection touches on only five aspects of our society. They are (a) the relationship of the Canadian majority with the aboriginal peoples of Canada, (b) some unintended social consequences of technological advances, (c) some thoughts about different types of privacy, (d) a dangerous shift in the meaning of elitism, and (e) the interplay of external threats and domestic social cohesion.

7.1 There Are Other Bridges

Canada is today in the process of coming to terms with its past treatment of its indigenous peoples. This has become a major focus of political discourse and has been a favoured area for gestures of reconciliation by the current government of Canada. Cynics, of course, usually advance the view that gestures of virtue signalling are a convenient way for the government to appear to be doing something when, in fact, not much is actually happening. But, in fact, something is happening, though it's not necessarily at the level of government. And the thing which is happening is that many more Canadians than in the past are actually thinking about issues related to our indigenous peoples, past and present.

Regrettably, the result has been considerable polarization. At one extreme are those engaged in a continuous and strident *mea culpa*, not for their own sins but for those of their forebearers, or, in many cases, for sins that were committed long before any of their relatives emigrated to Canada. At the other extreme are those who attribute the entire suite of difficulties faced by our indigenous people to the occasional corrupt hereditary indigenous leader, backward attitudes, and the politics of victimhood. Both extremes are wrong and toxic. In my limited experience of conversations with indigenous political leaders and opinion leaders, the vast majority have seemed to me to be well informed and inclined toward pragmatism rather than theory.

But if we ignore the noise of the extremes, some things remain true. There are problems. The resources allocated to solving them may well be insufficient, but it is also true that massive government bureaucratic inefficiency eats up a fair bit of the allocation, and some of what remains ends up being misdirected at the local level.

In my view, however, there is a bigger problem. A great fraction of the Canadian majority who are not indigenous are impatient and dismissive of these issues because they feel no great link with our indigenous population. That seems a natural consequence of the fact that so much of the current discourse centres on their majority role as oppressors and the victimhood of the minority. It seemed to me that a search for other links might be worthwhile. If the Canadian majority had a few more indigenous heroes in their pantheon, might that not do more for attitudes and true reconciliation than perpetual self-flagellation? Well, by accident, I stumbled across a highly suitable candidate. And for that, I must thank my old friend, the distinguished historian Donald Graves.

Donald Graves is perhaps the foremost authority on the War of 1812, and I've read all his books avidly. However, the first clue in my search did not come from one of Donald's own books but from a footnote in a reissued version of J. Mackay Hitsman's 1965 volume *The Incredible War of 1812: A Military History*. When it was first published, it was not the fashion to include extensive footnotes or endnotes in publications aimed at the general public, and so whatever notes Hitsman had made no longer existed when the opportunity presented itself for the book to be reissued in 1999. For that re-issue, Donald Graves set about to update the book, based upon the body of research since 1965, and to construct from scratch what he imagined would have been the roughly 1,000 suitably detailed endnotes.[35] It was in footnote #32 for chapter 9 of that book that I first met Black Hawk.

The quote from Black Hawk that Graves included in the footnote was extensive and incredibly illuminating and led me, in turn, to Black Hawk's own autobiography and the various commentaries thereupon. Black Hawk was a Sauk war chief in the late 18th and early 19th centuries, and a lifelong ally of the British. He was also the first North American aboriginal leader to produce a published autobiography (1833). He was also an extraordinary person.

When I first began reading about his life, I was serving as Principal of the Royal Military College of Canada and was very steeped in issues related to the profession of arms. It was instantly clear to me that Black Hawk's concepts and practices of the ethics of armed conflict aligned well with our notions now, in the early 21st century, but were so far ahead of those of his British allies of 1812, or of his American opponents of 1812 or 1832, that it almost felt like he was using a time machine. But it made me wonder. Perhaps his views were common among his people and their indigenous allies. We cannot easily know. But it is clear that, on these important matters, he was centuries ahead of our own forefathers. As far as I'm concerned, that makes him an important North American hero, not only for the First Nations but for all of us. It seemed to me that revelations about people like him had the power to change attitudes and caused me to speak and write about him. When I wrote, I consciously used terminology for roles and activities that would have been used for Europeans. For example, I routinely referred to Black Hawk's long career as a "soldier" and "military leader," rather than using the terms "warrior" and "war chief," because I wanted my military readers to understand how his role was, in fact, very much like theirs.

Some of these commentaries appeared in some of my speeches, as a book chapter[36] in 2007, and in an indigenous publication in Ontario at about the same time, but the definitive version[37] appeared in *Ottawa Life Magazine* on December 18, 2020, with the title "Two Centuries Ahead of His Time: Lessons from Black Hawk on the Ethics of Conflict." What I wrote was as follows:

Two Centuries Ahead of His Time: Lessons from Black Hawk on the Ethics of Conflict

Canada was defended by the British Army until 1871, four years after Confederation. In the latter part of the 19th century, the symbols, traditions, structures and ethos of the Canadian Army were essentially those of the British Army of the day.

CANADIAN SOCIETY—A BIT OF INTROSPECTION   269

Today, many of those symbols and traditions are still with us, but there has been a huge evolution of the values and ethos over time. Some of the evolution was driven by the conflicts we fought in, but a great deal of the change was just the process of aligning the values and ethos of our armed forces with the moving target of values and attitudes in Canadian society as a whole.

After some years of reading and reflection, I've come to the conclusion that the evolution of key elements of the ethos of the Canadian Armed Forces may well owe a substantial debt to the traditions of North America's aboriginal peoples.

But when one thinks about various modern legal and ethical precepts related to armed conflict which form part of the framework within which any Canadian military officer or non-commissioned member must act, most Canadians are blissfully unaware that North America's First Nations were a couple of centuries in the lead on these matters.

How did I come to this working hypothesis that the First Nations way of war in the early 19th century had important similarities to ours today? While preparing for a convocation address, I read the autobiography of one of the greatest North American military leaders of the late 18th and early 19th centuries, a man who was a soldier for 51 years, and who seemed almost to have a late twentieth century eye when observing the ethos of two centuries ago. His name was Ma-ka-tai-me-she-kia-kiak, which in the Sauk language means Black Sparrow Hawk, but we know him today as Black Hawk. He was the only enemy of the United States after which the US has ever named a major weapons system, the Black Hawk helicopter. Interestingly, a division of the U.S. army and a professional hockey team also adopted his name.

Black Hawk was born in 1767, and lived till 1838. Before his birth the Sauk nation to which he belonged had gradually migrated over more than a century from south of Montreal to

Michigan and thence gradually further south to the vicinity of present-day Rock Island, Illinois, though at the time of his birth it was named Saukenuk. This migration had been partly due to the pressures of the more powerful Haudenosaunee Confederacy, and of the gradual extension of French and British settlement. Saginaw Bay, in Lake Michigan is also named after his people. He and others believed that his great-grandfather, Thunder (or Nanamakee in the Sauk language) had been a key founder of the nation. The Sauk language is an Algonquian language and the Sauk had the closest of relations with another small nation of that language group, the Meskwaki (or Fox) nation, so as the most prominent military leader of the two allied nations, Black Hawk often led men from both nations. His military life began at 14, and from his later teens onward he was a military leader. While the armed units he led were often not large, they were frequently in the hundreds, and from time to time exceeded a thousand men under arms, which in the late 18th and early 19th century in the region of the Great Lakes or Mississippi watershed was a large force.

Black Hawk's military views aligned fairly well with those of his peers, but what was atypical was that he set them down and had them published in 1833, the year after the Black Hawk War. His was the first autobiography of a North American indigenous leader ever to be published. How he came to do so was interesting. Black Hawk didn't think what he was doing in 1832 was a war, and indeed he and modern historians would agree that it was a migration. Black Hawk was unhappy that the Americans were not honouring treaties. Furthermore, in his opinion they had, in some cases, used fraudulent and illegal methods to secure treaties. Consequently, he had given up on the Americans. Since he was a former ally of the British, and trusted the British, he was trying to migrate to any point north of the US border in order place his band in a British jurisdiction. But the US took his actions as a war, and defeated him with a field force of more than 4,000, which included in its number, curiously, Abraham Lincoln (as a lieutenant), Jefferson Davis, and Zachary Taylor. Despite his defeat, some of his actions are still viewed as among the most perfectly planned military manoeuvres of all time.

After Black Hawk's defeat, Jefferson Davis was appointed to escort him to Fort Monroe, where he was to be imprisoned. But there was significant sympathy for Black Hawk in the US, so shortly after Black Hawk reached Fort Monroe, the president decided not to imprison him, but to send him on a tour of major cities of the US, so he could see how many Americans there really were, and might see the wisdom in ceasing to make war on them. But the trip backfired. Black Hawk was accompanied by his eldest son, Nasheaskuk (Whirling Thunder) and his government translator, Antoine LeClaire, and, when he spoke in those cities, he drew increasingly large and sympathetic crowds. His son was evidently thought to be so handsome that large numbers of young women also tried to attend, a sort of early type of stage groupie. When he reached New York, he drew a larger crowd that did President Andrew Jackson, who was speaking in that city on the same day. This irked the president, who decreed that Black Hawk should just be sent home.

The tour was an epiphany for Black Hawk. Having discovered that his words had at least as big an impact as his weapons, he decided to fight the next round on paper. He dictated his life story to Antoine LeClaire, who did the translation into English. Interestingly, Black Hawk dedicated his autobiography to Brigadier General Henry Atkinson, who had defeated him in 1832, and in the dedication, couched in the form of a letter, he recalls his good treatment by Atkinson, and expresses his confidence that Atkinson will vouch for those facts in Black Hawk's narrative which are of the events of which Atkinson would have knowledge. He overtly draws Atkinson into what Black Hawk calls "the vindication of my character from misrepresentation." This shows that even by October 1833 Black Hawk fully appreciated that he had generated considerable sympathy and perhaps support from amongst former opponents.

Black Hawk was never a political leader, and carefully describes a separation of political from military decision making, even on the battlefield, that we would certainly recognise as modern practice, but was exactly the opposite of how the British were operating in Canada. Black Hawk was an ally of Britain through much of his life; he fought in the War of 1812 around western Lake Erie with British forces commanded by Henry Procter, and he grew to dislike the way the British and Americans made war. Writing in 1833, he recalled his reaction to Procter's blunders attacking Fort Meigs and Fort Stephenson, which caused Black Hawk to decide to lead his troops home (though he did rejoin the British forces late in the war in campaigns along the upper Mississippi River). Interestingly, his criticisms of Procter aligned closely with the findings in Procter's court marshal, which required the reasons for his discharge to be read out to every regiment in the British Army. But it wasn't just Procter's mistakes, grave as they were, and which later led to the death of Britain's most famous indigenous ally, the Shawnee leader Tecumseh. Black Hawk didn't think that the contemporary European way of war met any reasonable test for duty of care by officers or for ethics.

Remembering his visit to a friend's village on his way home from the War in 1813, Black Hawk retold what he had said even then:

> "After eating, I gave an account of what I had seen and done. I explained to them the manner the British and the Americans fought. Instead of stealing upon each other, and taking every advantage *to kill the enemy* and *save their own people*, as we do, (which, with us is considered good policy in a war chief,) they march out, in open daylight, and *fight*, regardless of the numbers of warriors they may lose! After the battle is over, they retire to feast, and drink wine, as if nothing had happened; after which, they make a *statement in writing*, of what they have done—*each party claiming the victory!* And neither giving an account of half the number that have been killed on their own side. They all fought like braves, but would not do to *lead a war party* with us. Our maxim is, "*to kill the enemy,* and *save our own men.*" Those chiefs would do to *paddle* a canoe but not to *steer* it. The Americans shoot better than the British, but their soldiers are not so well clothed or provided for."

The last sentence is really a separate observation distinct from his main criticism. Black Hawk knew that the tradition of gun ownership and use by Americans made them more practiced marksmen than the British, but that the American logistics system of 1812 was markedly inferior to that of the British.

Black Hawk had always commanded forces which included many of his relatives, and he detested the lack of concern that British and American officers showed for their men. His views on avoidance of unnecessary casualties, on close attention to the needs of troops, and on minimizing distinctions in comforts in the field between officers and men were at clear variance with British and American practice.

Black Hawk abhorred the mixing of alcohol with military operations, and also thought that the reports being made to higher headquarters were self-serving fiction. During the actions on the Detroit frontier, Black Hawk was enraged when other Indian allies of the British mistreated American prisoners of war, and he forced them to stop, which Major General Procter had not done.

Writing about his American opponents during the Black Hawk War of 1832, Black Hawk was critical of the American failure to distinguish combatants from non-combatants, the failure to honour flags of truce, and the failure to negotiate truthfully for cessation of hostilities.

Today, 182 years after Black Hawk's death, and 207 years after the battles on the Detroit frontier, the views we now hold of everything from rules of engagement to duty of care are much closer to those of Black Hawk than to those of the European or American generals of his era.

This is not completely surprising, since modern Canadian views on many social or ethical issues stem from our present egalitarian and cooperative model of society which would have been familiar to Black Hawk, but shocking and radical to his British contemporaries.

Which raises, of course, the broader question of the origin of the differences between European societies and those of Canada or the United States. North American society is clearly less rigid and less class-ridden than in Europe. It has been popular to attribute this to geography, the process of settlement and the diversity of immigration, but it seems just as reasonable to attribute some of it to the folks who were here first.

As I noted above, when reflecting upon Black Hawk's views and actions, we are fortunate to have his own account of his life. In the cases of other prominent indigenous persons in Canada during the late 18th and early 19th centuries, some of the key facts have only come to light in the fairly recent past. A fair amount is known about Joseph Brant (Thayendanegea) and his influential older sister, Molly Brant (Konwatsi'tsiaienni), but it is only since about 1970 that the significance of the contribution to the defence of Canada by Teyoninhokarawen (also known as John Norton) has become clear, since his journals only came to light at about that time.

In the two centuries since, there have been countless interesting heroes and role models from among the aboriginal peoples of Canada, and, in the majority of cases, their contribution was for us all, not just for the group from which they originated. They include scientists and scholars of considerable renown, artists, professionals of all sorts, and entrepreneurs aplenty. The more that the majority knows about them, the more the majority will not see the minority as "other." Nor are bridges of that sort a pressure for assimilation. The pressure for assimilation came from older notions of the pattern of human development, rooted in Victorian anthropology, that held that there was a single common route for cultural development, so anyone who was different was automatically backward. That hypothesis is, of course, completely outdated and discredited, but to keep it from rising from the dead from time to time, like a zombie, having a good supply of popular heroes from any group not of the majority is a pretty good vaccination against falling back into toxic ethnocentrism.

At the outset of this chapter, I promised a bit of introspection on Canadian society. It was never my intention that all of it would be historical in nature, and the rest of the chapter is more contemporary. This has a double advantage: The readers can test my hypotheses using their own experiences, and there is rather more opportunity to inject a bit of humour into the mix. You will doubtless recall my belief (from Chapter 1) that humour, especially the sort that is fairly gentle and not coarse, is a useful tool for drawing people toward the middle ground. Reading what follows, you can decide for yourself if it's working!

7.2 Sometimes It Works

The "pieces of eight" of pirate lore were the Spanish silver dollars worth eight reales. Such was their ubiquity and reliability that they were the original basis of the US dollar, and by extension, the Canadian dollar. Even the old slang term "two bits," to mean a 25-cent piece, or a quarter (i.e., a quarter of a dollar) drives from such antique terminology, implying that eight bits was a dollar. Till now. Now eight bits is a byte. And we have lots of bytes. Gigas of them (or billions, for older folk like me). They hang around in all our computing devices that are the consumer interface with the tech revolution.

I'm not a Luddite (though there is even some doubt that Ned Ludd ever actually existed), but, given my age, I do know quite a few of my contemporaries who are quite resistant to the charms of the tech revolution. Indeed, it is a bit of a fracture line in contemporary society. The current controversy over forcing anyone entering Canada to provide Border Services with data via the apparently not terribly useful ArriveCAN app underscores the divide on this matter. No, not everyone has a smartphone. And, no, the phones are not actually all that smart.

This is one fracture line that is largely, but not entirely, correlated with age. Furthermore, most of the critics of our huge reliance on the new technologies are those who have trouble using them, so the ones who are more expert are largely disinclined to listen to the critiques.

As someone who does use the new technologies but who is old enough to remember a world without them, I was aware of the plusses and minuses. A romp through them, for some perspective, seemed in order. To that end, I wrote, "Fruits of the Tech Revolution: The Good, the Bad, and the Absurd." It appeared on April 16, 2021, in *Ottawa Life Magazine*.[38] What I wrote was as follows:

Fruits of the Tech Revolution: The Good, the Bad, and the Absurd

The advances of the past few decades in the technology of communications and computing are wonderous and striking. Many formerly onerous tasks are much facilitated, and lots of novel capabilities have appeared and are being widely enjoyed. Canadians especially take huge delight in this revolution, because we have an ancestral memory of Canada as a nation of hewers of wood and drawers of water (except during the coldest season, when we became hewers of water and drawers of wood). Fiddling with a keyboard or touchscreen is much easier.

But not everything is better, and the road to better is not always obvious. There have been a few tricky wrong turns and cul-de-sacs.

Reflecting upon this has unleashed my inner curmudgeon, so perhaps a curmudgeon's tour of the less felicitous features of the new landscape would be in order.

Those of my age will remember that not so long ago, if you met someone in your town or city who you later wanted to contact, you could look up their phone number in something called a phone book. This task was made even more accurate if you knew their address, which was also listed, and would be confirmatory. Today however, even with online "phonebooks" this is a hopeless task, as they only list landlines, which are a sort of endangered species. The cell phone is dominant, and no directory exists for them (except the ones maintained by the intelligence services). So, your friends can't call you, unless you have made a point of giving them your contact information, but every scammer on earth will eventually reach out to you.

And, especially amongst the young, even cell phones are primarily for other things, and actual speech is much less favoured. Perhaps you recall a time when, if you needed to settle a small matter with someone, a phone call of less than a minute or two, with a few to-and-fro remarks from both parties, to reach an interpolated decision, would entirely suffice. That exchange today is a half-hour of texting.

In some circles there is such a bias against actually speaking that I sometimes get texts or emails from folk that I know, seeking permission to phone me.

And then there's parking. Years ago, when you sought to park, you would choose a spot equipped with a parking meter, you would get out, put a few coins in the meter, and go about whatever business you had stopped there to transact. Today, you get out of the car, figure out which solar powered ticket printer is withing a half a block or so, trundle down to it, wait behind two other folk, get to the unit (all the while worrying about whether it will actually give you back your credit card), only to find that it isn't working, so you climb over a snow bank, cross the street, climb another snow bank, go another half-block to find another ticket issuer, get the little paper slip, and, by the time you get back to your car to put the ticket on your dashboard, you have largely forgotten why on earth you wanted to park there anyhow. (Yes, I know that some cities have phone apps that cover some but not all of these spaces, but in some cases they are cumbersome. In one city I know, they only cover handicap parking spots. Furthermore, they compel the driver to own and carry a smart phone.)

And if your car is relatively new, it has quite a bit of computing power on board. That electronic package gradually drains the battery when the vehicle is not in use. Before these tech refinements, the battery decline was very slow, as it was due just to internal self-discharge of the battery, plus a tiny bit of power used by the electric clock. But today, the at-rest power drain is rather greater, and some car makers actually supply cute little smart 4-stage mini-chargers with new vehicles, to avoid a dead battery. But you need a place to plug it in. The electrician will need to put an electrical outlet where you park. (Hold on, aren't we Canadian? Don't we still have one of those from when we needed block heaters to get the damned car started in the winter?)

My next target is the ubiquitous personal computer. It is useful indeed, but it sure isn't perfect. It feels like an experimental technology that made its way into popular use before the experiment was complete. It's absolutely not a mature technology. You wouldn't tolerate similar behaviour from your dishwasher. If you washed your dishes exactly the same way every time, but once every two months your dishwasher ground your dishes up into subatomic particles, distributed them somewhere between Neptune and Pluto, and then locked the door on you until you disconnected all its hoses, and on reconnection, acted perfectly normal, you'd think it wasn't a mature technology. You might even think unworthy thoughts about the con artist that sold it to you.

I don't pretend to any great expertise in computing. I was near the leading edge of it in the 1970s, but got distracted for a few months, and haven't been able to catch up since. So now I'm a typical older, fearful computer user. Fearful, because, unlike younger folk, people like me remember when you could do real harm by pushing the wrong key.

Along with all the benefits of the computer revolution (and they are real) have come some negatives we should reflect on.

First, there is the waiting. A non-trivial part of total working time is lost by Canadians as they watch Bill Gates think, as exemplified by hourglass symbols, turning wheels, slowly advancing bar symbols, and a host of other devices all of which tell you to sit there and wait. And no system actually tells you how long you will have to wait, though many pretend to do so. These antics make me hope that my computer isn't just guessing at the answer to whatever question I asked it to solve, the same way it's guessing at how long it needs to complete its current manoeuvre.

We're subjected to this because, in the race between the hardware folks building capacity and the programmers using it up, the programmers always win. They always want to do more than is reasonable with the machine capacity, and we stupidly let them. So, we are all held hostage to the entertainment of a few thousand young geeks. Why not institute an industry standard that sets normal wait time for a single manoeuvre at no more than five seconds? Specialty software that doesn't adhere to the standard could be so labelled, and not bundled with the standard stuff. Millions upon millions of ordinary users who never explore most of the fancy features would be delighted.

Manuals are my next howl. Indeed, what manuals? You want to sell me something worth hundreds or thousands of dollars and you're too cheap to print a manual? I'm supposed to go online and print it with my own paper and ink? Wow, that's great customer relations. And, while no writer of a user's manual is ever a naive user, the custom used to be to at least try to imagine what a naive user would want or need to know.

Today's authors of computer manuals don't try to do that at all; they write for other experienced users, pointing out only the differences between what they've created and other similar systems.

As for the Internet, it's a hugely useful research tool, but it has also had a negative impact on what students and the public think is research. Rubbish and high-quality material are hard to separate, and often get presented with equal weight. Furthermore, the dross drives out the gold, as it's easier to produce. And e-mail, though handy, is the thief of literacy, the goad of the ill-considered reply, and the creator of flash points.

As for web-site builders, please take note of the three questions your firm is most frequently asked on the phone, and make sure they're answered on the website! It's not rocket science!

And then there's the economics of information technology, and the circular quest for an illusory holy grail. Our IT managers are comical indeed when they chant, "Our IT system could save us lots of time and money, if only there were enough time and money to get it running right." Well, there isn't, and will never be. I am, however, prepared to concede that it's much better than quill pens, and easier on the geese.

In addition, the tech revolution has profoundly influenced privacy. Privacy is now more fragile, and having any requires a certain low cunning to stay ahead of the forces fraying it at the edges. We need passwords, the more complex the better. But then we can't remember them. Some people store their passwords on their devices, a practice rather akin to leaving your wallet on the table in the restaurant when you go to the washroom. Others have somewhat better techniques, and there is doubtless a rather charming boom in pet ownership so that folk can use their pet names as easy-to-remember passwords.

The glitch there, however, is that we are exhorted by the experts to change our passwords often, and renaming a pet every few weeks or months might compromise your attempts to train it. In the end, most of us resort to a closely guarded hard copy of our list of passwords. It's time to buy and install a wall safe!

It is a delight, though, to have such a wide window to the world at large, via our devices. But the price we pay is that we can be importuned or conned from anywhere on earth. In days of yore the bad cats had to knock on our doors or stop us in the street. Now they come roaring into our homes and workplaces on a tsunami of electrons. I call this the flood of PPE. No, not personal protective equipment, but pickpockets, pirates, and embezzlers.

The ability of some systems to spoof a panoply of local phone numbers obviates much of the advantage of trying to block calls from specific numbers. We are fortunate, however, that most of the illicit importuning is done in such a completely incompetent fashion that it's hard to believe that it ever works. It's mostly just the annoyance. There was one recent period when it seemed that every few days I would get a call about "duct cleaning in my area," and would I like a deal on "duct cleaning." My house doesn't have ducts, so just responding that we had no ducts ended any such call. But one day, something in my head must have snapped, so instead of that usual answer, I replied, "Oh, the ducks are fine; do you do geese?" My interlocutor, who had a melodious accent of the Indian sub-continent, paused for a moment or two, before asking me, "Oh, and how many geese do you have." He then burst out laughing. In a way, it was charming to find that the intrusions were being made by folk who could find joy in a joke.

Receiving importuning by email is less fun. No matter how I tune to reject spam, some gets through. Years ago, I would even sometimes get spam purporting to be marketing a better spam filter. I can safely say that if one key on my computer wears out before the others, it will be the delete key.

To be fair, while the pace of electronic solicitation and deception has skyrocketed with the coming of the internet, its beginnings do go back to the era of the rotary dial telephone. The first mass solicitations to residential land line phones in Canada seemed to appear in the early 1950s. It was more genteel than today, and the canvassers felt obliged to use the phone books to try to target their interlocutor by name. My earliest recollection of these was an incessant campaign by Arthur Murray Dance Studios to get additional custom by telling those that they called that they had won a few free dance lessons.

My father had a terrifyingly imaginative sense of humour. I have a vivid recollection of his response to one of these phone solicitations. When he answered the phone, he heard his caller say, "Mr. Cowan, this is the Arthur Murray Dance Studio, and you've just won three free dance lessons." He answered, "No, this is not Mr. Cowan, I'm Mr. Stratavobarobalinski." This prompted the caller to try to pronounce the fictitious name. My father coached him patiently, first pronouncing it slowly, and finally spelling it. After a few minutes of training, the salesman finally got the name right, and got right back on track, making the original offer to "Mr. Stratavobarobalinski." My father's counter to this was to feign weeping softly into the phone. The puzzled salesman then asked, solicitously, why he was weeping. His reply: "Don't you think it is cruel to offer free dance lessons to a man with one leg?" The caller fled the scene. My father most assuredly had two legs, and was a fine tennis player and a pretty decent dancer. And clearly, he had figured out how to get himself on the 1950s equivalent of a do-not-call list, long before such things were invented.

Today, stopping the plague of begging and scamming is not so easy. It is unfortunate that the automation of the importuning enabled by modern technology largely precludes the use of the power of embarrassment to check it. But sometimes I give it a shot.

Of course, one of the standard fringe benefits of curmudgeonhood is the right to make fun of the more ineffectual bits of modernity. But when it comes to the tech revolution, the plusses are quite substantial. For example, I'm a big fan of the audio-visual technologies for remote meeting attendance. I don't have to look for a parking spot, and I can mute my microphone when I am about to sneeze.

It seems that the best recipe for coping is adopting what's useful and gently ridiculing the rest, in the hope that the ridicule will bring about change. But coping is not the whole story. The other aspect is that every change causes a change somewhere else. I hinted at a part of it in the lighthearted tales about how to handle scammers and solicitations. But an underlying change is that the tech revolution has created a whole new geography separate from the physical world, and, in that new geography, we may be too visible or not visible enough, or both. That is a portion of the subject dealt with in the next section of this chapter.

7.3 When Rights Collide

Canadians have historically been less attracted than Americans to extreme libertarian viewpoints. Various hypotheses have been cited to account for this, from a more severe climate driving a need for greater cooperation and collective effort by the inhabitants of Canada to a lingering impact of the Revolutionary War on the American psyche, but the real reasons are likely more complex, multifactorial, and subtle.

Thus, the expectation of compliance in Canada with any action or disclosure deemed necessary for public safety has always been high. And yet Canadians value their privacy just as much as Americans do. So, what happens when these two public goods collide? Perhaps the answer lies in deconvoluting what privacy really is. Perhaps privacy is not as simple as we thought. Is there, perchance, a hierarchy of slightly different privacies, with some entitled to greater protection than others? If so, it may be an error to lump them all together. I had wondered about these questions before, but the Covid-19 pandemic brought the question into tighter focus for me, and on careful reflection, I concluded that there were, indeed, quite different privacies. That thought prompted me to write "The Privacy Paradox: We Have Both Too Little and Too Much Privacy."

It appeared on December 28, 2021, in *Ottawa Life Magazine*.[39] What I wrote was as follows:

The Privacy Paradox: We Have Both Too Little and Too Much Privacy

Privacy was never an easy matter. Most humans want a reasonable degree of privacy, but want to be nosy too. It has always been a tricky balance.

Privacy is intimately connected to rights, and, in our society, there is a constant swinging of the pendulum back and forth between emphasis upon individual rights and emphasis upon collective rights. A case could be made that in recent times the pendulum has swung a bit too much towards individual rights and a bit too far from collective rights, but that is a discussion for another day.

Nonetheless, debates about rights contain some very important lessons that can inform debates about privacy as well.

We have lots of jurisprudence about rights and their boundaries. One boundary where rights cease is the point at which harm to another person begins. No-one has the right to harm another. The old adage that the right to swing one's arms stops just short of someone else's nose is a folksy and pithy expression of this well-tested principle.

So how could it be possible to have both too little and too much privacy? The debate about rights holds the clue. It is entirely likely that there are two distinct types of privacy. The first type would be privacy about matters dear to you but which will not harm others. Perhaps we should call this type of privacy "NEB privacy." The NEB stands for Nobody Else's Business. But there is also the matter of the sort of privacy which many desire, out of guilt, embarrassment or the risk of disadvantage, which would be privacy about something which has a non-trivial risk of harming others. Perhaps we should call this type of privacy "ROID privacy." The ROID stands for Risk to Others of Injury or Death. There can, of course, be questions about a grey zone between these two types, but more on that later.

It seems to me that today we have too little NEB privacy and too much ROID privacy. I'll deal with the easy one first.

The decline of NEB privacy is fairly obvious, as it has been considerably exacerbated by the communications revolution. Some of that decline has been accepted as a fact of life. We have largely acquiesced to having our shopping (and window-shopping) tastes tracked on line, with internet data mining having become a major industry. But there is also a profoundly seamy side to it as well. Hackers and fraudsters have a vastly easier time engaging in identity theft than was once the case, and slightly naïve folk are frequently amazed to see private electronic communication with friends, especially on social media, end up being distributed to an unlimited audience. The unwary can find that reputations can become quite fragile when a few ill-chosen words delivered to a relative or close friend a decade or so in the past can be resurrected with a few clicks and held out to be both contemporary and meaningful.

Intrusions into NEB privacy by electronically enabled fraudsters has resulted in not only an extraordinary amount of financial loss, but also in a remarkably low arrest and conviction rate for such offenses. At some point government will need to mandate the deployment of both passive and active countermeasures to prevent things like phone number spoofing and identity and site hijacking. There has long been a reluctance on the part of government to impose on the purveyors of electronic communications services the obligation to cleanse and insulate their networks from a wide range of illicit and fraudulent activities, because of the difficulty and cost of doing so. And there will always be a technological race between the crooks and the regulators, but that is hardly an excuse not to try to regulate.

High-school age children are especially vulnerable to the loss of privacy in the cybersphere, because they often combine poor judgement in what they thought was private speech and lack of resilience when their words or images are amplified by malicious electronic distribution. Hence the huge uptick in cyber-bullying.

And at the less damaging end of the spectrum, loss of NEB privacy can still be thoroughly annoying. A few months ago I did write a piece in this magazine which touched, in a more lighthearted way, on some of the intrusions caused by the tech revolution (*see section 7.2 above*). Our inability to block the intrusions has, of course, created a sort of verbal arms race, and I find myself having to invent new responses to the apparently unstoppable flood of spam and scam phone calls, always from new (spoofed) numbers. My latest favorite retort is, "Do your parents know that you are playing with the telephone?"

But if the erosion of NEB privacy is annoying and sometimes harmful, the rise of ROID privacy risks dramatically more harm.

Of course, the Covid-19 pandemic has brought the issue of new and exaggerated ROID privacy to the fore. It is worth noting, however, that spreading a communicable disease is not the only way in which individuals may be dangerous to those around them. Nonetheless, I will begin with some Covid-related analysis and then broaden the discourse.

Last summer a friend of ours needed to take her car to the dealership for some service work. The dealership offered a courtesy shuttle service to take her home. The shuttle consisted of a van with some passengers and a driver. A cautious person of an age for which Covid can be very dangerous, she asked if all had been vaccinated. The passengers affirmed that they were, but the driver became irate, claiming that she had no right to ask him that question.

While I am convinced that he was wrong, many in our society share his peculiar belief that asking them public health related questions like their vaccination status, health status, or travel history is an invasion of their privacy. They also expect that their exaggerated privacy rights will extend to their employment setting. Furthermore, they believe that the modern trend to ask them such questions is a new encroachment on some long-established privacy right. Many of those who believe in such forms of privacy are so strident about it that some organizations in our society have acquiesced to their views, albeit a bit reluctantly, and have allowed them to be present or to work without answering such questions.

And, unsurprisingly, many of the folk who think that their public health status is a private matter are the same ones who feel that compliance with public health rules is a matter of individual choice.

However, their dearth of historical knowledge is striking. Their alleged privacy rights with respect to ROID privacy are not of long standing. To the extent that they exist, they are recent and informal. I recall that even over 60 years ago, when I travelled, I had to carry my yellow vaccine passport and present it when requested. Furthermore, the much-vaunted confidentiality of the so-called doctor-patient relationship has never been absolute. Indeed, obligatory reporting with respect to certain communicable diseases is of long standing. But other reportage is required as well, so if a physician feels that some health condition, be it cardiovascular, metabolic or neurological, might make it unsafe for a person to drive, that too is reportable.

Furthermore, the questioning of apparently well persons about where they have been, with the possible outcome of a period of quarantine, is also not a new "invasion of privacy," as some have claimed, but has an extraordinarily long history.

Quarantine orders based not upon symptoms but merely based on where one had visited have been widely used in Europe for well over six centuries. The plague that swept Europe from 1346–1353, and returned periodically thereafter made early legislators somewhat aware of patterns of disease transmission. On July 27, 1377, in the Republic of Ragusa (centred on what is today the city of Dubrovnik, not the city of Ragusa in Sicily), the governing council passed an ordinance requiring all those aboard visiting ships to first spend 30 days (a "trentine") on a nearby unpopulated island. In general, quarantines first became widely used during that century to protect port cities from plague. Venice, for example, required ships coming from infected ports to stay at anchor for forty days (quaranta giorni), hence quarantine. The vast majority of communicable illnesses have much shorter incubation periods, of course, but the biblical importance of forty days gripped the imaginations of the time. After all, the first great quarantine was Noah's 40-day highly diverse couples cruise, during which time the rest of the planet was disinfected. There has been some modernization since then, and, today, the word is applied to isolation periods tailored to actual incubation periods.

So, it does indeed bother me when I hear of folks invoking privacy rights as an excuse for not answering reasonable questions that bear on the probability of them being infectious, and hence dangerous to those around them. It is perhaps instructive to take note of the questions one is asked on entering a hospital or vaccine clinic site. Logically, anyone ought to be able to ask and get an answer to those questions if they are expected to be anywhere near the person they are asking, especially indoors.

But dubious expectations of ROID privacy are not exclusively about risks of injury or death related to the transmission of communicable diseases. Some of it relates to risk of injury or death from assault, in all its forms. Causing another person physical harm intentionally is a criminal offense, and convictions for doing so are a matter of public record. There is an exception in those cases where the perpetrators are under the age of 18, and the Youth Criminal Justice Act (YCJA) applies, usually conferring anonymity to assist rehabilitation. However, even under the YCJA, in rare cases, youths are given adult sentences, in which case their identity is known. Occasionally, as well, a judge may declare that the name of a convicted juvenile should be made known because of risk to the public.

So, we have a legal system the original intent of which was that a person's history of conviction for violence would be known to those with whom they will subsequently interact, except for the above-mentioned exception for the very young.

There are good reasons for this, not the least of which is risk mitigation, because of concern over possible recidivism. Simply put, there is a greater likelihood that those who have already been convicted of violent offences will reoffend than there is that some average member of the public will commit a similar act in the first place.

However, over the past few generations, the safeguards that came from knowing who was inclined to be violent eroded, as population increased and we gathered in larger and larger urban areas. Cities confer anonymity. Villages do not. The anonymity of the city conferred a sort of informal de facto privacy, so that an inconvenient or embarrassing history of criminal violence might well not be known to the neighbours of the person with that history. This accidental conferring of ROID privacy for violent offenders is of recent origin, because, historically, our towns and cities were so small that every knew everyone else, and knew pretty much everything about them. I live in Kingston, Ontario. During the War of 1812, it had a population of 2,250. Toronto (then called York) was smaller, at 1,460. Even by 1834, Toronto still only had 9,252 residents. Four years after Confederation, in 1871, our capital, Ottawa, boasted only 21,525 inhabitants. Clearly, back then, the communities were small enough that everyone knew so much about every one else's business that no ROID privacy related to any history of violence could possibly have existed. Thus, this sort of ROID privacy is, by historical standards, something of a new fad. No doubt, a case could be made that a modicum of ROID privacy of this sort is a good thing, helping folks put the past behind them. But it is my view that it has now gone rather too far in the urban setting. After all, if I knew that a neighbor had a prior conviction for flying into a rage and injuring or killing someone, I'm pretty sure I would mitigate my risk by not complaining to him about his dog crapping on my lawn.

Another context in which there is a risk of inappropriate ROID privacy being generated relates to occupations which have some duty of confidentiality. I won't address the issue of the secrecy of the confessional in the Catholic Church, as there are a sufficient number of mystery novels and films that explore the moral dilemmas that priests encounter. But lawyer-client privilege, physician-patient confidentiality, the press custom of protection of the identity of sources, and the confidentiality expected of ombudspersons all raise questions about ROID privacy. For each occupation, the confidentiality is important, but there is always a delicate balancing act if something is learned, perhaps accidentally, which presages possible harm to others, or to the client.

Of the four occupations, I have a sense, based upon reading, and a few interviews, that, for the most part, the lawyers handle the tricky balance fairly well. They are all trained to reflect upon three questions before using the public safety exception to break privilege, specifically:

(a) Is there a clear risk to an identifiable person or group of people?

(b) Is there a risk of serious bodily harm or death?

(c) Is the threat of danger immediate or imminent?

If they answer yes, they know they can break privilege. But the problem they face is that the questions don't specify how much risk. It's always a guess. Plus, they're really going to irk the client, who is sometimes a scary character. Looking back, I think most get it right. But a handful do not.

Physicians seem to have more difficulty with the tricky balance. For them, there are two categories of exceptions to their obligations to protect confidential patient information. One is the range of matters where they are explicitly required to report, and compliance is very much the norm in such situations. More problematic for them are the matters where they are permitted to disclose, but not required to. Canadian courts, including the Supreme Court, have not imposed a mandatory duty on physicians to alert third parties of a danger posed by a patient. But while they are not obligated to, they may disclose confidential information when they have reason to believe that there is an imminent risk of serious bodily harm or death to an identifiable person or group. While it is hard to gather any statistical material on this, it seems likely that many practitioners are quite reluctant to exercise their right to warn when it is not explicitly mandated.

Journalists, for the most part, feel strongly that the maintenance of a free press means that they have the unfettered right not to disclose their sources. Often that is true. But not always. It is eleven years since the Supreme Court of Canada (SCC) found for the Crown in R v. National Post. It is now clear that confidential sources must be disclosed in those fairly rare cases where the needs of law enforcement trump the interests of the media, despite the recognition of the important role that confidential sources play in making sure that stories of the public interest are brought to light. I remain uncertain that all of our journalists fully accept the tricky balance, and I suspect that in some cases their understandable desire to protect sources sometimes causes them to choose confidentiality over public safety and effective enforcement of the law.

Ombudspersons are in an even more difficult situation, as their potential clientele may be scared off if there are doubts about the confidentiality of their discussions. But sometimes ombudspersons have a duty to warn of impending danger. Carrying out that duty can be hard on them, and can, in some cases, compromise their ability to carry on. There are a couple of pages on just such a case in section 2 of my report to the Board of Governors of Concordia University of the extensive Board of Inquiry that I conducted there in 1994 (The Cowan Report[6]). It convinced me that ombudspersons may be substantially disadvantaged if they perceive a duty to warn, and break ROID-type confidentiality in the interests of public safety. It is only logical, then, to assume that this occurs somewhat less frequently than it should.

It is also worth noting that there is something of a privacy movement, or privacy lobby, in Canada. There are, as well, federal and provincial privacy commissioners, who are expected to be essentially privacy regulators, though some have come close to being privacy advocates.

Privacy advocates largely consider themselves to be progressives. When the privacy movement and its advocates press for increased NEB privacy, I consider them to be on the side of the angels. But, because my quaint notion that there are two distinct types of privacy is not shared by all, when advocates press for strengthening ROID privacy, it feels to me a bit like trying to recreate the lawlessness and turmoil of Wild West. I indicated earlier that I thought the pendulum had swung a bit too far towards individual rights, and away from collective rights, and ROID privacy is part of that overswing.

So that brings me back to my original hypothesis about having too little NEB privacy and too much ROID privacy. But in the paragraph where I introduced this odd notion of two distinct types of privacy, I did hint that this sorting into two bins might be an over-simplification, and that there was doubtless an indistinct grey zone between them. Of course, this must be so. There are other forms of harm that are not physical, but I nonetheless opted to define the ROID privacy bin as limited to a connection to risk of physical harm. Furthermore, one needs to ask questions like, "How great a risk (probability)?," and "How much harm?". It is clearly not possible in an article of this length to parse out what parts of the grey zone should see improved or weakened privacy. But the stimulus for reflecting on this came in the first instance from some folks' dubious privacy claims related to the Covid pandemic we are living through. So, reflecting upon communicable diseases only, I can say at least that I'm confident that a person's Covid and vaccination status is a ROID type of privacy issue, and their athlete's foot status is a NEB privacy issue.

It is no easy business to identify the optimum balance point between individual rights and collective rights. My comments about the swing of that particular pendulum did not explicitly identify where I thought the bottom centre point of that arc lay. I took the easy route by only observing that a particular form of privacy that might well cause injury or death to others was obviously too far into one extreme of the pendulum swing, but that, by itself, does not tell us where the centre of that arc lies. Finding that spot and stopping the swing right there is an ideal, but a hard thing on which to achieve consensus.

I gave no examples of the other side of the arc, examples where collective majority rights have been overweighted, but I hardly had to, because we've surely learned of plenty of them from history and sometimes from current news. Gerrymandering by temporary majorities to perpetuate their rule is surely one example that's been seen often enough, while history is replete with tales of regimes that forced an official religion upon all.

However, when I expressed the view that we were experiencing a period where society was erring by having moved a bit too far toward the protection of individual rights at the expense of the whole, I was reacting in part to exaggerated freedom movements, especially in the United States, that are partly the result of a self-indulgent mindset after more than three quarters of a century since a major global war, and which bespeak a lack of duty of care for one's neighbour. They represent the triumph of desire over duty and of expectations of privilege over responsibility. That the fallacious freedom movement seems to have its greatest appeal and resonance among the least educated and least accomplished is unsurprising, as such groups are somewhat more susceptible to untruthful or untested hypotheses and have a normal desire to seek persons or forces other than themselves to blame for their failures and inadequacies. The demonization of "the elites," is a predictable consequence, which leads us to the next section. But, as we shall learn, not all elites are the same, and the ones that we read about in the history books didn't get there by the same routes as the putative "elites" of today.

7.4 A New Political Tool: Demonizing Knowledge

People who feel strongly about something usually construct a forceful narrative for themselves that justifies their stance. Not all those narratives are equal; indeed, they range from impressive to bloody awful. The best narratives are rich in verifiable facts, coherent in their organization and logic, contain hypotheses that can actually be tested, and are free from excessive exaggeration. The worst narratives are conjectural, reliant upon provable falsehoods, chaotic, and wildly overstated.

It should surprise no-one that the middle ground is something of a magnet for the better narratives, while toward the extremes one usually finds narratives that fail almost every test implied above. And it is a fairly smooth continuum. The most extreme stances are typically accompanied by the wackiest narratives.

But sometimes the narratives contain themes that echo not only across much of the political spectrum but also across time, and, when those themes appear in the narratives of the protagonists, it sometimes requires some careful inspection just to ascertain that they haven't taken on meanings that diverge in problematic ways from their original underpinnings.

One theme that crops up in the narratives of both left and right extremes is anti-elitism. This was touched on at the very beginning of this volume, in Section 1.1 (A Middle Ground Manifesto). In that introduction to the theme of this book, I had argued (in "The Curvature of Political Space") that the extremes of right and left shared many common features. In that piece, written in early 2019, I had begun to decry the beginnings of the drift in the meaning of "anti-elitism." But, in the ensuing three years, the shift in what the extremists take "anti-elitism" to mean accelerated and has become so pronounced that it has very nearly entirely reversed the meaning of the term. Because it crops up so often in the discourse of extreme groups, I felt that the hijacking of the meaning needed to be highlighted. To that end, in the spring of 2022, I wrote, "Anti-Elitism Ain't What It Used to Be." It quotes from the earlier piece[2] but goes substantially further in setting out the harm that the drift in meaning is causing. It appeared on March 1, 2022, in *Ottawa Life Magazine*.[40] What I wrote was as follows:

Anti-Elitism Ain't What It Used to Be

My parents were adults during the Great Depression. While solidly middle-class, they had a deep appreciation and sympathy for the plight of the less fortunate and the dispossessed.

I was born in Toronto during the Second World War, and I have strong memories from the 1950s of my intellectual and quite progressive father holding forth about the undue influence and machinations of the "elites." But the elites of which he spoke were defined by money and bloodlines. Indeed, in those days Ontario was still largely dominated by a WASP elite who were very much the inheritors of the Family Compact of pre-1837 Upper Canada. And he was probably right that wealth and "class" garnered extraordinary influence in public affairs in the Ontario of 65 years ago. After all, the Canada of the 1950s was only a generation removed from the British honours system that had perpetuated a titled aristocracy, and some Canadians of the 1950s still carried titles awarded before the Nickle Resolution of 1919.

Somehow, the long and winding road of the 65 years from then till now has managed to bend our language a bit out of shape. Were my father still alive today, he would be shocked at the new meanings of the word "elites."

Today in the liberal democracies we are witnessing the emergence of a new reactionary populism that is very vocal in its anti-elitism. This movement is much stronger in the US and in some European nations than in Canada, but nonetheless it was strong enough in Canada to enable the Truckers Convoy protests, though it is unlikely to have much of an impact at the polls on election day. It was, however, fascinating to listen to the members of the Goofy Pilgrimage and Winter Camping Extravaganza in their attacks upon the "elites," because the things they objected to made it clear that the definition of "elites" has changed.

Yes, there were still the references to an elite of wealth (though the references were tinged in their discourse with a bit of racism here and there). And I can readily accept the notion that very wealthy individuals may have easier access to the corridors of power than others, and we do know that sometimes influence is bought and sold (though not as often as is usually feared). But it is clear that, in Canada at least, the old upper class defined by bloodlines is no more. The family names of our cabinet ministers no longer belong to one small geographic or ethnic group, but sound like a selection from around the world. And in that, the social experiment that is Canada is a great triumph, proving that inherited class is a pretty much a dead issue here, except perhaps for the rare cases of dynastic politics, where name recognition has value.

But the "elites" who draw the most fire these days from the populists are a new group. They are people who came from all walks of life, but studied hard. They dedicated themselves to both acquiring knowledge and generating new knowledge, and over many years of hard work became the top experts in their respective disciplines. They are the people who we all turn to when we desperately need advice on things with which we are unfamiliar. They are the scientists who generate and teach new knowledge, or the skilled practitioners who apply it, or the logistics experts who make it available to all, or the top analysts who predict effects by observation, data collection and extrapolation. They are the people who know stuff.

Complaining about people with high expertise by describing them as a new self-interested, exploitive elite is evidence of a double disaster. It tells us that the complainers think that they can function and run things without knowledge, or that they can simply substitute their biases for actual knowledge. And it also underscores the catastrophic failure of our education system, which not only doesn't provide a good underpinning in terms of real knowledge, but has also failed in its currently fashionable modern objective of "teaching people how to learn."

The delusion that the "elite" of experts is engaged in a widespread, perfectly coordinated plot to massively inconvenience the citizenry with Covid restrictions, for the sole purpose of elevating their own sense of self-importance also has an important psychiatric dimension, and, in a way, is a substantial health crisis all by itself. It is a bit of a shock to realize that, instead of just feeling anger towards those who block arteries of commerce and disrupt residential neighborhoods in order to try to compel governments to cancel various public health measures, we should probably also feel pity for them.

There is, of course, a larger issue about this sort of anti-elitism. At this point, I'd like to quote two paragraphs from an article that I wrote in this very magazine about movements of the extreme right and extreme left, and their surprising convergence. It was published on April 8, 2019, well before the Covid pandemic.[2]

"Yes, the elites have had it their own way for a damned long time, even if those who comprise the elite changed with each era. But within those bastions of privilege, be they economic, social or academic, are stored the accumulated knowledge that humans have amassed over a few thousand years. To believe that all this knowledge is really conspiracy, and that there are "alternate truths" just a click away, scripted by a fantasist in a basement, perhaps, but just as good as knowledge tested in the fires of debate or experiment, of peer review and reconfirmation, is to throw away civilisation and any chance of improvement in the human condition or uplifting of the spirit.

But today's extremists, in occupying the pretend moral high ground, are inclined to insist that the discourse of virtually every public official, every scientist or scholar or other expert, and every person of means is suffused with blatant self-interest, and indeed conflict of interest, and that there are no facts, only opinions. Thus, facts can, in the new parlance, be countered by "alternate facts." Hence the anti-vaccine movement and the like. Such folk cannot dare to believe that those with special expertise, even if privileged, might speak actual truth out of genuine public interest, out of concern for others, and out of a sense of public duty, because it clashes with their world view."

It is interesting that in writing about extremism in April 2019, (pre-Covid), I had used the anti-vaccine movement as an example of the rise of anti-knowledge feelings. I could not have known then how soon that particular manifestation of "anti-elitism" would become enormously consequential.

Furthermore, those protesters seem to me to be remarkably innocent of the usual political verities, because they also blame the politicians for over-reacting to the advice of the experts, and consequently imposing unneeded public health restrictions which the protesters believe to be excessive, crippling and motivated by nefarious objectives. In a democracy with frequent elections, political axiom #1 is, "Don't do things that inconvenience or annoy large numbers of voters, if you can possibly avoid it. And if you can't avoid it, delay as long as possible, do as little of it as possible, and stop doing it at the first hint that you might be able to ease off."

The application of this axiom to government decisions on restrictive public health measures during a pandemic is a virtual guarantee that the restrictions imposed for public health reasons will always be inadequate. Inevitably they are a little too mild, a little too late, and end a little too soon. This will be true for democratically elected governments of all political stripes, with slight variation. That is to say that all will err in the same direction, but those with libertarian inclinations will err a bit more than the others.

This verity about governments of all stripes normally being (as my father would have said) "a day late and a dollar short" on all such inconvenient but important protective measures, means that any protest to get the measures lifted or abated sooner than the government's own plan is almost certainly on the wrong side of history and the wrong side of logic.

But the same folks who have transformed "anti-elitism" into an anti-knowledge ideology have, inadvertently, done violence to other bits of language. The word "research" has also taken a bit of a drubbing, and migrated considerably down-market.

My occupation from the mid 1960s until the late 1980s was research and teaching in a faculty of medicine. I studied and prepared for years to be able to carry out my research, competed for resources to carry it out, collected and analyzed the data myself, wrote up my findings and their justification, subjected those reports to the judgement and criticism of top experts, and reported my findings in highly rated journals.

But these days it has become something of a joke when someone says, "Oh, I've done my research!," just before they are about to announce some insane notion that is easily disproven. What they mean by announcing that they've done their research is that they've asked Dr. Google to search out a couple of sites that, given how they posed the question, will obligingly cater to their confirmation bias. If you ask such people what primary sources they used, they look at you slightly puzzled, because they think you've asked them whether they've consulted someone in primary school. But I suppose I must be slipping into curmudgeonhood if their etymological and epistemological sins bother me. After all, language does change.

In the end, it's not the corruption of the words that really saddens me. It is the lost potential in all those people who have so much energy and so much desire to influence events, but have so little inclination to learn enough to have a middling grasp of the subject they are addressing. I guess they fear that if they listen too long to anyone in the knowledge elite they will be sucked into some unseen and sinister vortex, and will become what they have decided to oppose.

A cynical reader might be tempted to suspect that my compassion for the deluded, as expressed in the last paragraph above, is not entirely genuine and is just an additional rhetorical device to further categorize them as lost souls. That cynical reader would be at least partly wrong. I am embarrassed by the extent to which those who govern us have not taken the people entirely into their confidence. We owed the members of the public, including the somewhat deluded ones, a lot more than they received. We owed them better educations, and we certainly owed them better and more open leadership, and complete and candid explanations during times of crisis.

In my own personal experience, when I took the time to discuss matters more fully with people that I had thought were intractably wedded to counterfactual notions, some of them became quite receptive. Even if they didn't necessarily make it all the way back to my version of the middle ground, they certainly got a good bit of the way there.

It is the dearth of transparency and candour that enlarges the space in which nonsense and conspiracy theories can thrive. The inarticulate, self-serving blather that passes for articulation of government policy, or is proffered as explanations when things go wrong, is so simplified and sanitized that it just cries out to be disbelieved. Especially at the federal level, even entirely true pronouncements have suffered so much cosmetic surgery from the spin doctors that, while they remain largely true, they are also almost unrecognizable, even to the experts that created them in their unadorned state, before the facelift was done and the makeup applied.

Early in the Covid-19 pandemic, when we were faced with a tangible set of problems, many of them science-based, there was a brief period when it seemed that society might experience a sea-change in which the status of and regard for genuine expertise might rise to levels not seen in many decades. It did, briefly, but the moment didn't last.

It could have. Some of the public is still very keen to hear the real story from the most knowledgeable sources. Why it didn't last is complicated and multifactorial. But one of the factors that has militated against trust in expertise, and the opportunity for better discourse, was that some governments squandered the opportunity because they preferred an oversimplified and sanitized narrative, underestimating the ability of the public to understand facts and ideas. There was so much talking down to people that it actually encouraged the rise of noxious myths, the proliferation of contempt for expertise, and the new form of anti-elitism that equates knowledge with bias or self-interest.

If the middle ground is to hold, we need to reclaim some of the folks who have drifted to the extremes. The best way to reclaim some of them is to make the effort to give them the entire story, warts and all, and then answer all questions truthfully (if, indeed, we actually have answers). Starting now would be good.

But, while giving the full story and answering questions fully and candidly can facilitate convergence within a society, there can be external factors as well that sometimes predispose societies toward convergence and social cohesion, and that is the topic of the next section.

7.5 Convergence in a Dangerous World

The liberal democracies have often demonstrated strong social cohesion and consensus when at war or during periods of substantial external threat. The most extensive large-scale conflict within living memory was the Second World War, and there are myriad accounts of how everyone "pulled together" during that dreadful six years. It is perhaps a bit ironic that such bad times often produce more social cohesion than good times. This is not just a Canadian experience and has been well documented. But that example did cause me to reflect on three topics: the origins of my own biases, the possible domestic impact of the current international tensions and conflicts, and how we might routinely induce people to be less fractious and more inclined to cooperate with and help others.

To that end, I wrote "Fracture Lines and Glue: The Interplay of External Threats and Social Cohesion." It appeared on December 5, 2022, in *Ottawa Life Magazine*.[41] What I wrote was as follows:

Fracture Lines and Glue: The Interplay of External Threats and Social Cohesion

I was born towards the end of the Second World War and grew up during the 1950's and 60's. Naturally, my parents and all of my early mentors had strong memories of that war, and strong views of the tense world that succeeded it. The Cold War was a central feature of that era, and for my generation, there seemed to be nothing more important than finding ways to maintain peace, especially since the alternative seemed to imply a sort of global self-immolation. Isolationism was very much out of fashion, and internationalism was widely held to be at least one reasonable route to a less dangerous future. Starting in the 1950s, Canada invested some considerable effort into trying to make supranational bodies like the United Nations into effective peace-makers and peace enforcers. Some early partial successes encouraged my generation to think that, gradually, the world might become more peaceful as nation states ceded tiny bits of their sovereignty to supranational entities that would damp down the exaggerated fires of nationalism and make wars gradually obsolete, replacing them with negotiation.

A key feature of that era was that many of the nations of the northern hemisphere had gathered themselves (in one case) or been coerced (in the other case) into two great camps, NATO and the Warsaw Pact. Yes, the two great camps were, to a considerable degree, in dispute, but it was a frozen dispute, replete with ritual and ideological mudslinging as a substitute for actual conflict. And within at least one of those two great alliances, folks got along pretty well. European peoples, who had fought one another for two millennia, now cooperated, created an economic free trade zone, and eventually a sort of half-assed political union, with a European parliament (albeit with very limited clout) and, eventually, a common currency. For my generation, it did seem that our assumption of higher and higher levels of aggregation of human groupings was actually taking place.

And then a strange thing happened. By 1989, the Cold War had ended. That's when slightly naïve optimists and progressives like me began to discover how wrong we had been about the path towards the unity of humankind. We had failed to notice that some of that coming together of various different peoples in the previous forty years had been due not to maturity, or to respect for others who were slightly different, but rather due to fear. Within each of the two great camps, the disparate groups in each had huddled together and made common cause under their respective nuclear umbrellas out of fear of the other camp, and of an apocalypse held at bay by the terrifying nuclear standoff called deterrence, or MAD (Mutually Assured Destruction). When, somewhat suddenly, that fear abated, the horrible truth which started to come to light was that people sometimes didn't like their slightly different neighbors very much.

Countries started to blow apart along ethnic lines, sometimes peacefully (Czechoslovakia), and sometimes less so (Yugoslavia). Today, Belgium, created as a democratic state in 1830, is essentially two states, living like a separated couple that still shares a house. Separatist movements are flourishing in many lands. The so-called United Kingdom isn't entirely united, or so the SNP would have you believe.

But even within developed countries that are not actually splitting up, consensus has become a rarity. Canadians watch with a combination of horror and smugness as polarization surges in the US, with some of the most extreme on both sides employing physical force rather than the ballot box as their tool of choice. Fortunately, Canada lags behind a bit in such matters, with our long tradition of making a mad dash for the middle, but even that is weakening. Both extremes have begun to make inroads in their shared project to shout down the centrists. And hate, of various types, is in the air, at both ends of the spectrum.

The discouraging conclusion that one might draw from all this is that social cohesion is bolstered by external threats, and has trouble sustaining itself when those threats are not especially evident. As reluctant as I am to say it, it seems that people need someone or some group to be angry at, and, if a suitably fearsome external entity is not available, they'll find some entity at home to feel that way about, and make a new fracture line (or exacerbate a small existing one).

Thus, we arrive at the slightly disturbing hypothesis that fracture lines in social cohesion will normally arise with even inconsequential stimuli when people don't have bigger things to worry about. As a corollary, significant external challenges can be part of the glue that repairs the fracture lines.

So, does that mean that Mr. Putin's ill-considered and disastrous invasion of Ukraine, in addition to being a great tragedy and a great foolishness, may also be an opportunity? Certainly, it has already reinvigorated NATO and unified Europeans. That war may not end soon. It has ramped up tensions, with a few echoes of the Cold War, and its aftermath will require some rejigging of our postures abroad and enhancement of our defence preparedness. It is not a small matter. So, one wonders, might it be the external stressor that provides some glue to bind up some of the internal fracture lines that we now experience, all related to issues of minimal consequence that have assumed undue importance of late in Canada?

Is it possible that a degree of solidarity on what we must do to meet external challenges might cause some of our fellow citizens to stop making a whole meal out of tiny differences at home? Will the loony right perhaps stop calling Mr. Trudeau a communist, or stop displaying bizarrely exaggerated anger over nearly every action taken by a duly elected government, when, in fact, they have every right to replace that government at the ballot box very soon, if they can so persuade the electorate. And might the loony left stop pretending that they are deeply offended or terrified every time anyone says something with which they do not entirely agree, and so they wish to curb that speech.

In real life, when there are tangible threats and urgent tasks, as opposed to imagined crises, no-one has time for nonsense like that.

In fact, a non-trivial part of the great tragedy of the fracture lines and the decline of social cohesion is, in fact, wasted time and wasted effort. The wasted time and effort of the thoroughly wacky truckers' convoy protests is an example. And similarly, at the other extreme, we watch putative progressives waste the precious hours and minutes of their lives in the elaborate vilification of long-dead corpses whose great sin appears to have been their failure to invent and use a time machine, in order to modernize their opinions to meet the expectations of the present day. And, both the right and the left could profitably stop wasting time and effort on their new (but also old) hobby of gratuitous and pointless antisemitism.

Indeed, the very fact that these two polar opposite pseudo-political groups have the surplus time and energy to invest in such nonsense probably tells us a great deal about the real nature of the fracture lines of which I speak. What is clear is that, for the most part, the creation and exacerbation of the fracture lines is an amusing activity and a found purpose for people who haven't got much else to worry about, have leisure time, and are reasonably well-fed. That is to say, essentially a First World luxury item for the bored, ill-informed, and self-righteous. These manufactured conflicts appeal especially to those who would like to feel more important than they are, but will not engage in the harder tasks associated with building cohesion, either because they do not feel a sufficient sense of community or they lack the skills, or both.

The external threats that seem to damp down such nonsense are not actually a complete cure for that particular malaise, but rather just suppress and diminish it, because, as we respond to grave external challenges, the public opprobrium levelled against those who encourage internal division increases. When we are under pressure from abroad, we tend to see our compatriots in a better light, if only because, as the old adage goes, "The enemy of my enemy is my friend."

But it would be so much better if only we could find ways of convincing people not to "sweat the small stuff," and maintain a civil dialogue, even when there is no external threat. It seems, though, that people don't know how to identify issues as "small stuff" if they have not, within recent memory, been exposed to genuinely serious challenges.

I recall, some two decades ago, being in an administrative meeting where some of the players who were in disagreement were obdurate, vehement, and testy. I was just getting ready to slip into mediator mode when a somewhat more junior colleague entered the fray, and with great brilliance and aplomb, cooled the situation right down, and worked the set of problems in such a way that all the protagonists got something they wanted, and nobody was irked. He seemed immune to the thinly-veiled insults flying about and made all the players feel valued. He took none of the imprecations or dubious behavior personally. The meeting ended with consensus, and I'd had to do absolutely nothing to help it get there. I was very taken with his handling of a fractious situation.

On leaving the meeting, I was walking along a corridor with that junior colleague, and I complimented him on keeping his cool in the face of obvious provocation, being the soul of moderation, and guiding the crankier players into a safe harbour, and I asked him how he had learned to do that while maintaining such a benign manner. He responded that it seemed pretty easy, because, after all, nobody was shooting at him, and his airplane wasn't on fire. I thought to myself, "Well, there's a chap who knows the difference between big stuff and small stuff." Indeed, I had briefly forgotten that his prior occupation did encompass a fair bit of that big stuff.

So, now, as some big stuff looms on the horizon, and might require our focussed attention for a few years, perhaps it would be a useful to ease up on "sweating the small stuff." There is serious work ahead of us; endless acerbic bickering about minutiae won't get it done.

I suspect myself of being an unrepentant optimist, but, to my eyes, in Canada, at least, the fairly widespread consensus about aid to Ukraine is already evidence of external pressures creating some repair of internal fracture lines in the political arena. And while political competition still requires the usual ritual bickering over questions of style, the major political parties do not, at this instant, seem to be very far apart on what we should be doing on the world stage, but rather have confined their disagreements to differing views of our competence and alacrity, as well as disagreeing about which particular bit of virtue signalling should get top billing on any given day.

And then, of course, there is the natural life cycle of governments in Canadian politics, such that, as governments get a bit long in the tooth and exhibit increased risk aversion, they become especially platitudinous and dithery, which invariably attracts increased opprobrium from opposition parties and other critics. Sometimes a government that faces a near-death experience reinvents itself and goes through a sort of renewal that restores its early vigour, but not always.

Furthermore, retail politics is always partly about the appearance of things, and sometimes finding substance is not an easy task, but during the last part of 2022 and the early parts of 2023 it seemed to me that the march toward exaggerated polarization had abated. But we won't have any certainty about such political trends until after the next federal election. The nature of the rhetoric during that exercise will tell us whether there is any movement toward the middle ground, and, if so, we may get hints of the extent to which it will spill over into sectors other than politics and how soon. Regrettably, there are fewer signs yet of potential convergence in our neighbour to the south, the United States, but we shall see if the run-up to 2024 gives any such hints.

Meanwhile, whatever vitriol may be displayed in the realm of political theatre, I'm not noticing it very much in the street and in normal discourse. Indeed, I am sensing that the Covid pandemic, now having evolved into a Covid-cautious new steady state, has left Canadians even more considerate of those they encounter. Possibly it too counts as an external stressor that acts as glue for some fracture lines.

AFTERWORD:
THE OPINIONATED
MIDDLE GROUND

EACH EDUCATED PERSON'S WORLDVIEW is somewhat skewed by their first discipline because their first intensive exposure to a field of study has a non-trivial influence on how they analyze things. There is a charming expression for this phenomenon in French, and it is at the same time a pretty decent pun. In French, the term for one's professional training is one's "formation professionnelle." But the descriptor for the biases generated by that training is the slightly adjusted term "déformation professionnelle" (which is also a pun), because it implies that our professional training may well deform how we see things, and, yes, it does mean a predilection toward certain ways of thinking due to the effects of our training. The techniques of analysis, and even the biases, ingrained by our training may well be useful, but we need to be aware of them. I have often used the expression, in English, that we are all, to some degree, captives of our first discipline.

I know that I am. My first discipline was physics. After that, I still stuck with the experimental sciences and did two further degrees in physiology, with a very strong biophysics slant. As you can imagine, I got very used to wanting facts and insisting that hypotheses be "proven," at least to some degree of statistical significance, using the scientific method and good experimental design, followed by withstanding a reasonable amount of peer review. So, people like me don't necessarily cope well with sweeping, unproven generalizations, or great dollops of conjecture.

Fact addicts like me tend to aggregate in the middle ground, because the more one learns about a subject, the less convincing the extreme views of it become. That doesn't mean that, in science, the majority view is always exactly right. There are plenty of examples of revolutionary findings that, at least to a degree, upend the majority view. That's part of the process of discovery and progress. But such revolutionary findings invariably come with testable evidence. That's why people with my background are uncomfortable with stuff that isn't evidence-based. Big, bold, unsupported claims, including conspiracy theories, hold no appeal for fact addicts like me because the automatic sorting system in our science-conditioned brains dumps them in the trash when they fail to clear the first hurdle of the verification process.

If my "déformation professionnelle" predisposed me to the middle ground, another one of my activities cemented the tendency. Starting in 1974 I became very involved in labour relations, and, over the ensuing 40 years, I did a huge amount of negotiation, mediation, and arbitration. I was a chief negotiator for labour and for management and resolved dozens of collective agreements and some 350 grievances. I never came even close to a strike, and (so far) I have been on the winning side of every grievance that went to arbitration, though I have conceded a number of them before getting to that point, when I concluded, on listening to their arguments, that the other side was right.

I learned from all that. Perhaps the most important thing that I learned was that behind every silly allegation or unworkable proposal is somebody's worry, discontent, or fear. The best solutions invariably find some more sensible way to address the worry, discontent, or fear without validating the silly allegations or adopting the unworkable proposals. This taught me that the middle ground need not be just soulless compromise. Indeed, it routinely consists of much more than just mechanical interpolation between competing interests.

And then an interesting thing happened to me. I retired. There are two things you should know about retired people. The first is that they no longer need to be quite so careful with their words. They can say exactly what they think, and nobody can fire them, and, furthermore, nobody is obliged to do as they say. This means that they can be much more candid in what they say or write. It is a special form of freedom for the elderly. They can be as opinionated as they want. That freedom led to "opinionated" in the title of this book.

The second thing you should know about retired people is that retirement takes away most of the platforms from which they normally spoke during their working lives and diminishes the reach of their discourse. One of the ways to get back some of that amplification is to avoid being too circumspect. In short, being opinionated gets us back in the game.

So, retirement allows one to be opinionated, and, if one wishes not to become invisible, it also requires that one become opinionated. So, best to just go with the flow and admit to being as opinionated as all get out.

For me, then, the opinionated middle ground was not exactly a choice. It seems to have been preordained by training and by age. I admit that the terms "opinionated" and "middle ground" do not typically appear together, but, in this case, it seems to have been inevitable.

Not every occupant of the opinionated middle ground is retired. And sometimes the ones who are still working do quite well at provoking convergence. I have seen arbitrators and mediators use carefully crafted bluntness to jar two parties in conflict toward convergence. I've done it myself from time to time. Seeing or even initiating that process taught me some important lessons about handling people who were stranded at one or another extreme. The key was not so much dictating to them where the middle ground lay (though, if necessary, arbitrators' decisions can do so), but, rather, it was creating the conditions that encouraged the parties to want to locate it themselves.

I well remember a remarkable experience in the late 1970s. I was serving as a member of an arbitration board that was adjudicating a complicated grievance against the dismissal of a high-profile senior employee. The setting was a small industrial Canadian city, and, clearly, the community was very much riven over the issue. The behaviours of both the counsel for the grievor and the counsel for the employer were extraordinary: They both carried on, in a very theatrical fashion, using the most inflammatory language imaginable, and aiming much of their discourse at the audience of locals, rather than at the arbitration board. Each was trying, quite successfully, to get their own faction of the local community thoroughly enraged. After some eight days of this, the chair of the arbitration board insisted upon a closed-door meeting with the two lawyers. His opening words, behind closed doors, were, "What the hell is going on here?" After a bit of discussion, it became clear that there was no secret agenda. It was just that the parties were unhappy. I mean really unhappy. Wildly unhappy.

The chair of the arbitration board stopped them from bickering for a moment and explained:

> You must understand one thing: it is not in our power to make you happy. Your clients made that impossible. The parties had screwed up their relationship, and managed to make themselves and everyone around them impressively unhappy long before I and my two colleagues got here. Given the state of affairs on our arrival, our job will be to make sure that both parties are exactly equally unhappy.

The two lawyers looked a bit stunned. A cross between surprise and embarrassment, sort of like the reaction one might have after just stepping into a pile of dog poop in the street. They cleared out and came back 25 minutes later with a settlement. It was an unusual settlement and very fair. It calmed the community right down. Strangely, the parties must have been impressed with what he said, because the settlement, which we then endorsed, retained an oversight role for the arbitrators for months thereafter.

Usually, it takes quite a bit longer to guide warring parties to where or how they might find a middle ground. But, as in that example, a suitably direct telling of the plain, unvarnished facts can be a big part of the answer.

Not a huge shock, when you think about it. After all, it's nothing more than the observation that sanity, moderation, and civility will flourish if the majority of those who operate in public fora just stick to telling the plain truth. Yes, there will always be differences of opinion as to exactly what is true and what its nuances are. On the other hand, there will be far fewer disagreements about what is patently false.

So, there you have it. It's not that complicated. Just tell the truth. Do not tolerate those who lie. Give full explanations, not sound bites. Favour others who do the same. Treat opponents with respect, if their behaviour is civil. Listen and read, because you might learn something. Be open to being persuaded in areas you didn't expect. Don't reward people for false truculence. Don't pass on rumours without verification. Exhibit a bit of wariness about fads.

Does all this sound vaguely familiar? Is there some resonance with what our parents told us? Indeed, seeking the middle ground is surprisingly similar to becoming a real adult. And, if you live long enough, you can be opinionated too.

NOTES

1. From Bad to Verse: Seriously Unserious Pieces in Verse or Short Story Form *Plus* Something in the Air: A Memoir of My First 22 Years of Flying. Kerr House Publishing, 2021, 106 pp, ISBN978-1-7778144-0-3. Hardcover from Novel Idea, Kingston, or soft cover or Kindle from Amazon Canada.
2. http://www.ottawalife.com/article/the-curvature-of-political-space?set_lang=en
3. https://www.ottawalife.com/article/why-isis-and-its-friends-must-be-opposed?c=9
4. https://www.ottawalife.com/article/carbon-taxes-fine-idea-terrible-marketing?c=1
5. https://www.ottawalife.com/article/gun-crime-gun-tragedies-and-a-plan-for-real-gun-control?c=13
6. LESSONS FROM THE FABRIKANT FILE: A REPORT TO THE BOARD OF GOVERNORS OF CONCORDIA UNIVERSITY. An independent review of the employment history of Valery Fabrikant at Concordia University, with particular emphasis on concrete measures to enhance the future ability of the university to deal with a wide range of issues raised by the case in question (42 pp.). It can be found at https://www.concordia.ca/content/dam/concordia/offices/archives/docs/cowan-report.pdf

7. https://www.ottawalife.com/article/the-archduke-game?c=1

8. https://www.ottawalife.com/article/coronavirus-two-nations-two-systems-one-pattern/

9. At the date of publication of that piece, the incumbent president was Donald Trump.

10. https://www.ottawalife.com/article/covid19-telling-half-truths-never-ends-well/

11. https://www.ottawalife.com/article/covid-19-reflections-on-the-end-game?c=13

12. https://www.ottawalife.com/article/covidiots-and-their-cure?c=1

13. https://www.ottawalife.com/article/unspoken-causes-of-vaccine-avoidance-and-public-health-noncompliance?set_lang=en

14. https://www.ottawalife.com/article/free-speech-and-academic-freedom-in-universities-challenges-and-a-solution?c=13

15. Argument, Vol. 24, n° 1, automne-hiver 2021–2022, pp. 13–20

16. https://www.ottawalife.com/article/education-information-and-democracy?c=1

17. https://www.ottawalife.com/article/the-long-decline-of-university-undergraduate-education-causes-and-remedies?c=13

18. https://www.ottawalife.com/article/funding-scientific-research-sometimes-targeted-research?c=13

19. Is a War on Terror Possible? Lessons from the Long War against Piracy, by John Scott Cowan. *Queen's Quarterly*, Volume 114, Number 1, Spring 2007, pp 72–85.

20. A War on Terror: Is It Possible, by Dr. John Scott Cowan, *Canadian Military Journal*, Volume 8, Number 2, Summer 2007, pp 43–50.

21. Absolute Rates of Glucose Production, Accumulation, and Utilization in the Dog at Pancreatectomy and Thereafter. G.A. Wrenshall, A.M. Rappaport, C.H. Best, J.S. Cowan and G. Hetenyi Jr.: Diabetes 13, No. 5, 500–508, 1964.

22. https://www.ottawalife.com/article/tigers-rabbits-and-foxes-the-physiology-of-international-tensions?set_lang=en

23. https://www.ottawalife.com/article/canada-and-china-neither-seems-to-get-what-makes-the-other-tick?c=1

24. https://www.ottawalife.com/article/delusions-of-adequacy-how-russia-and-pakistan-lie-to-themselves-in-similar-ways/

25. https://www.ottawalife.com/article/how-lt-gen-currie-turned-the-canadian-corps-into-a-national-army/

26. https://www.ottawalife.com/article/risks-from-biocontainment-labs-a-puzzling-lack-of-realism-about-human-fallibility-prevails?c=13

27. https://www.ottawalife.com/article/science-and-politics-always-a-stormy-marriage?c=1

28. https://www.ottawalife.com/article/designs-and-democracy-the-politics-of-imperfectly-levelled-playing-fields?c=1

29. https://www.ottawalife.com/article/the-spectacularly-awful-leaders-debates-causes-and-a-remedy?set_lang=en

30. https://www.ottawalife.com/article/a-fairer-capital-gains-tax?set_lang=en

31. https://www.ottawalife.com/article/memo-to-canada-pay-your-insurance-premiums?set_lang=en

32. https://www.cgai.ca/canadas_capacity_to_engage_tough_questions_to_ask_and_hard_answers_to_address

33. https://www.ottawalife.com/article/ukraine-is-our-wake-up-call-canadian-forces-lack-capabilities-to-be-operational?set_lang=en

34. https://www.ottawalife.com/article/canadian-nuclear-power-different-from-the-others?set_lang=en

35. The Incredible War of 1812: A Military History, by J. Mackay Hitsman, updated by Donald Graves, Robin Brass Studio, Toronto 1999, 398 pp.

36. Aboriginal Peoples and Military Participation: Canadian and International Perspectives, edited by P. Whiney Lackenbauer, R. Scott Sheffield, and Craig Leslie Mantle, Canadian Defence Academy Press, 2007, *see* Chapter 6: Black Hawk: A Model for Today, by John Scott Cowan, pp 153–160.

37. https://www.ottawalife.com/article/two-centuries-ahead-of-his-time-lessons-from-black-hawk-on-the-ethics-of-conflict?c=13

38. https://www.ottawalife.com/article/fruits-of-the-tech-revolution-the-good-the-bad-and-the-absurd?set_lang=en

39. https://www.ottawalife.com/article/the-privacy-paradox-we-have-both-too-little-and-too-much-privacy?set_lang=en

40. https://www.ottawalife.com/article/anti-elitism-aint-what-it-used-to-be?set_lang=en

41. https://www.ottawalife.com/article/fracture-lines-and-glue-the-interplay-of-external-threats-and-social-cohesion?c=1

ABOUT THE AUTHOR

JOHN SCOTT COWAN (B. 1943, Toronto) attended Upper Canada College and then studied physics (BSc) and physiology (PhD) at the University of Toronto. A postdoc at Laval University preceded 24 years at the University of Ottawa as a professor in the Faculty of Medicine, Chair of Physiology, and as Vice-Rector (Vice-President). He was Vice-Principal at Queen's University before becoming Principal of the Royal Military College of Canada (RMC) in 1999, where he served until 2008. He has been President of the Canadian Federation of Biological Societies, the Canadian Physiological Society, and the Canadian Association of University Business Officers. Also active in labour relations for over 40 years, he has been a negotiator, arbitrator, and teacher (including teaching at the national Senior University Administrators' Course) and was the first Senior Advisor on Labour Relations to the Association of Universities and Colleges of Canada (now Universities Canada).

Despite having an extensive research career in physiology, he has also had a long involvement in defence issues, starting with a monograph on defence policy in 1963. In the period 1999–2014 his writings were mostly focused on defence and security issues (including asymmetric threats, terrorism and piracy), but since 2014 he has written frequently about many other topics, including universities, Covid-19, international and strategic issues, domestic public policy, and some history.

He was President of the Conference of Defence Associations Institute (CDAI), 2008–2012, and was Chair of the Defence Science Advisory Board of Canada (DSAB), 2010–2013 (now called the Defence Advisory Board of Canada). He has received the Queen's Golden Jubilee Medal (2002) and Diamond Jubilee Medal (2012), the Sovereign's Medal for Volunteers (2018), and the Canadian Armed Forces Medallion for Distinguished Service (2008). His current RMC status is Principal Emeritus, and in May 2009 he received a Doctor of Military Science (*honoris causa*) from RMC for his contributions to the profession of arms. He was also the Honorary Colonel of the Princess of Wales' Own Regiment till early 2017. He is Vice-Chair and Director of Research of the Hill 70 Memorial project.

He has also flown over 60 aircraft types and is a bit deaf from a few thousand hours of flying the Harvard (known as the T6 in the United States), and so he does not mind at all if people shout at him. He is married to Dr. Marie-Anne Erki, Professor Emeritus of Civil Engineering at RMC.